Isabel Kuhl

Egon Schiele

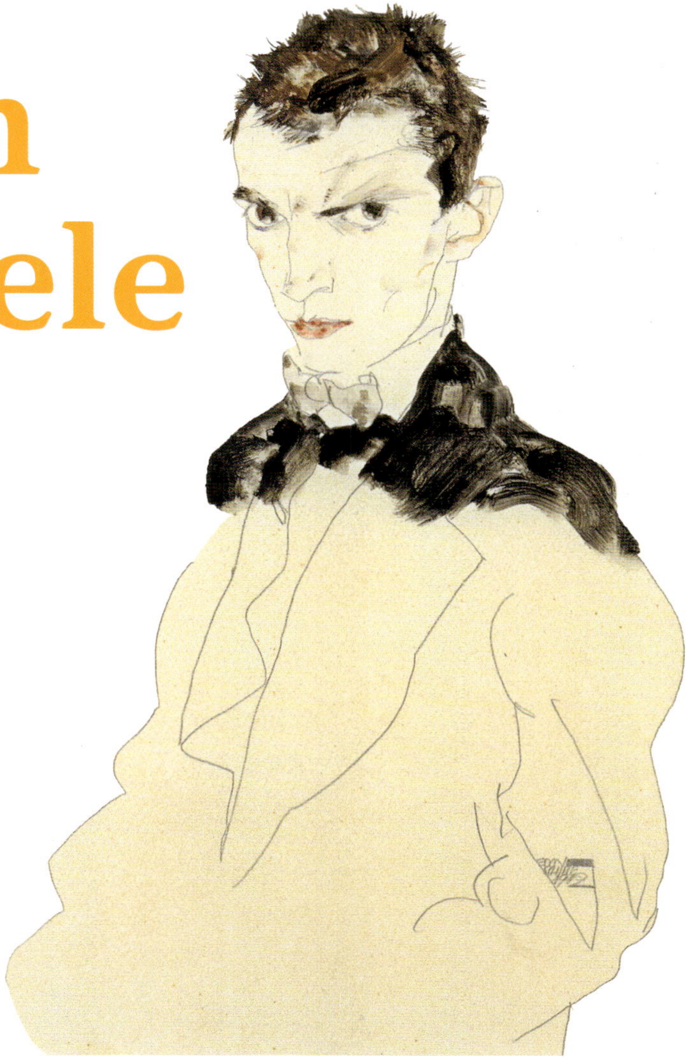

Prestel
Munich · Berlin · London · New York

Contents

p. 4 Flashback
Light and Shadow

p. 16 Fame and Honor
The Rise of a "New Artist"

p. 34 The Art
Before the Mirror and On the Ladder

p. 56 The Life
A Child of the Railroad on an Artist's Track

p. 90 The Loves
Two Is One Too Many

p. 110 Today
Late Fame

Flashback

“Our native city of Vienna is,
as has often been recognized …
the birthplace of
the art of
our time.”

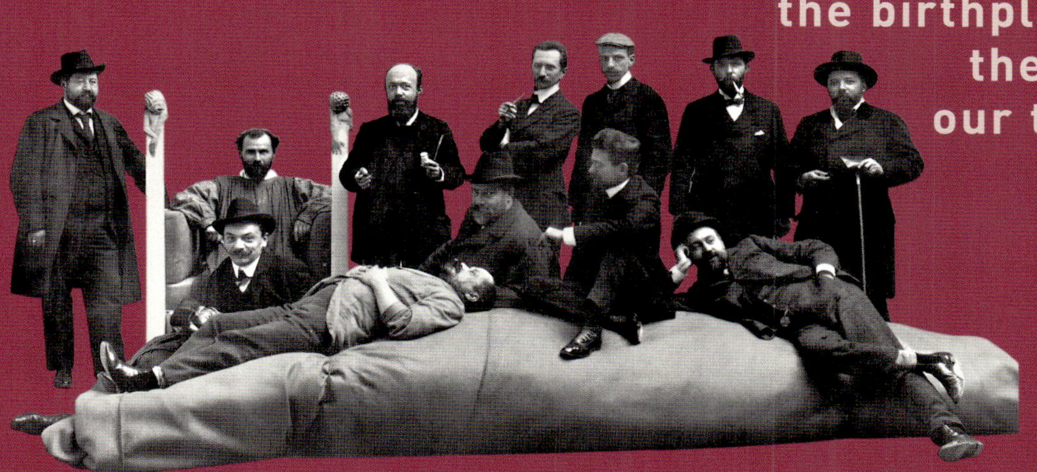

Otto Wagner, 1903

Between the Waltz and the World War

Though drawn to the countryside, Vienna was Egon Schiele's town, and was where his unparalleled artistic career began. At the time, the imperial capital was being transformed into a modern metropolis, and countless creative artists were a part of its modernization: Arthur Schnitzler with a pen, Gustav Mahler with his baton, Gustav Klimt at his easel.

The painter of women

At the turn of the century, painter Gustav Klimt was the brightest star on the Austrian art firmament. Klimt was the co-founder and first director of the Vienna Secession, whose first years coincided with what is referred to as the "Vienna Spring." In 1905, he left the artists' union and dedicated himself primarily to portraiture of Viennese high society. In both drawings and paintings, Klimt focused on surfaces and ornamentation, and his work was considered exemplary of the decorative Jugendstil movement. In addition to his elegant portraits of women, Klimt earned renown with his large-format wall decorations such as the *Beethoven Frieze* in the Vienna Secession building.

Gustav Klimt's portraits of women were a great inspiration to Egon Schiele. Klimt often painted his close friend and companion Emilie Flöge, here in a blue and gold celestial gown.

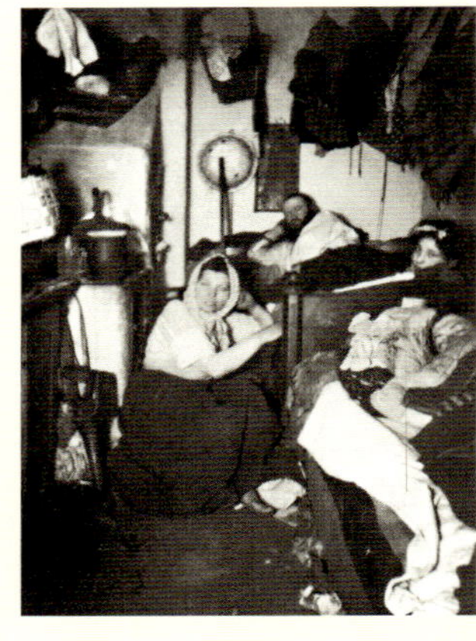

Almost half …

--> of the population of turn-of-the-century Vienna worked in industry.

--> of the Viennese workforce were immigrants from every corner of the multinational state.

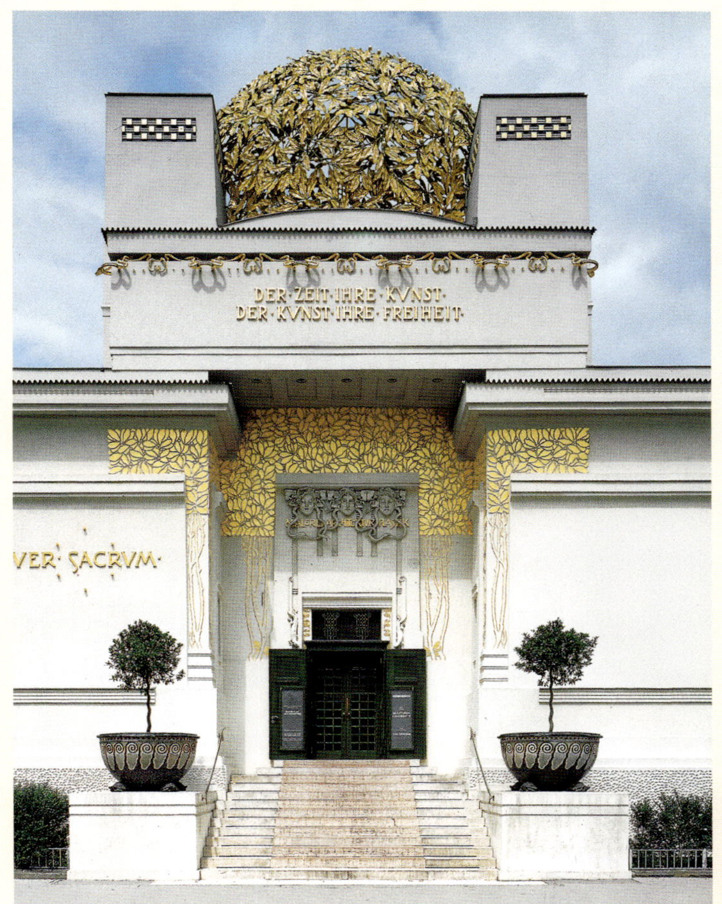

Spring in Vienna

The German term "Jugendstil" for the turn-of-the-century artistic movement had its roots in the avant-garde Munich magazine *Jugend;* elsewhere it was known as Art Nouveau, the Modern Style, et al. In the Vienna of 1897, visual artists from diverse creative fields banded together in the dawning modern period. The name Secession symbolized a "disassociation" (from the Latin *secessio*) from the academic tradition. The Viennese Secessionists were privately financed and thus represented an independent art scene—a novelty in the still old-world Austria-Hungary. The Vienna Secession still exists today as an exhibition space for modern art.

"In Austria everyone becomes what he is not."
Gustav Mahler

Sissi's homeland

In 1867, the weakened Austrian ruling house of Habsburg was forced to enter into a dual monarchy with Hungary, with both states retaining their independence. The Austrian-Hungarian Empire, with a population of some thirty-six million, was a multinational state, comprised of around a dozen nations with countless different languages and dialects. National tensions, above all in the Hungarian part of the dual monarchy, become the trigger for conflict. The two nations shared a head of state, Emperor Franz Joseph I, who was also the king of Hungary. Other crowned heads were the unforgettable Elisabeth, or "Sissi," empress of Austria and queen of Hungary, and of course the waltz king Johann Strauss, who made the Viennese waltz acceptable at court balls.

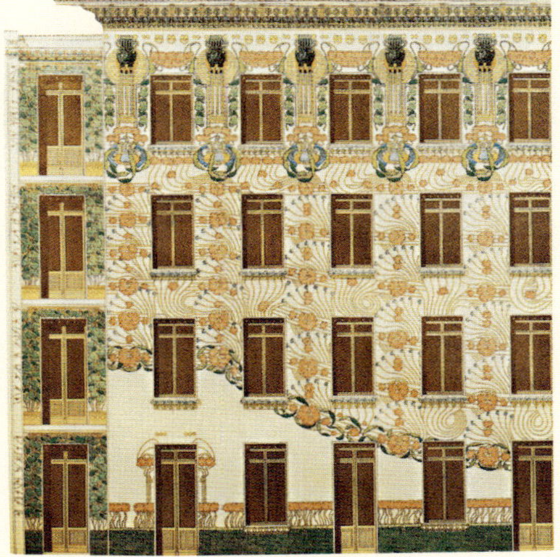

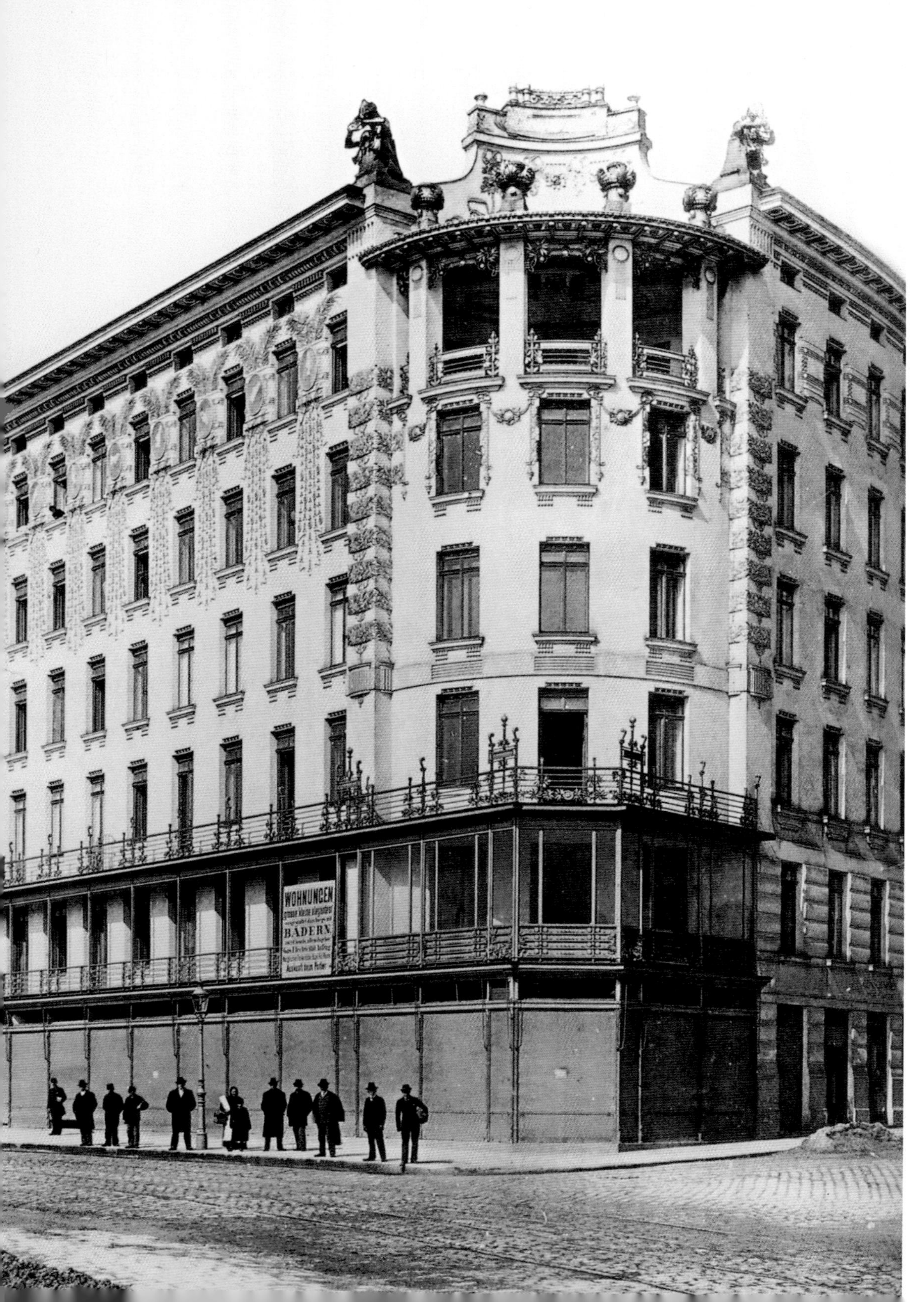

This residence at number 38 Linke Wienzeile caused a stir in its time with its rounded-off corners. The gold ornamentation on the façade is by the Jugendstil artist Koloman Moser.

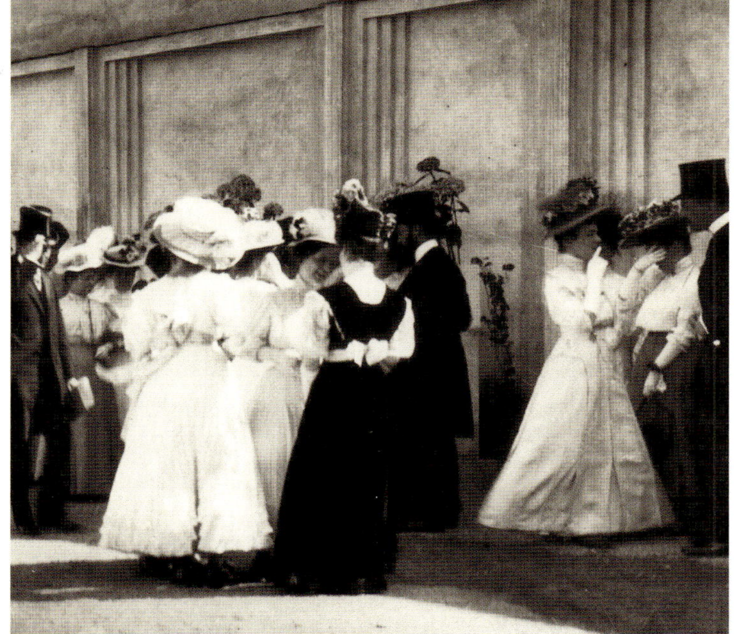

In 1908, the Viennese attended the *Kunstschau* in droves. Gustav Klimt was the star of the exhibition.

Light and Shadow

Where there is a lot of light, there is also a lot of shadow. This is certainly true of many cities, but particularly so in the case of turn-of-the-century Vienna. Around 1900, the city on the Danube was bursting at the seams. In a short time, Vienna became the fourth-largest city in Europe, and in the wake of industrialization workers were in great demand. Yet while industry celebrated their great success, entire social classes suffered and slipped into poverty.

"Tradition means passing on the fire, not worshipping the ashes."

Gustav Mahler

In the splendor of the arts

A veritable building boom and a downright population explosion shaped the era's cityscape, but in this fast-moving climate many inhabitants were left at a disadvantage. The artistic avant-garde constantly ran up against the oppressive moral corset of the outdated monarchy. "Viennese modernism," as the two decades before and after 1900 are known, served up plenty of tension and scandal—and, above all, a great deal of new art. Under the rule of Emperor Franz Joseph I, Vienna became a metropolis, the center of Austrian music and theater, and the birthplace of new philosophical ideas and literary forms. In the countless

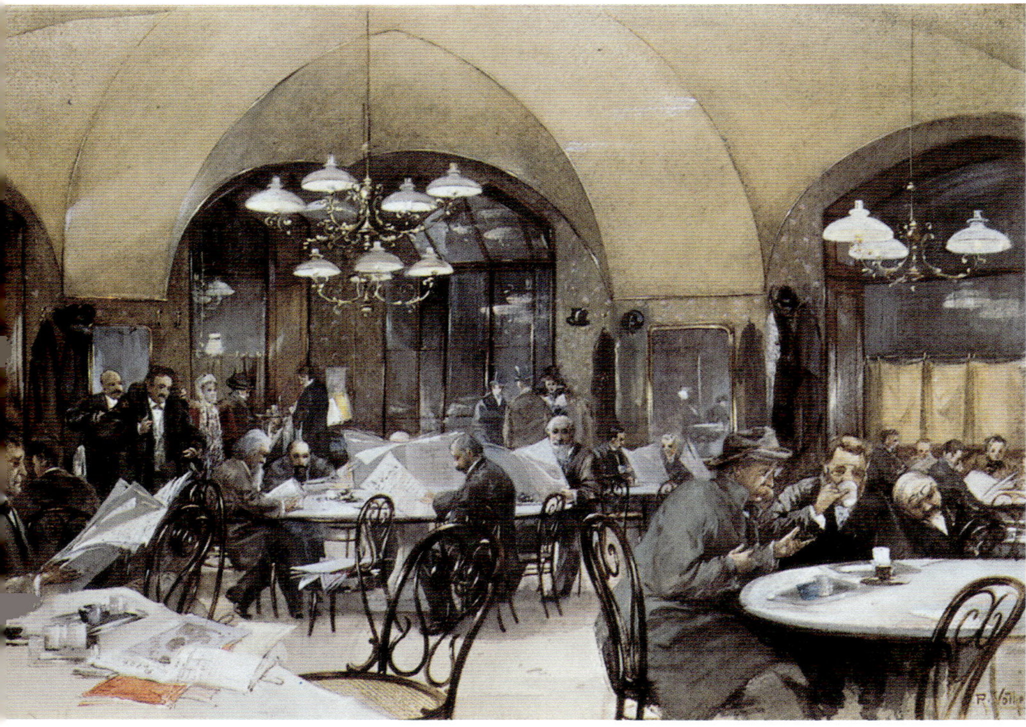

The coffeehouse, a home away from home—whether to read the newspaper, sip melange (similar to cappuccino), or take part in a discussion. A veritable institution of Viennese modernism was (and still is) the Café Griensteidl on Michaelerplatz.

coffeehouses, rich, upper-class patrons and intellectuals met to converse or read one of almost fifty daily newspapers then published in Vienna. A number of projects contributed to the modernization of the rapidly expanding city. Developing along the newly created Ringstrasse were building and artistic projects of unprecedented dimensions. Museums, an arts academy, city hall, a university, an opera house, and Hofburg Palace were all to be found on this historic avenue. Some 850 imposing structures, public and private mansions, lined the Ringstrasse, where artists were in demand to fit them out in the incredibly popular historicizing.

A society in upheaval

Turn-of-the-century Vienna was a city of contrasts, torn between a spirit of optimism and an atmosphere of decadence. The glittering world of the Ringstrasse existed side by side with a working-class population facing rapid impoverishment. The number of illegitimate births rose despite, or rather because of, the strict bourgeois morality. Prostitution flourished, not least as a result of unemployment and starvation wages for women. Around 1890, women became politically active and began demanding rights, and the General Union of Austrian Women formed to campaign for women's suffrage, and equality in education, the workplace, and in social matters. Fashion was another important indicator of these changes: the stiff corset gave way to comfortable cuts and fabrics.

The *Gesamtkunstwerk* was the ultimate goal of the Jugendstil artists. Advertising posters were no exception, such as this one by Maria Li Karz for the Wiener Werkstätte.

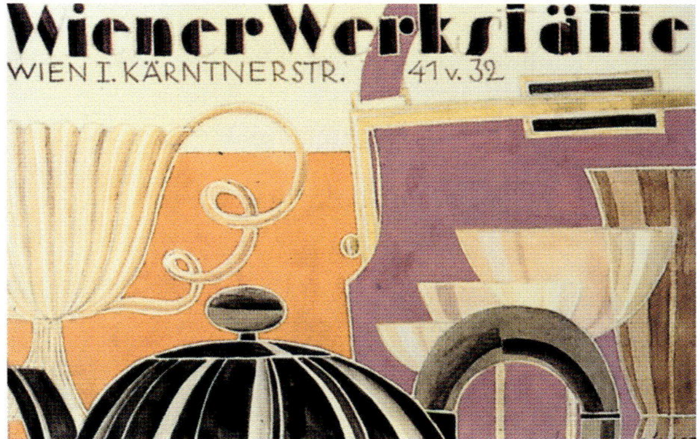

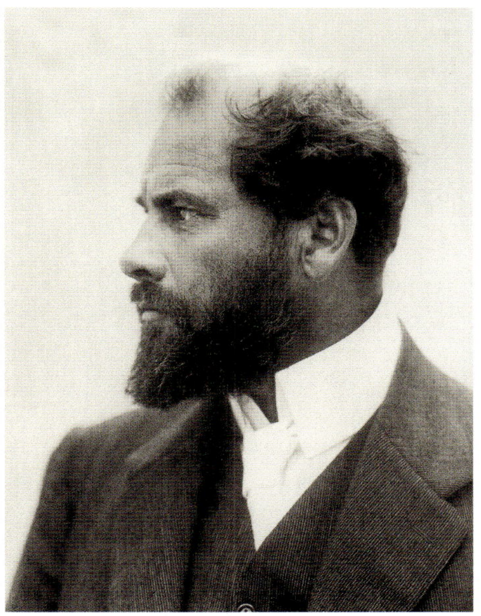

Schiele self-confidently described himself as the "Silver Klimt"—which would presumably make the original, here in a 1910 photograph, the Golden one ...

Slowly but surely the winds of change began to blow through Viennese society. Around the turn of the century, The Jugendstil movement gradually gained a foothold, and modernism influenced architecture, painting, music, and literature. Characteristic of Vienna at the time was the cross-pollination of all forms of art—the declared aim was the *Gesamtkunstwerk*, the total work of art.

Nature and art

Whether in houses or paintings, tableware, or clothing, plant motifs and undulating lines dominated the works of the Jugendstil artists. In around 1900, against the backdrop of industrialization, the movement began forming groups that drew its vocabulary of organic forms from nature. In the Vienna of 1897, the Jugendstil artists broke with the academy that until then had controlled the arts. Numerous painters, architects, and craftsmen presented their works in their own exhibition building, the Vienna Secession. "Half mosque, half blast-furnace," was the comment in the *Illustrierte Wiener Extrablatt* on the newcomer in the heart of the city. Undoubtedly, the first exhibition building in Europe dedicated exclusively to modern art was a daring architectural achievement. Its designer, Joseph Maria Olbrich, reveled in erecting a contrast to the grandiose structures of Vienna's city center, looking to unite art and nature with the building. The "Secession's" dome resembles a laurel tree, and its gilded leaves earned it the nickname "the golden cabbage." Olbrich's design for the exhibition space was unpretentious, a novelty given the richly decorated museum spaces in Vienna's temples of art. Gustav Klimt was the star of the Secession, and was elected its first president. For its 1902 exhibition, he designed the monumental *Beethoven Frieze,* a representation of the cycle of life.

Slippers on the pulse of the times

Klimt was also connected to the Wiener Werkstätte, which was founded by architect Josef Hoffmann, painter Koloman Moser, and businessman Fritz Waerndorfer a year after the *Beethoven* exhibition. In response to

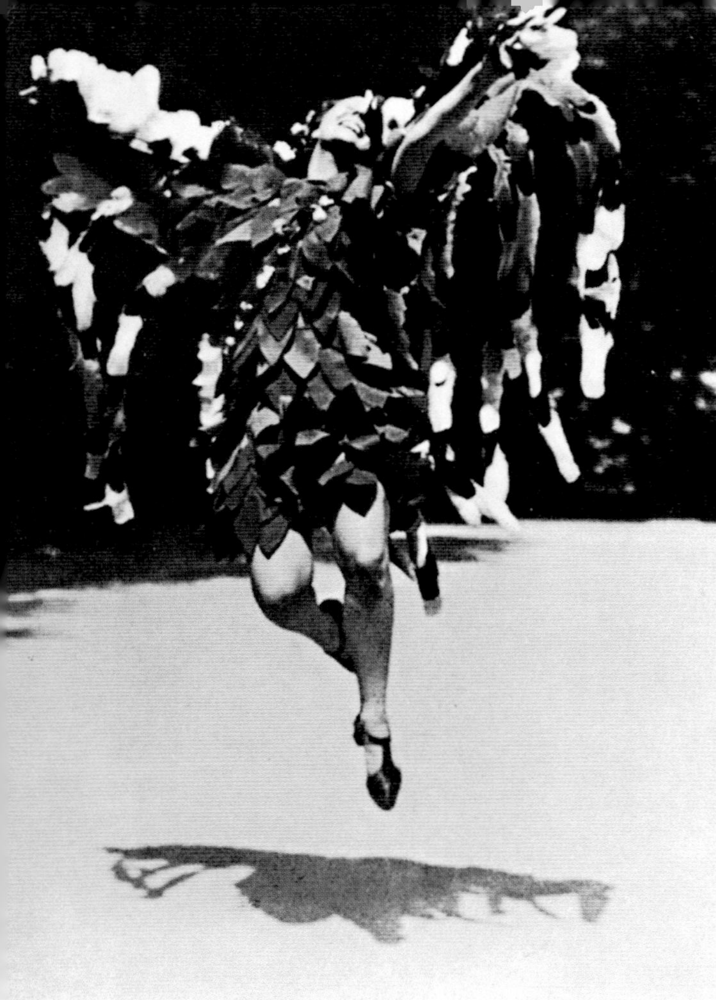

The Viennese dancer Grete Wiesenthal breathed new life into ballet. Here she dances Richard Strauss's waltz *Voices of Spring.*

industrial mass production, their motivation was to raise the reputation of the applied arts with artisan craftsmanship, which had long stood in the shadow of the so-called fine arts, such as painting. Adherents to the Wiener Werkstätte provided all of life's necessities, from architecture to bedroom slippers, and even crafted children's toys. Everything was to be functional and accessible, whether it was interior decoration, clothing, or jewelry ...

The world of yesterday had served its time

Viennese modernism, however, was by no means restricted to the art of the Secession. In the two decades before and after 1900, there was a buzz of excitement everywhere. Even in the venerable Viennese opera house! Around the turn of the century, the composer and conductor Gustav Mahler directed the Viennese Court Opera, and under his directorship the staging of opera was modernized. Many artists were sympathetic to his reforms of the operatic form. The Viennese composer and music theorist Arnold Schoenberg took a step even further toward modernism and "New Music." Exploring the boundaries of tonality, Schoenberg developed his twelve-tone technique in the first decades of the twentieth century.

One of the leading representatives of literary modernism in Vienna was the author and dramatist Arthur Schnitzler. He focused on the emotional world of his fictional characters, and his criticisms of Austrian society—such as the common double standard concerning sexuality—are readily apparent in his works. Another writer dedicated to portraying the inner life of his characters was Stefan Zweig. His autobiography *The World of Yesterday* (1944) offers a fascinating look at turn-of-the-century Viennese culture.

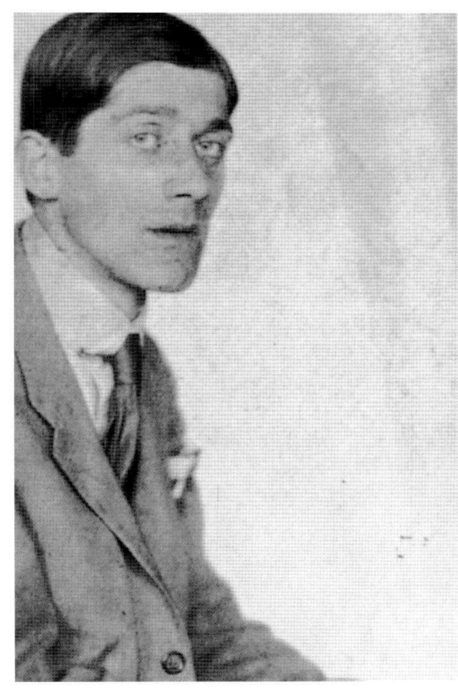

Oskar Kokoschka had little time for the Jugendstil. He became one of Austria's most important Expressionist artists.

Sigmund Freud's exploration of the human psyche, in particular the unconscious and the world of instinct, proved influential for the artists of the time.

Escaping 3/4-time

In any discussion of the pursuit of the *Gesamtkunstwerk,* dance must be included. In 1902, Expressionist dancer Isadora Duncan shook up the home of the waltz when she appeared at the Vienna Secession. Duncan introduced a new sense of the physical to dance. The three Wiesenthal sisters, Grete, Elsa, and Bertha, went even further, dancing at Secession and Wiener Werkstätte events. They formulated a countermovement to the rigid rules of classical ballet in an attempt to return to natural expression in movement and authentic body language. Painters like Egon Schiele were not alone in responding to the dance created circa 1900. Self-realization and self-liberation, whether on a movie screen or a stage, were the central concerns of countless turn-of-the-century artists.

The soul

At the center of the new Expressionist art was an exploration into the world of emotions. In paintings and graphic art, as well as literature and music, artists delved into their psyches and souls as a response to the rules of the academic world. Rather than mere representation or a simple portrayal of the beautiful, their works were "expressions." Classical nudes gave way to deformed bodies; hard contour lines and bold colors replaced naturalistic portrayal. For the Expressionists, bourgeois ideals of beauty were passé. The artists' group Die Brücke, founded in 1905 in Dresden, were the German representatives of Expressionism. In Austria, in addition to Egon Schiele, the painter Oskar Kokoschka and the poet Georg Trakl were leading representatives of this artistic movement.

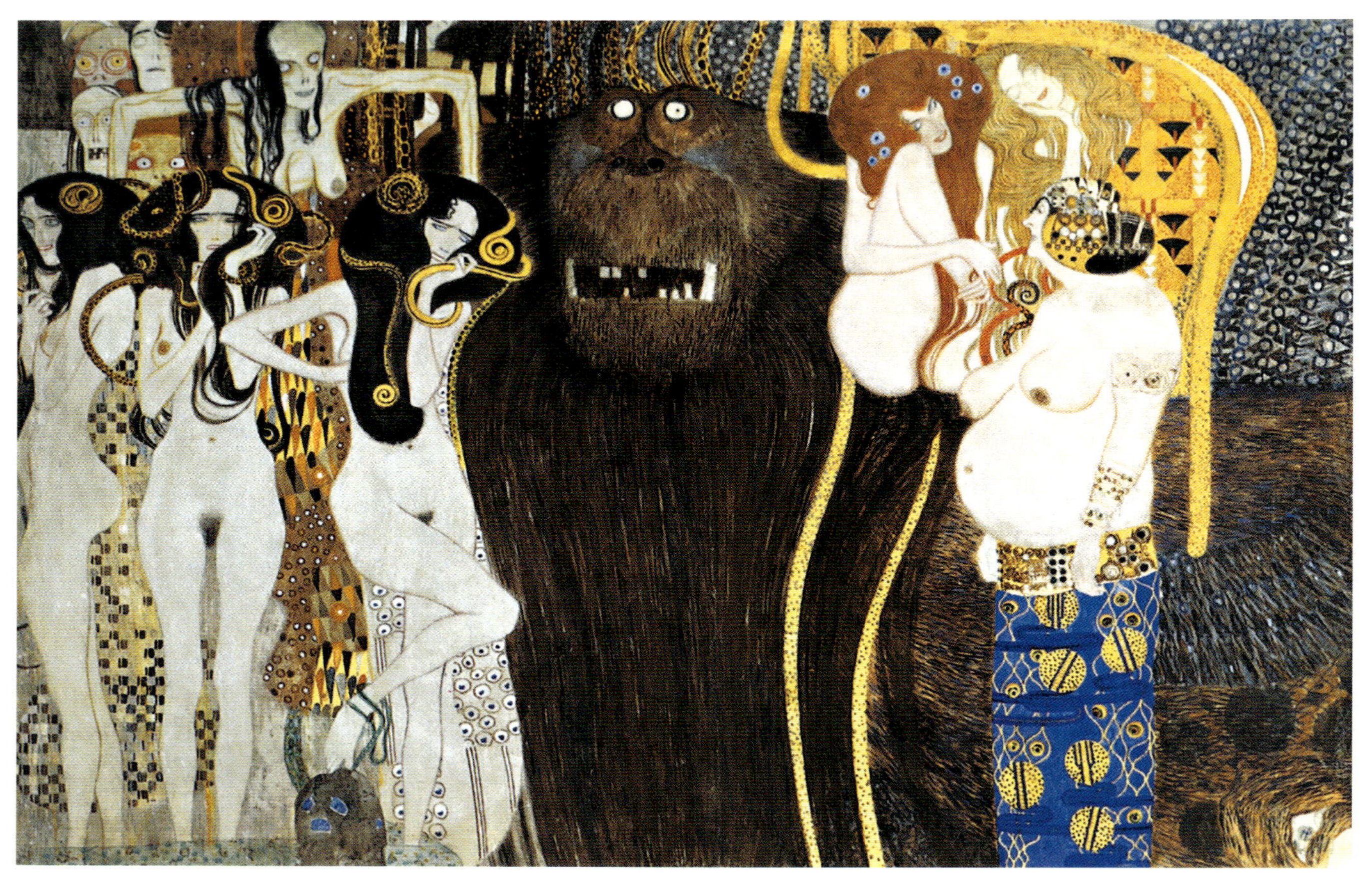

Rejection Gustav Klimt's monumental *Beethoven Frieze* found few admirers. For most observers, the twenty-four-meter-long wall painting in the Secession was neither beautiful nor sufficiently sublime. The *Beethoven* exhibition, for which Klimt created this work in 1902, was a financial disaster.

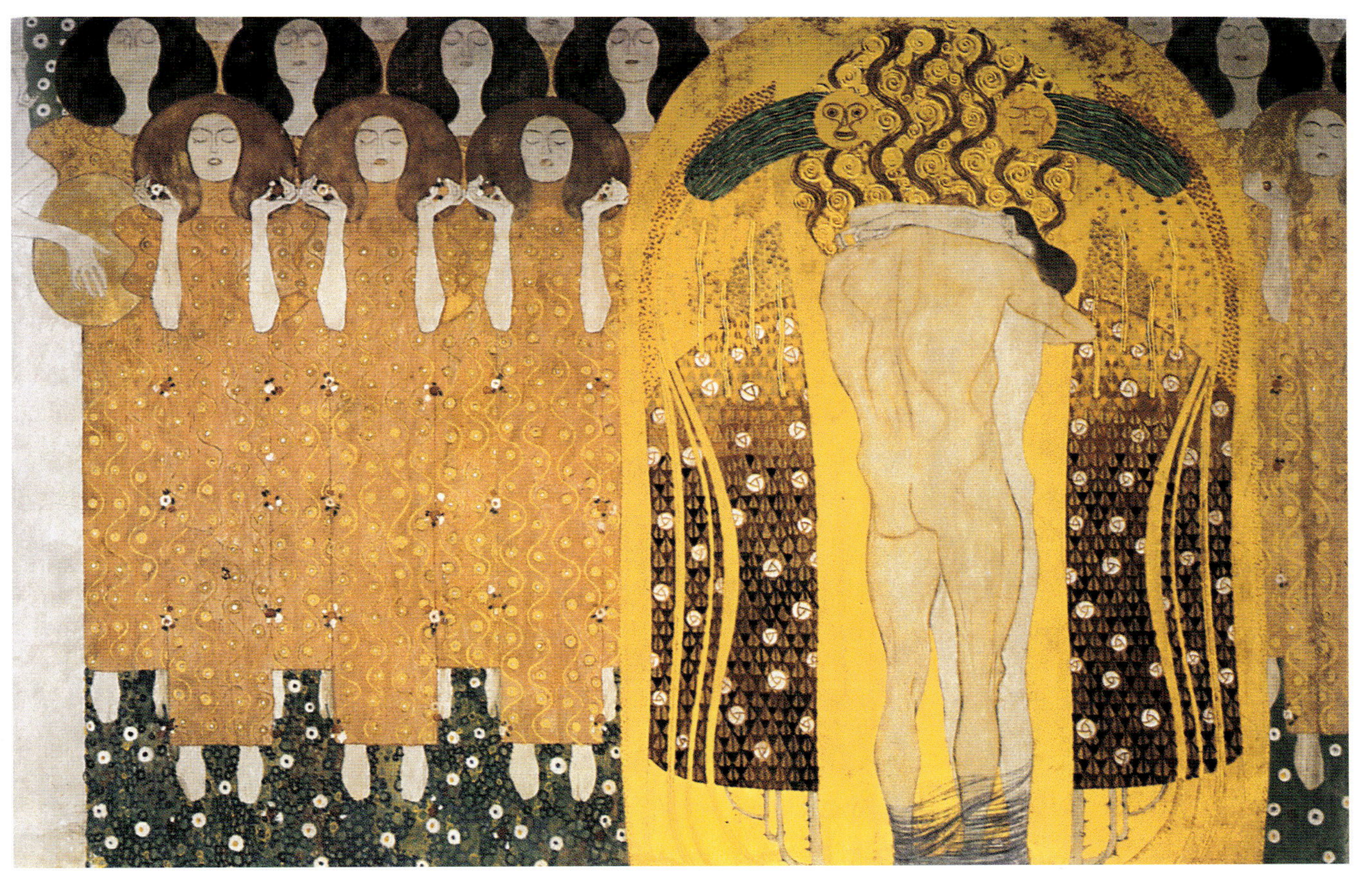

Utopia This frieze, dedicated by Klimt to Ludwig van Beethoven, took as its theme the utopia of the artist—the salvation of mankind through art and love. The hero survives the dangers posed by hostile forces and is redeemed in the embrace of his beloved.

Fame and Honor

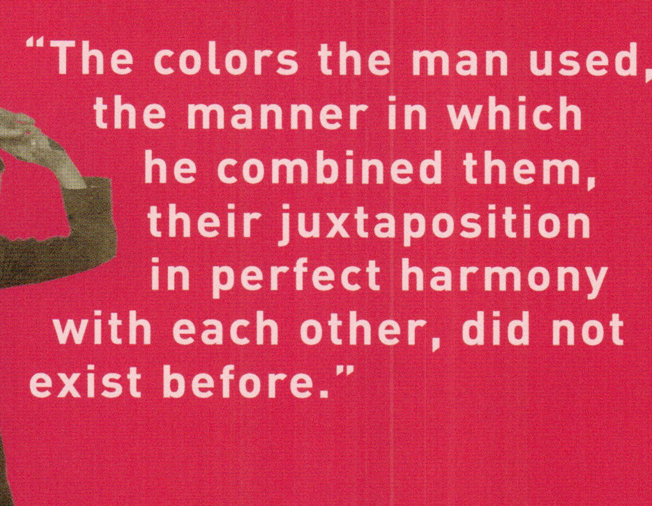

“The colors the man used, the manner in which he combined them, their juxtaposition in perfect harmony with each other, did not exist before.”

Heinrich Benesch

An Artist with Airs and Graces

At the tender age of eighteen, the self-assured Egon Schiele exhibited his works for the first time. In fact, at no time could the painter have complained of a lack of public interest. While his close family circle may have had little appreciation for his work, Schiele could count on loyal and enthusiastic patrons—and an exaggerated sense of self-confidence.

A true fan

"A poor imitation of Klimt." That was what Heinrich Benesch first thought of Schiele's work. But he quickly changed his mind on the occasion of Schiele's first exhibition in 1908, and built up a large collection of the artist's drawings and watercolors. In 1913, he had his portrait, together with his son Heinrich, painted by the artist. Yet even before that, he told Schiele of his enthusiasm for even the littlest of his works: "Let me ask one thing of you, dear Herr Schiele, don't throw any of your sketches in the stove, whatever they are, even the smallest, most unremarkable things. Please write in chalk on your stove the following equation: 'Stove = Benesch'."

As early as 1917, Heinrich Benesch, collector and friend of the artist, proudly owned seventy drawings from Schiele's hand.

Photographic art

→ In 1914, the Vienna painter, sculptor, and photographer Anton Josef Trčka produced a series of portraits of Schiele.

→ Schiele experimented enthusiastically in front of the camera.

→ He touched up some of the images himself with a paintbrush.

A portraitist with money problems

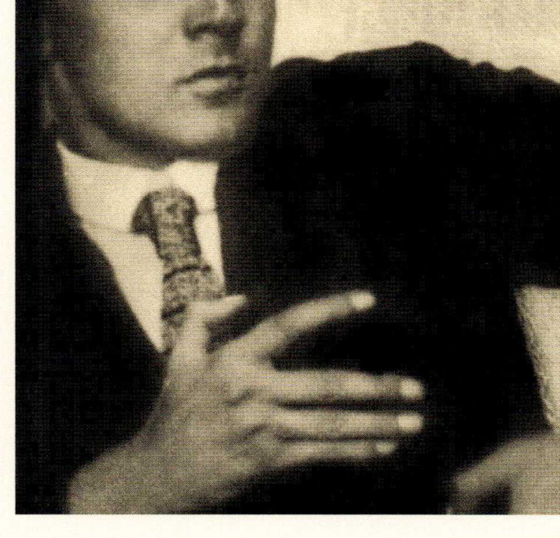

Schiele earned a living from above all portrait commissions. More or less, anyway, for his clients sometimes rejected the paintings—Oskar Reichel, for example. Unlike Gustav Klimt, Schiele did not have great success as a portraitist. A bit of a spendthrift, Schiele was constantly concerned about money.

At home in the museum

That Schiele saw his works in museums during his lifetime was of great importance to him. In the spring of 1917, the director of the Modern Gallery in Vienna, today the Austrian Gallery Belvedere, acquired several drawings for the collection. The following year, he purchased an oil painting, a portrait of Edith Schiele. However, he had the young woman's colorful checked skirt, in his opinion too bohemian for a state museum, overpainted with something plainer (p. 31).

A star's prices

Schiele's first exhibition was a modest one: a group exhibition of painters from Klosterneuburg in the monastery's Kaisersaal (Imperial Hall). But Schiele's ideas about pricing could hardly have been more exorbitant. The bold youngster demanded 800 kronen for one of his works. Even years later such sums were an absolute exception. The public hardly felt inspired to snap up his work and Schiele did not sell a single painting. Yet the exhibition did have an upside: Schiele's mother and his guardian Leopold, otherwise unsparing in their criticism, were silent for the first time. Today, with his work commanding millions, Schiele's aplomb would finally seem to be vindicated. In June 2006, at Christie's auction house in London, Schiele's *Autumn Sun*, a work long believed lost, saw the hammer fall at the princely sum of nearly $22 million.

"I am everything at the same time, but I'll never do everything at the same time."

Egon Schiele, ca. 1910

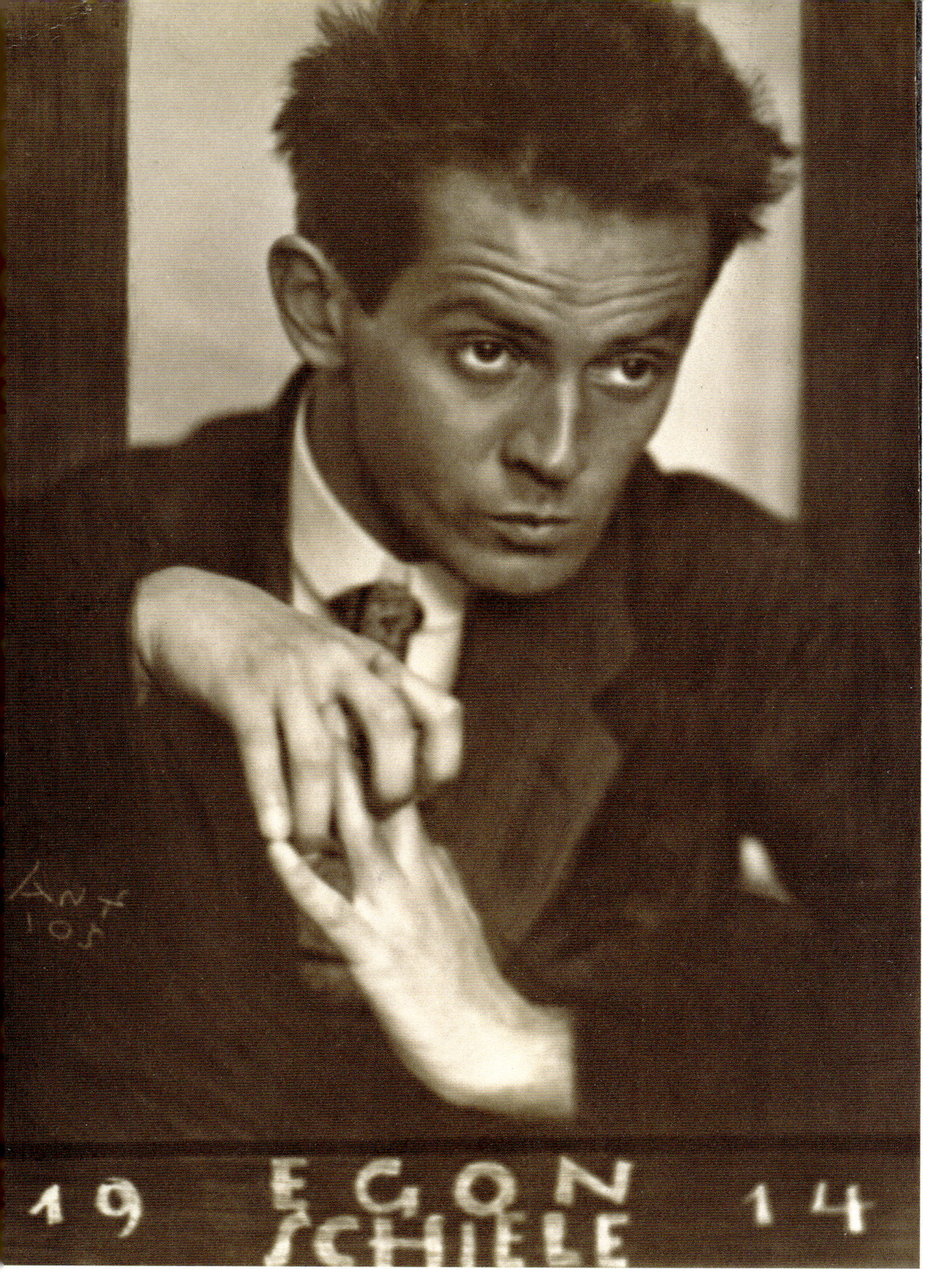

Schiele's pleasure in posing for the camera is evident from this 1914 photo.

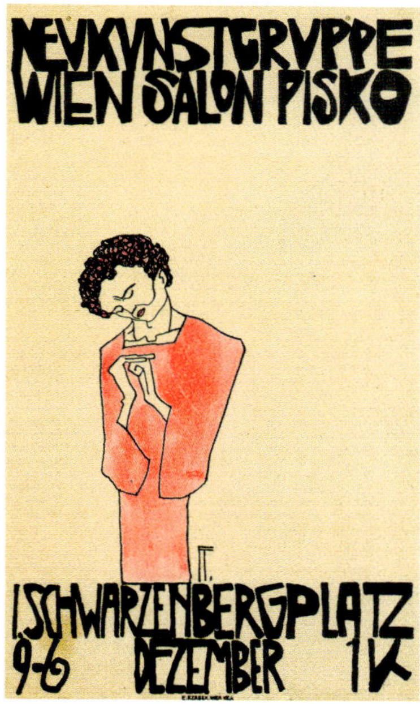

The New Artist Group started to exhibit immediately after it was founded. This exhibition poster was designed by Anton Faistauer.

The Rise of a "New Artist"

Egon Schiele's time witnessed a transforming art market. The traditional patronage system that had long prevailed in Vienna, and which had provided Gustav Klimt with a rather good living, gradually gave way to an art market organized and maintained by gallery owners. Schiele nevertheless succeeded in building up a network of patrons and backers capable of easing his financial concerns.

Creative self-determination

At the age of nineteen, Schiele stepped onto the uncertain road to artistic independence. With his collaboration the Neukunstgruppe (New Art Group) was born. Schiele made it clear that creative self-determination took precedence over formal programs.

"... we want the flight of talent from our country to stop so that all of those whom Austria has produced may be able to work for Austria's honor."

Egon Schiele

Schiele wrote of their aims in the group's manifesto: "The new artist is and must at all costs be himself, he must be a creator, he must build the foundation himself without reference to the past, to tradition. Then he is an artist." In December 1909, having recently formed, the "New Artists"

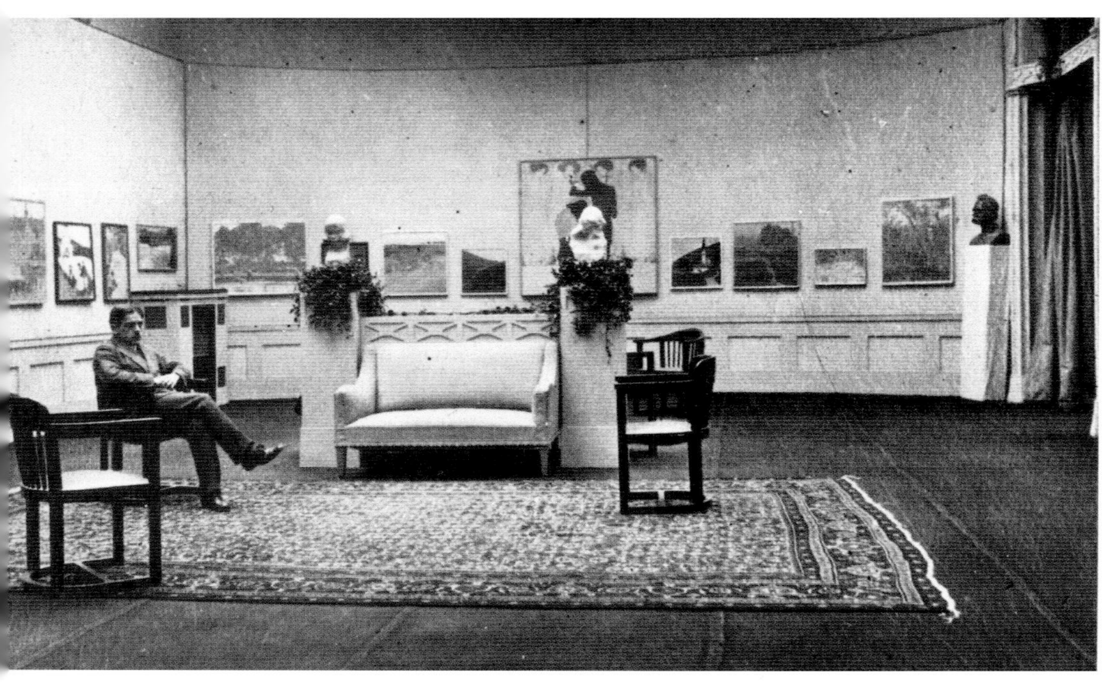

The New Artists presented their works for the first time in the rooms of the Viennese art dealer Gustav Pisko.

put on their first exhibition. The Viennese art dealer Gustav Pisko put his space at their disposal. Further exhibitions followed in Vienna, Prague, and Budapest.

The first collectors

In the summer of 1909, Schiele received an important invitation: Gustav Klimt asked the young painter to exhibit at the second *Kunstschau*. Schiele's paintings hung side by side with the works of illustrious contemporaries from all over Europe, among them Edvard Munch, Paul Gauguin, and Vincent van Gogh. Though his works were lost in the abundance of works on display, for some they left a lasting impression. His first commissions followed. Oskar Reichel, a prosperous physician, ordered a portrait from Schiele. And while he rejected the painting, over the following years he would buy a total of a dozen drawings and fifteen oil paintings by the young artist. Schiele also managed to draw the attention of one of the most important modern art collectors in turn-of-the-century Austria: the industrialist Carl Reininghaus. The collector wanted to commission Schiele to carry out monumental erotic wall paintings for his new apartment in Vienna, but the painter was not interested. However, Schiele knew how to humor his collectors. He wrote to Reichel in January 1911, "Without flattery, I know no one in Vienna who knows more about art than you." And a few lines later he again laid it on thick, this time about one of his own paintings: "It is undoubtedly the best of what has been painted lately in Vienna .... Why should I remain silent, when it is the truth."

Working tirelessly

Modesty was not among Schiele's virtues. But perhaps it was exactly this self-conviction that appealed to his fans. Arthur Roessler, art critic and journalist, had as little doubt about Schiele's talent as the artist himself. In the Social Democratic *Arbeiter-Zeitung* of December 7, 1910, he wrote about the Neukunstgruppe exhibition of that year: "Many will probably fall by the wayside, but I believe some to be inwardly and outwardly strong enough to 'come through.' Among

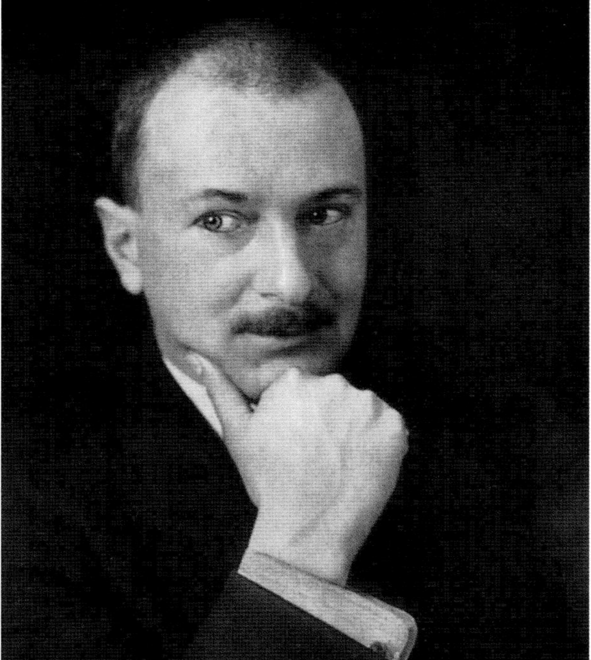

Faithful companion, enthusiastic patron: the journalist and art critic Arthur Roessler.

these I count the exceptionally gifted Egon Schiele, Toni Faistauer, Franz Wiegele, Hans Ehrlich, all four painters ... In all the aforementioned, the feeling for style is quite astonishingly pronounced."

The critic bought drawings by the young artist, and Schiele painted his portrait. Apart from several drawings, Roessler left a total of twenty-three oil paintings to the Historical Museum of the City of Vienna. And after Schiele's death, he became his biographer. In Roessler's essays, Schiele sometimes comes across to the reader as a starving, at-times martyred artist suffering from the world's incomprehension. Yet given the support Schiele received from his patrons, and the opportunities he had to his exhibit his work, this would appear to be a somewhat distorted image. Nevertheless, Roessler's untiring dedication to the painter was impressive. Not only did he follow Schiele's career with generous reviews, but when Schiele submitted a poetically conceived résumé for publication, Roessler also served as his editor (see p. 61). As a precautionary measure, in the "Sketch for a Self-Portrait"

Arthur Roessler discovered Schiele very early on. Here the two enjoy summer holidays at the Traunsee.

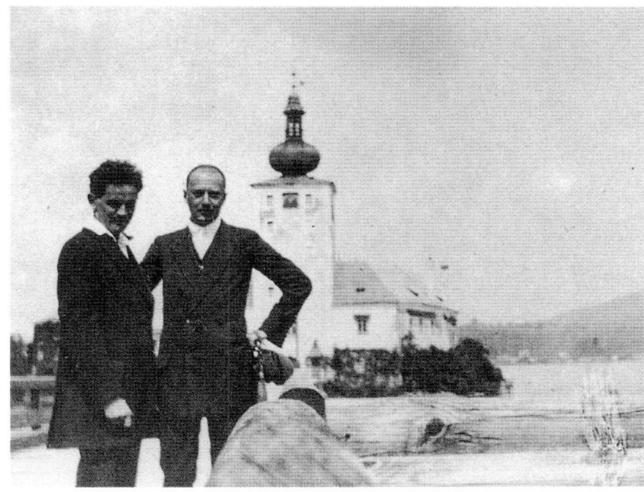

Roessler added both a lawyer and a mayor to Schiele's family, and reintroduced scholastic stages omitted by the artist. Even with this polished-up biography, Roessler couldn't succeed in making Schiele famous beyond Austria's borders.

Father and son

Heinrich Benesch's enthusiasm for Schiele was equally enthusiastic. Even his moderate budget—he was, after all, a railroad inspector—could not dampen his collecting fever. Not only was he one of Schiele's

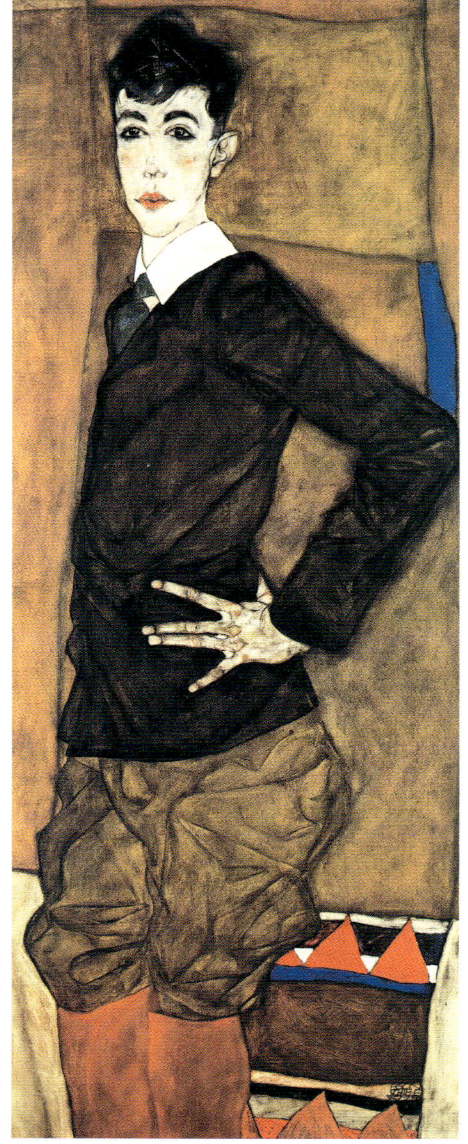

The wealthy liquor manufacturer August Lederer commissioned Schiele to paint a portrait of his son Erich.

first buyers, but also a fatherly friend who tried to calm the storms Schiele stirred up. When the young artist had a falling out with his guardian Leopold, Benesch went to him—unsuccessfully—to ask for money for the undernourished Schiele. His commitment to the artist was contagious, and his son Otto often accompanied him to Schiele's studio. Though six years younger than Schiele, the teenage Otto supported the artist. In 1915, he would write the introduction to the Egon Schiele retrospective exhibition. Given the criticism his laudatory foreword provoked, he later clarified: "Herr Schiele, you were once one of 'Klimt's circle.' The transformation that diverted you onto other paths could have been either a step up or a step down. Undoubtedly it was a step up, proven by your art's reputation among true connoisseurs."

A solid network

Collectors and companions such as Reichel and Reininghaus, Benesch and Roessler, played a significant role in Schiele's life. By the age of twenty, he had already made numerous contacts and weaved an impressive web of patrons. In comparison, art dealers played a mere supporting role. His first long-term representation by a gallery was with the Munich art dealer Goltz, but lasted only until 1913.

The Lederer family

Nineteen-twelve was a difficult year financially for Schiele; the following year the situation became disastrous. Klimt put him in touch with the Wiener

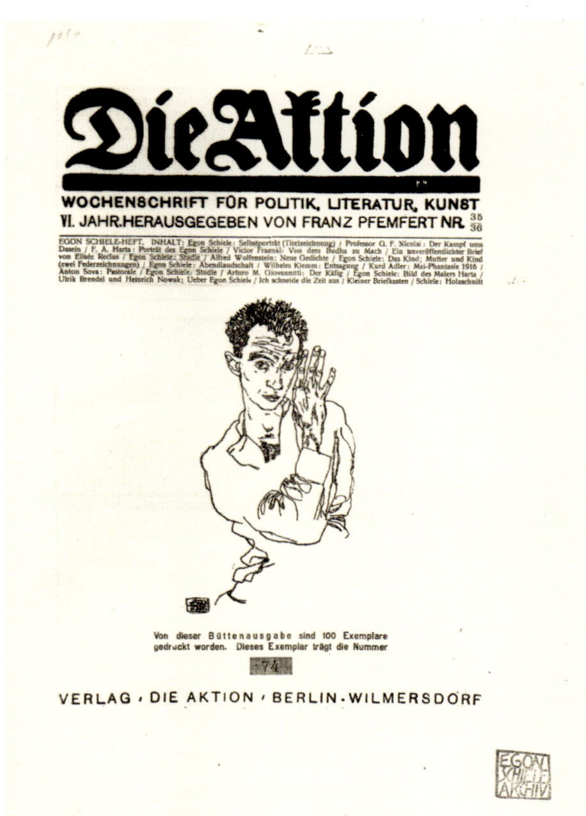

Die Aktion

WOCHENSCHRIFT FÜR POLITIK, LITERATUR, KUNST

VI. JAHR. HERAUSGEGEBEN VON FRANZ PFEMFERT NR. 35/36

EGON SCHIELE-HEFT. INHALT: Egon Schiele: Selbstporträt (Titelzeichnung) / Professor G. F. Nicolai: Der Kampf ums Dasein / F. A. Harta: Porträt des Egon Schiele / Victor Fraenkl: Von dem Budha zu Mach / Ein unveröffentlichter Brief von Elisée Reclus / Egon Schiele: Studie / Alfred Wolfenstein: Neue Gedichte / Egon Schiele: Das Kind; Mutter und Kind (zwei Federzeichnungen) / Egon Schiele: Abendlandschaft / Wilhelm Klemm: Entsagung / Kurd Adler: Mai-Phantasie 1916 / Anton Sova: Pastorale / Egon Schiele: Studie / Arturo M. Giovannitti: Der Käfig / Egon Schiele: Bild des Malers Harta / Ulrik Brendel und Heinrich Nowak: Ueber Egon Schiele / Ich schneide die Zeit aus / Kleiner Briefkasten / Schiele: Holzschnitt

Von dieser Büttenausgabe sind 100 Exemplare gedruckt worden. Dieses Exemplar trägt die Nummer 74

VERLAG · DIE AKTION · BERLIN-WILMERSDORF

EGON SCHIELE ARCHIV

In 1916, the magazine *Die Aktion* devoted an entire issue to Schiele's poems. The magazine contributed significantly to the diffusion of Expressionism.

Werkstätte, for which Schiele produced postcards, among other works, in order to keep his head above water. Schiele did in fact earn a few portrait commissions. The recently formed Hagen Union of Artists, which was slowly emerging from the Secession's shadow, invited the young artist to exhibit his works. But Schiele's money worries persisted. Once again Klimt lent a hand, introducing him to one of his major patrons, the liquor manufacturer August Lederer. Schiele visited the family in Hungary at the end of the year and was impressed by their lifestyle. "The carriage is always waiting," he hold his mother. He even asked Roessler's advice on how much he should tip the servants. Schiele enjoyed the luxurious surroundings, and Lederer in turn was enthusiastic about Schiele's work and became a regular collector. He had his sixteen-year-old son Erich's portrait painted by Schiele. Erich himself became a great admirer of the artist and even took drawing lessons from him, though he did later admit his main objective was getting to know Schiele's models.

Private lessons

Through his contacts with the Wiener Werkstätte, Schiele also met the art-lover Heinrich Böhler, who hired the twenty-four-year-old artist as a private teacher and paid for his materials and models, thus providing Schiele with a regular monthly income. The artist also received some portrait commissions from Böhler's circle of friends. His situation had improved, and he had no reason to fear the end of his good fortune. Schiele wrote to his mother, "I have the feeling I have finally extricated myself from my precarious existence."

A member everywhere

Even during his youth, Schiele sent his works to exhibitions all over Germany, including those of the Blaue

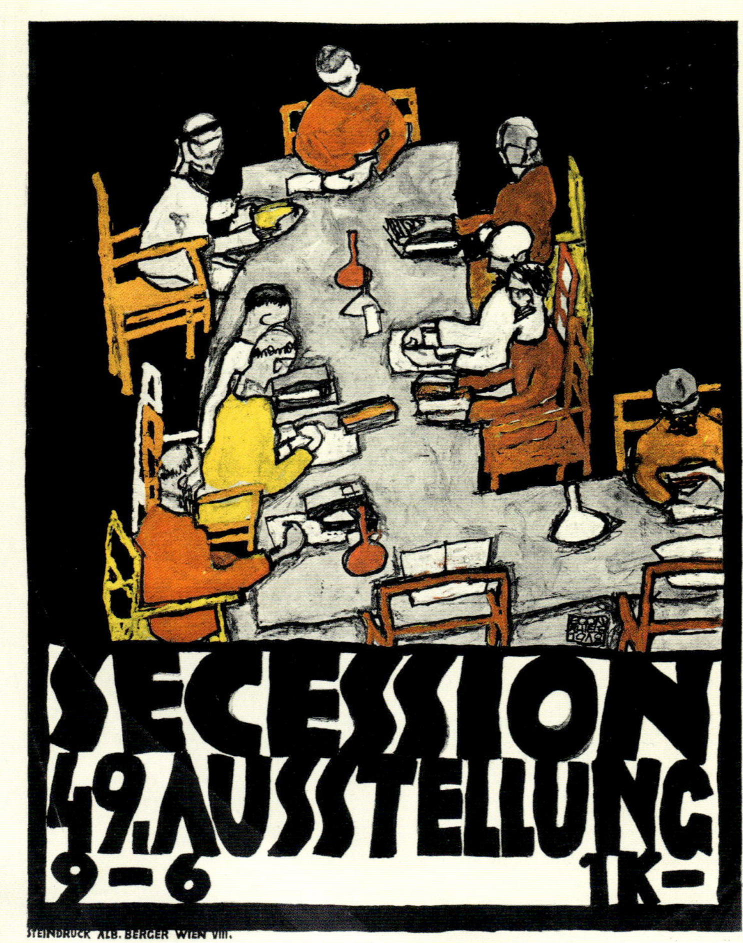

For the poster of the 49th Vienna Secession exhibition, Schiele portrayed himself in the company of friends. An empty chair was reserved for Klimt, who had died at the beginning of 1918.

Reiter group. He was also a member of the Munich artists group Sema. Even during the war years, Schiele participated in numerous exhibitions, including outside Austria's borders. In 1917, the first portfolio with reproductions of his works was printed. In the same year, Schiele promoted the "Kunsthalle" project: against the backdrop of World War I, musicians and painters such as Arnold Schoenberg and Klimt attempted "to gather together the forces of all areas of art that have been shattered by the war." This joint venture was to be an "intellectual meeting-place," "offering painters, sculptors, architects, musicians, and creative writers the opportunity to make connections with a public which, like them, is ready to defend itself against the accelerating disintegration of culture." While the project failed, new opportunities immediately opened up for Schiele.

In Klimt's footsteps

The Vienna Secession contacted Schiele with an offer of membership. At first, he hesitated. For the forty-ninth annual exhibition in March 1918, Schiele was not only invited to participate, but also commissioned to design the exhibition poster.

On February 6, 1918, Gustav Klimt unexpectedly died. The magazine *Der Anbruch* published Schiele's obituary of his friend and patron: "Gustav Klimt / An artist of incredible perfection / An individual of rare depth /

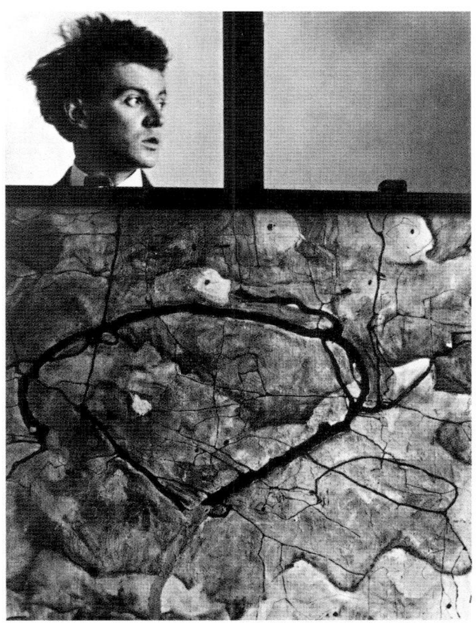

Schiele often painted atmospheric autumn landscapes with bare foliage. Here he stands behind one of them.

His work a temple." Klimt was the star of the newly founded Secession, and with his death Schiele inherited his legacy as Austria's leading artist. In his exhibition poster, Schiele made reference to the gap left by the great artist. He designed a color lithograph after an uncompleted oil painting of the previous year, showing him and his friends sitting around a table. Georg Merkel, Paris Gütersloh, Anton Faistauer, Felix Albrecht Harta are gathered—only Klimt's seat remains empty.

The Secession exhibition was a complete success for the young artist. The prestigious central room of the building, measuring an impressive fifteen by fifteen meters, was devoted entirely to his works. Schiele exhibited nineteen of his oil paintings, as well as drawings and watercolors. His works enjoyed spectacular sales, new commissions came in, and his financial worries receded ever further into the background.

"This time it is a gathering of young painters who have been invited by the Secession to exhibit in their rooms, most of them members of the so-called Klimt group ... The large main room is occupied—rightly—by Egon Schiele, one who has what it takes to be a great artist, but who uses his gifts in such a way that, when one day the zeitgeist has dissipated, he will probably be considered a mere monument to the pathologically perverse way of seeing and feeling of a certain era—a monument, admittedly, that shows unusual artistic qualities ... and this too is how these romantics of decay and degeneration will fare" (Franz Servaes, *Neue Freie Presse,* March 9, 1918).

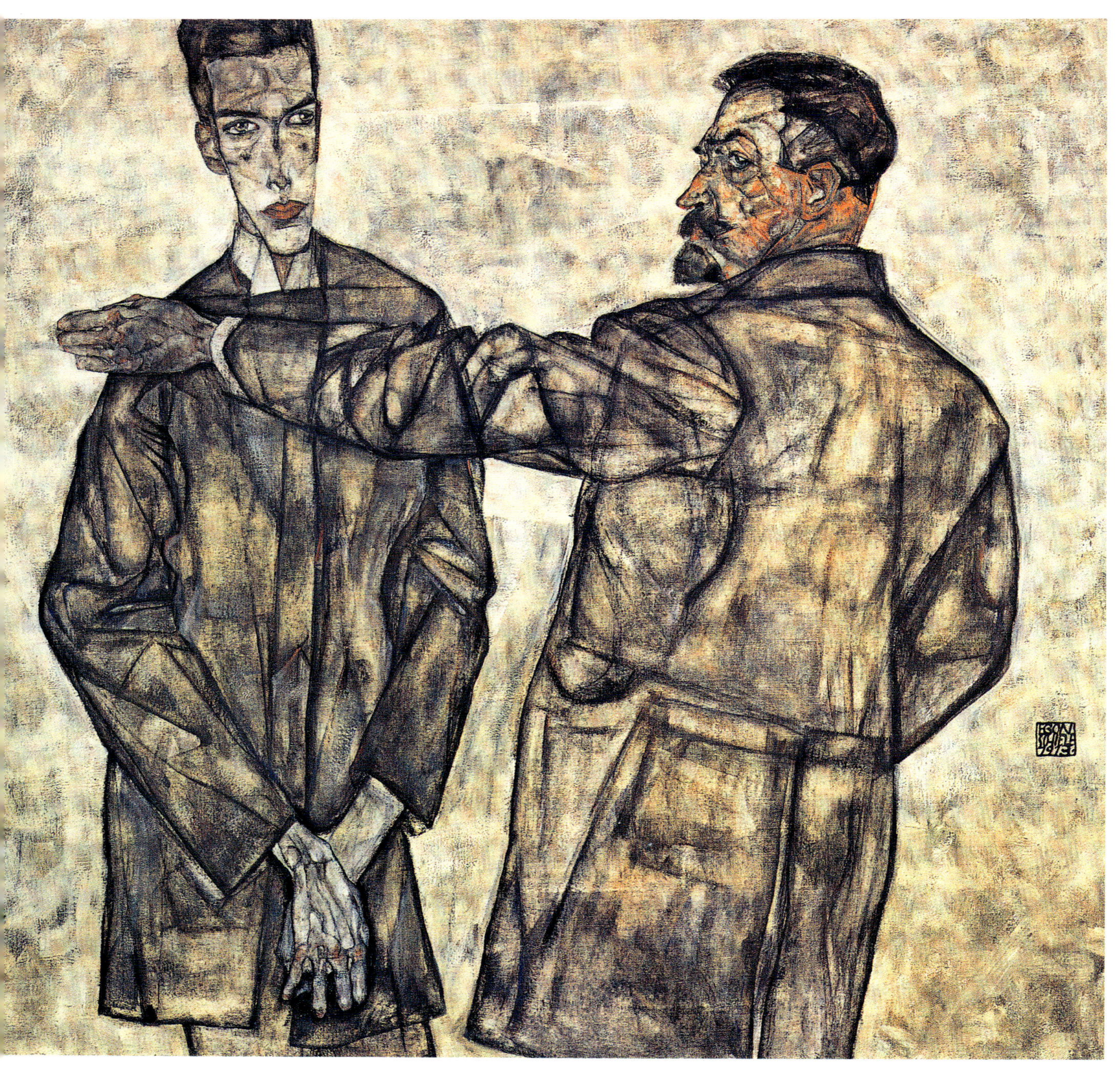

Father and son Schiele's first collectors prove to be faithful companions. This double portrait of Heinrich and Otto Benesch was composed of geometric forms. Typical for Schiele's work, the subjects' skin is unnaturally colored.

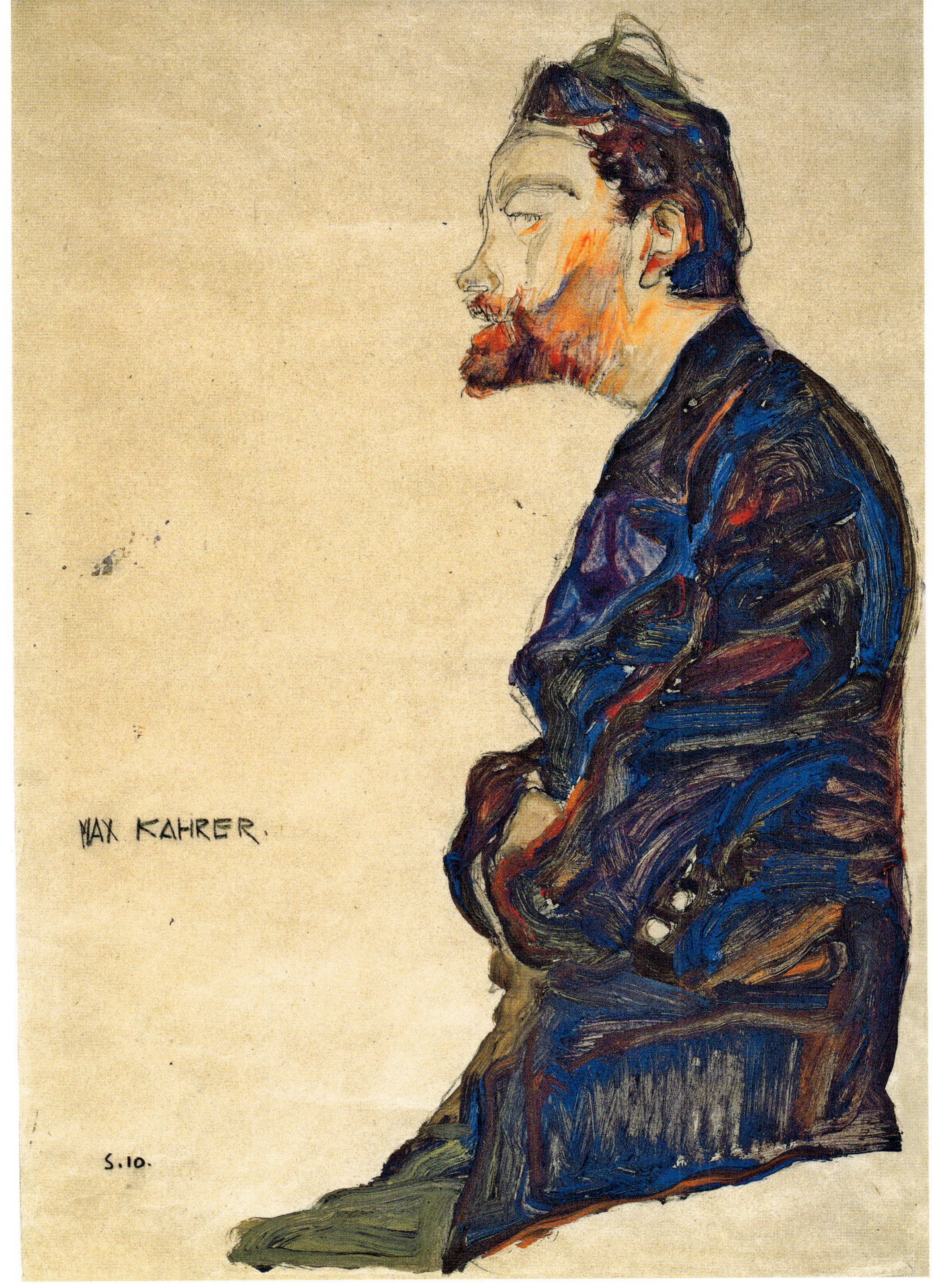

From teacher to model One of Schiele's early Expressionist portraits was of Max Kahrer, his former drawing teacher in Klosterneuburg. Schiele positioned his teacher on the right side of the page, leaving the left side empty.

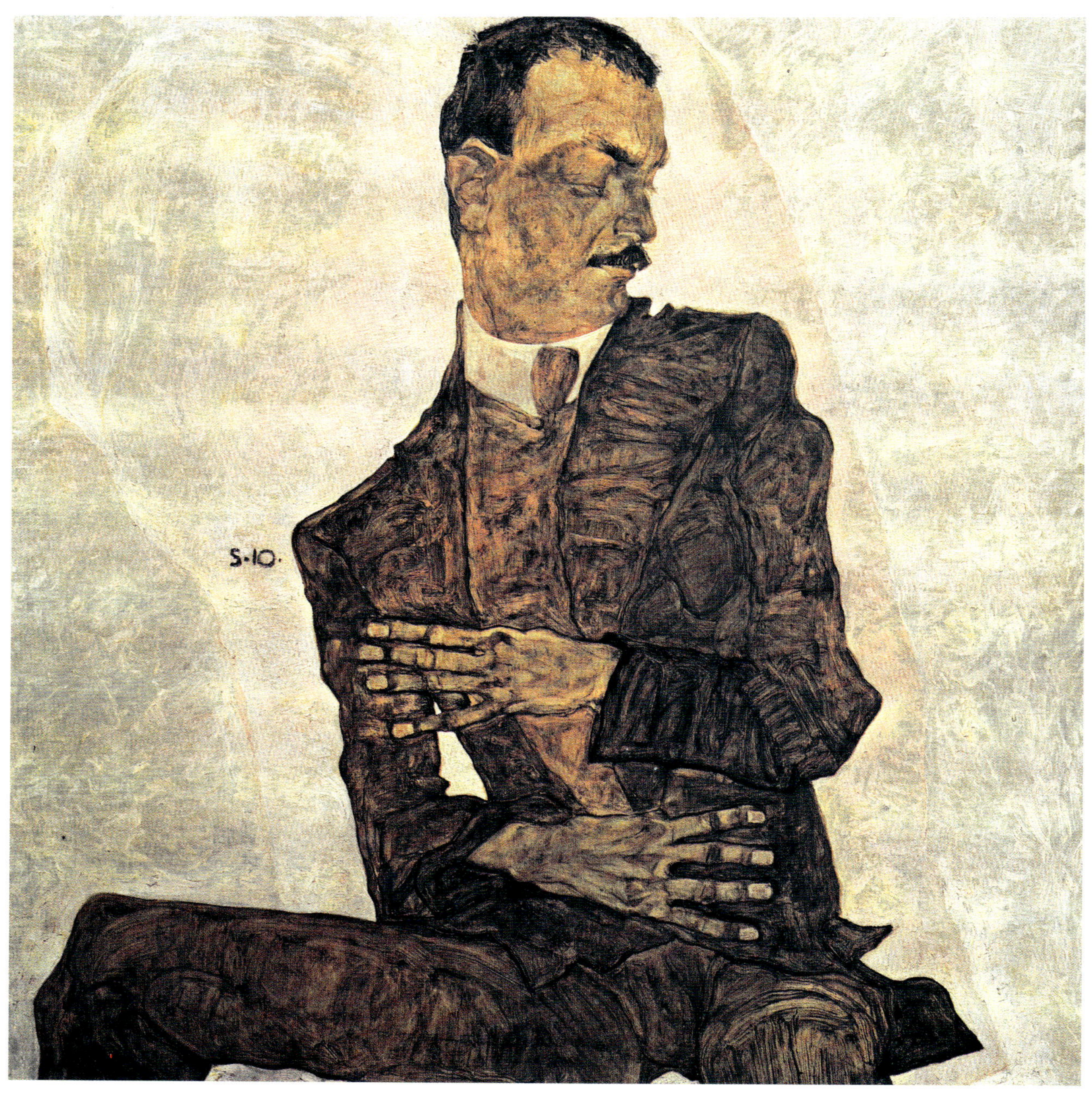

Friend and patron Arthur Roessler also commissioned Schiele to portray him on canvas. As the painter situated him in the frame, he appears withdrawn, bathed in earth colors. The man's large hands, spread across the middle of his body, draw the viewer's attention.

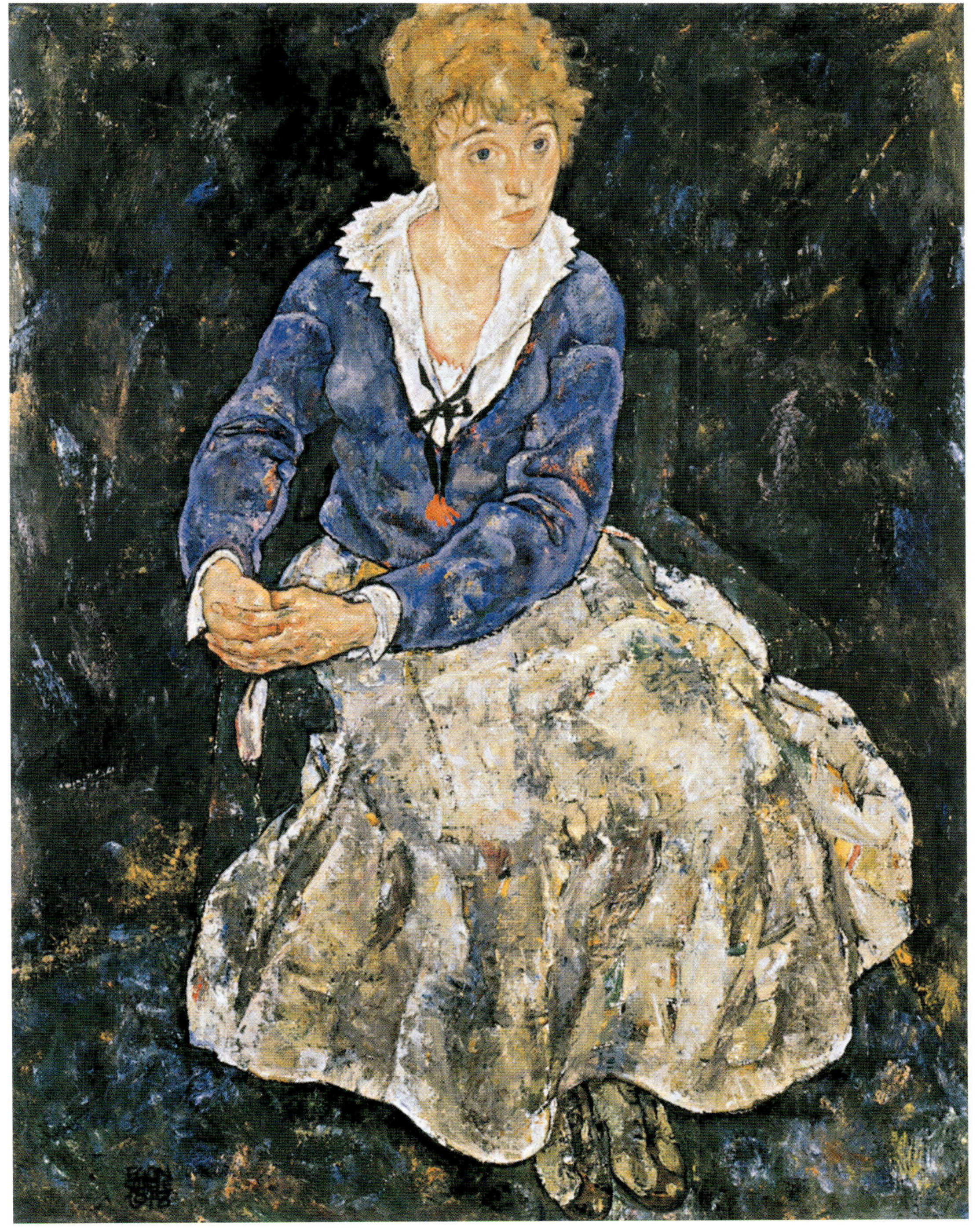

Change of clothes Schiele's wife Edith in an unpretentious skirt. The purchaser had asked for the check pattern in the first version of the painting to be painted over—after all, he was the director of the Belvedere in Vienna. He found the article of clothing too bohemian for a state museum.

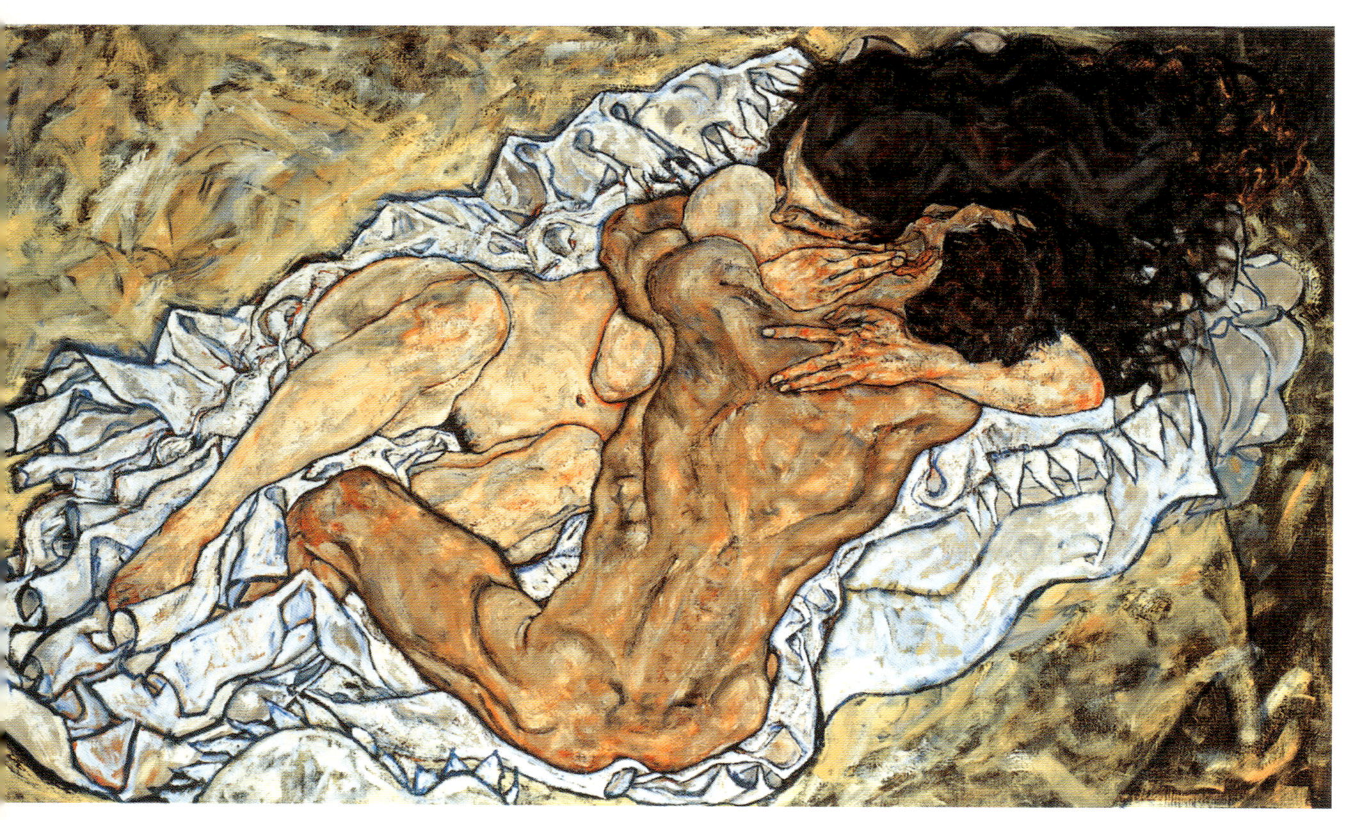

Intimately close In this *Embrace*, Schiele dispenses with the greenish skin tone of his early portraits and nudes. He displayed this work in the large exhibition at the Secession in 1918. Is it Egon and Edith romantically entwined?

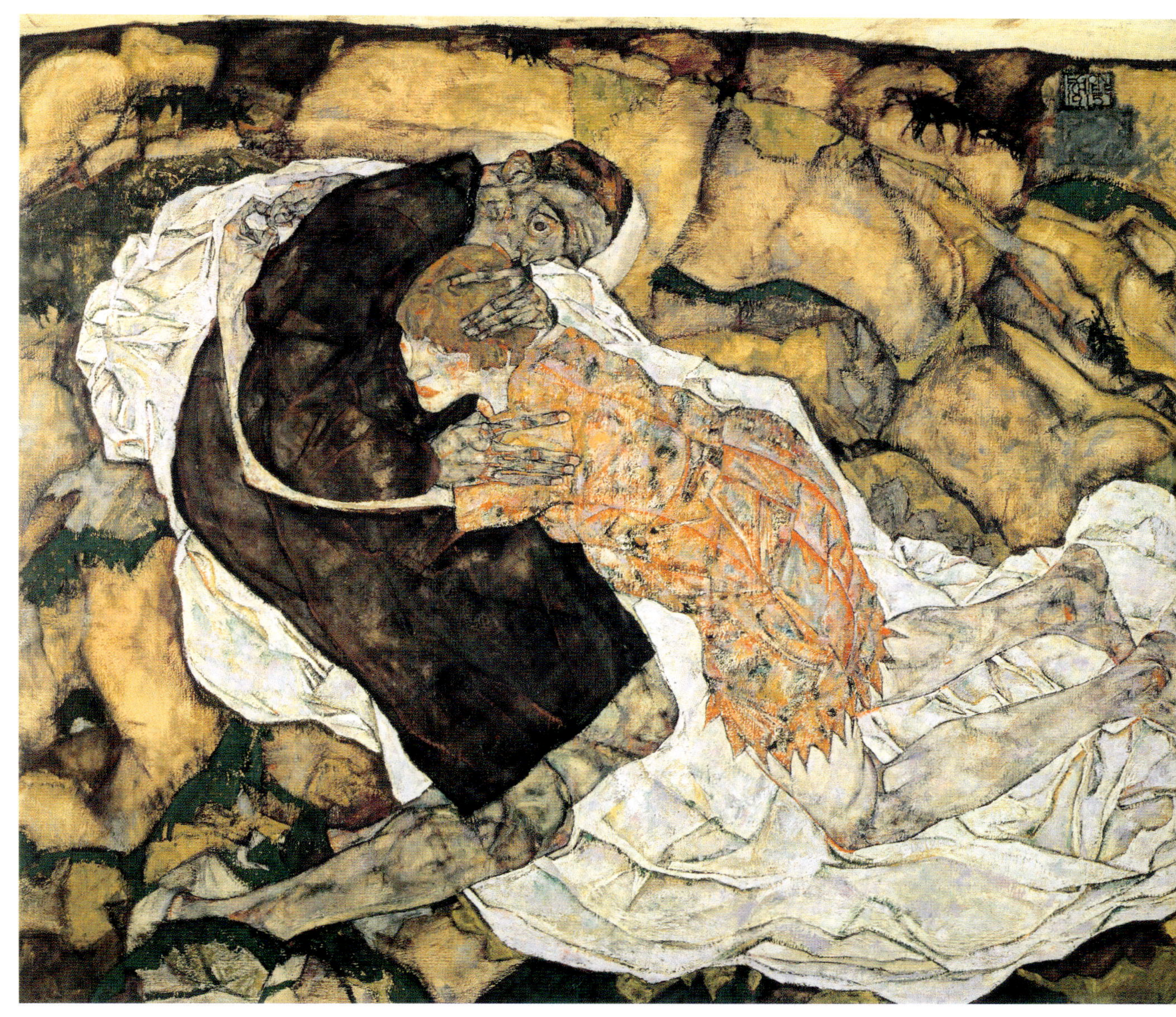

Somber vision Schiele also exhibited this large-format oil painting, *Death and the Maiden,* at the Secession in 1918. The model for the strawberry-blonde girl was probably his mistress Wally Neuzil.

The Art

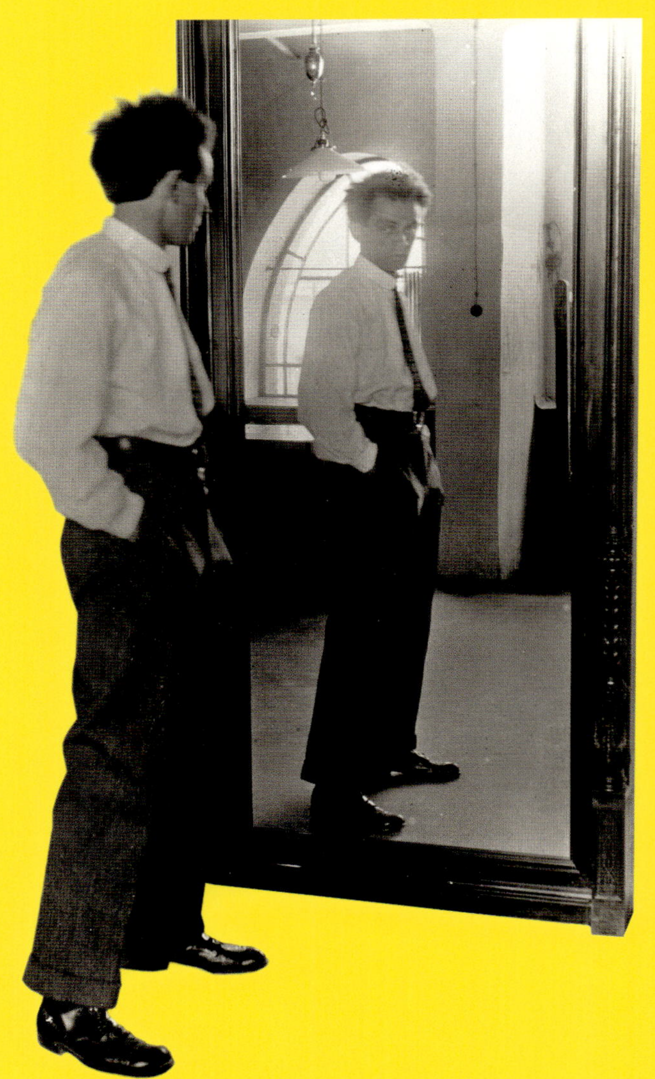

“Art cannot
be modern;
art is timeless.”

Egon Schiele

Opening Up New Horizons

One of Egon Schiele's virtues was diligence: in twelve years of artistic creativity he produced two thousand works on paper—drawings, watercolors, and graphics—and three hundred paintings, as well as a considerable number of poems. A certain degree of vanity on his part is undeniable. Schiele's interests were his art—and his own ego. The young artist left behind some one hundred self-portraits. He was his own favorite subject.

Self-portraits

Schiele was just twenty years old when he "dissected" his own naked body in a series of self-portraits. By doing so he had entered new terrain: not only were male nudes uncommon next to their female counterparts, but until then there was hardly an artist who had thought of combining the self-portrait and the nude. Nor did Schiele shrink from portraying ugliness. He not only depicted individual body parts as abstract forms, but his color choices were often reminiscent of decomposition.

Bold statements

--> are often found in Schiele's letters. In 1911, for example, he wrote to his guardian Leopold: "If the artist loves his art more than anything, he must be able to abandon even his dearest friend."

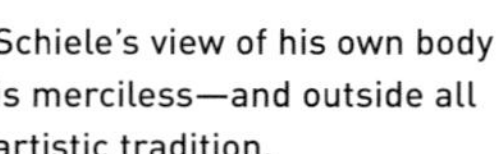

Schiele's view of his own body is merciless—and outside all artistic tradition.

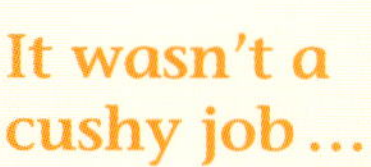

It wasn't a cushy job ...

... Schiele had when he began graphic work on the advice of Arthur Roessler: "In the time it takes me to etch a plate, I can draw fifty to sixty pages, well-done and effortlessly; in fact even more, certainly up to a hundred pages."

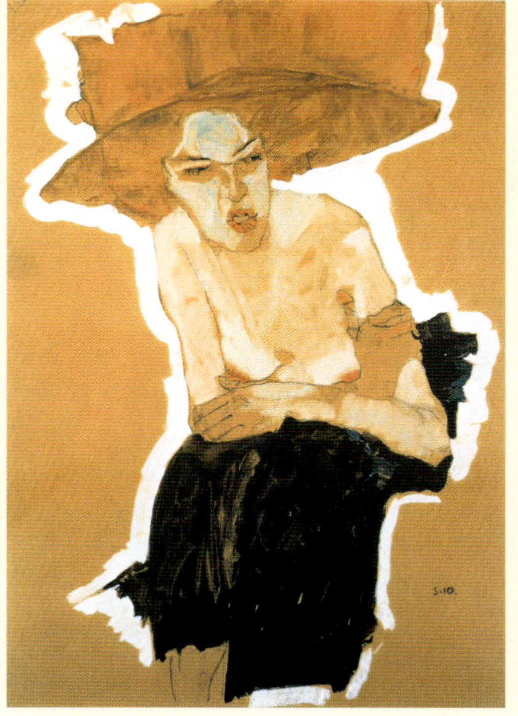

Expressionism

Gustav Klimt provided the impetus for the treatment of themes such as sexuality, illness, and death. Not only Schiele, but also Oskar Kokoschka and numerous other artists took up these motifs. They developed a two-dimensional, intensely colorful style containing a strong psychological and emotional component that became characteristic of this artistic movement. Expressionism influenced not only painting and visual graphics, but also literature. Its importance waned with the end of World War I.

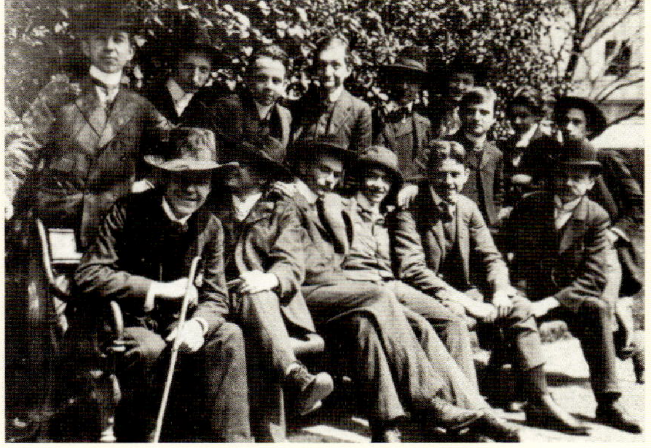

Vienna Academy of Fine Arts

The oldest art academy in Central Europe was distinguished by a rather conservative and traditionalist spirit. At the turn of the century, the Academy was the predominant authority in Austria. The academic curriculum began with classes in anatomy and drawing. Painting students began by drawing from plaster casts of classical statues from the Academy's collection, followed by drawing "from life," i.e., from models. Egon Schiele was not the only one who had problems with the outdated teaching methods. This image shows a photography session in front of the Academy: Egon Schiele is second from the right in the second row, and on his left, Anton Faistauer, his future colleague in the New Artist Group.

Studio or café?

While Schiele retreated to his studio on the outskirts of Vienna to paint, many writers were attracted to the cafés in the center. The works composed there were referred to as "coffeehouse literature." The writer Stefan Zweig, who in his youth preferred to spend the days in Café Griensteidl rather than at school, saw the coffeehouse as "the best educational establishment for everything new." Some of the typical Viennese coffeehouses still exist today.

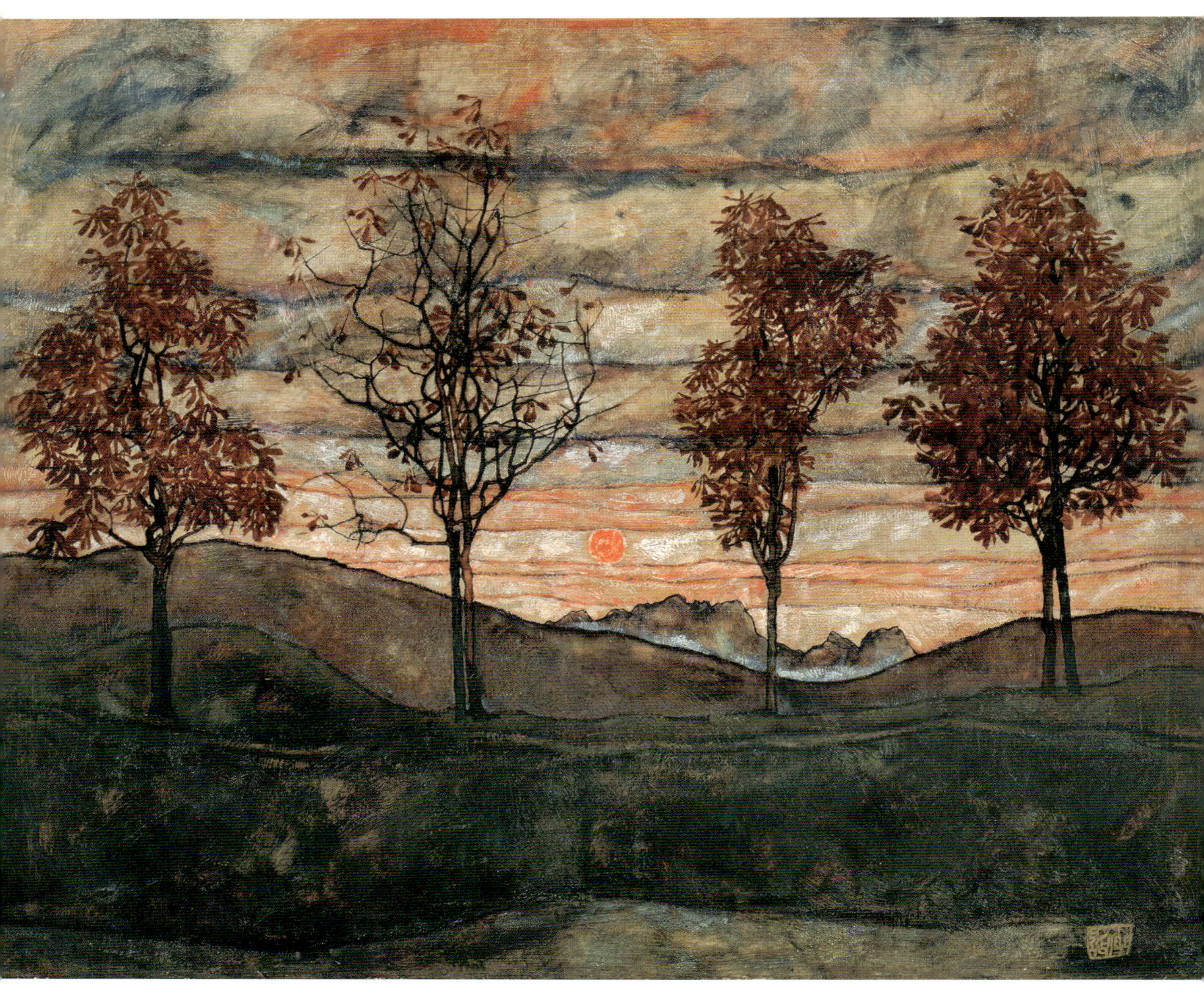

Schiele's landscapes long stood in the shadows of his scandalous nudes—undeservedly, as can be judged from his *Four Trees at Sunset*.

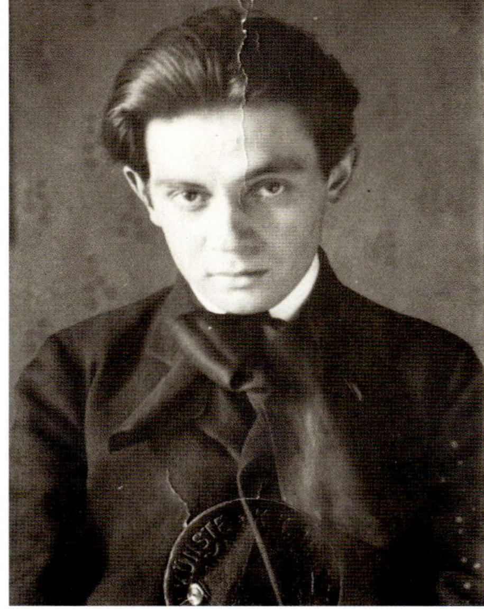

Schiele's photograph from his Academy of Fine Arts student card

Before the Mirror and On the Ladder

Schiele's artistic development was nothing short of spectacular. The staid drawings he was producing when admitted to the Academy in Vienna quickly gave way, with his introduction to the Jugendstil, to an amazingly dynamic visual language. However, his allegiance to the decorative style was short-lived, and he instead began to experiment with bold colors, jagged contour lines, and a radical formal language that gave a strong expressiveness to his works.

A focus on the body

By the time he was twenty, Egon Schiele had already found his own powerful style. He focused on the human figure, isolated, often fragmented, and typically in empty space, depicted with brusque gestures and grotesque facial expressions. Schiele presents his own body in a number of self-portraits—painted, drawn, or in watercolor—as deformed (and at times seemingly horrified because of it). He also worked in landscapes, but as independent motifs rather than as backgrounds.

> **"Since the bloody horror of war broke out over us, many people have probably realized that art is more than a matter of bourgeois luxury."**
>
> **Schiele to Anton Peschka, March 2, 1917**

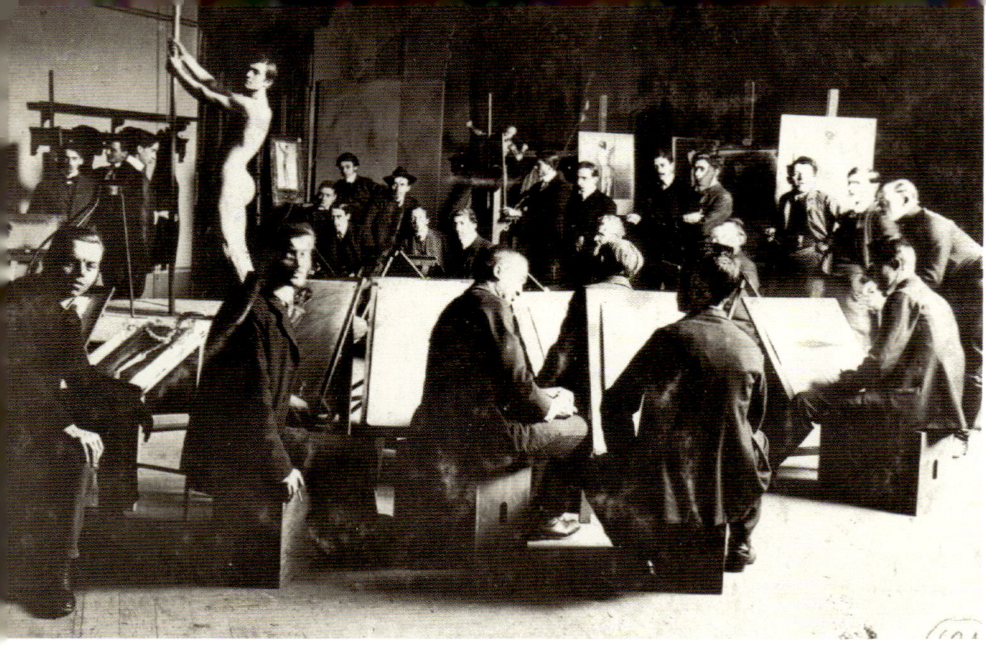

Schiele in life drawing class at the Vienna Academy of Fine Arts. He is standing at the back on the left, next to the man in a hat.

First sketches

Egon Schiele first tried his hand at drawing from a window of his parents' apartment located in the Tulln station building; his early sketches feature trains as the principal motif. But his horizons soon widened when his family moved to Klosterneuburg, and Egon documented his new surroundings on a sketchpad as he wandered through the natural landscape in the shadow of the Vienna Woods. Art teacher Ludwig Karl Strauch fostered the young man's talent and pushed Schiele, who by then had begun to experiment with watercolor, to try his hand at oil painting.

Dusty traditions

Schiele had not yet reached his sixteenth birthday when accepted to the Vienna Academy of Fine Arts. Having achieved brilliant marks on his entrance examination, he entered the class of Professor Christian Griepenkerl. No champion of progressive art movements, Griepenkerl was more interested in keeping to the program, having his students work first from plaster casts and later from models. Indeed it was only because of the life drawing classes that Schiele continued to attend. What he was missing was color—in the first years at the Academy, oil painting was simply not allowed. In Griepenkerl's eye's, Schiele made scant progress, and the professor went so far as to ask his student not to tell anyone with whom he studied!

Enthusiasm for Jugendstil

Nearby the venerable academy was the Secession, the exhibition building of the Viennese Jugendstil artists. For Schiele, who had lost interest in his classes, this was a welcome distraction. He regularly read the Secession magazine, *Ver Sacrum* (Sacred Spring), and in 1907 met its co-founder, Gustav Klimt.

Professor Griepenkerl was not particularly fond of the Jugendstil, and he forbade his students to attend Secession exhibitions—in vain, at least in Schiele's case. An aspiring artist simply couldn't have passed up the chance to contemplate contemporary Austrian

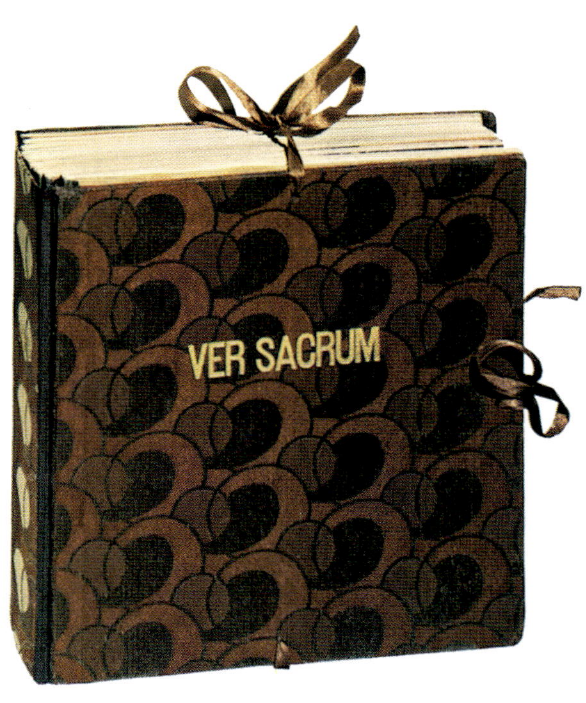

The magazine *Ver Sacrum*—shown here is the first volume in a fabric binding specially designed by the artists—was the mouthpiece of the Viennese Secessionists.

art at the first *Kunstschau* of 1908. With the Jugendstil artists pursuing the elusive *Gesamtkunstwerk*, all the artistic genres (architecture, sculpture, painting, crafts) were represented at the exhibition.

Gustav Klimt's works, displayed in a single room devoted exclusively to him, attracted a great deal of attention. The work for which he is probably best known today, the golden shimmering *The Kiss*, was present. And Schiele was enthralled. But he was not so easily convinced by the Jugendstil idea of the *Gesamtkunstwerk*. In 1910, he expressed his hopes for a next *Kunstschau* comprised only of painting and sculpture: "Each artist has his own room—Rodin, Van Gogh, Gauguin, Minne ... Only the visual arts."

New Artists together

After Schiele's forays into the world of the Secession, once again dutifully committing himself to his studies proved difficult. And he was not alone. In 1909, a small group of students plucked up the courage to criticize the academy's outdated methods, and were immediately threatened with expulsion from its sacred halls. Schiele was ahead of the game; after three years of study he abandoned his academy training. Thus Schiele, along with painter colleagues Anton Faistauer and Anton Peschka (his fut brother-in-law), his schoolmate, the musician Arthur Löwenstein, and others founded the Neukunstgruppe (New Art Group). From then on, Schiele would have complete artistic freedom.

The nineteen-year-old Schiele suddenly found himself on his own, both artistically and financially. And he had an auspicious beginning: his first year after leaving the academy he completed six large oil portraits, five of which were commissioned works, including the portrait of his collector Arthur Roessler.

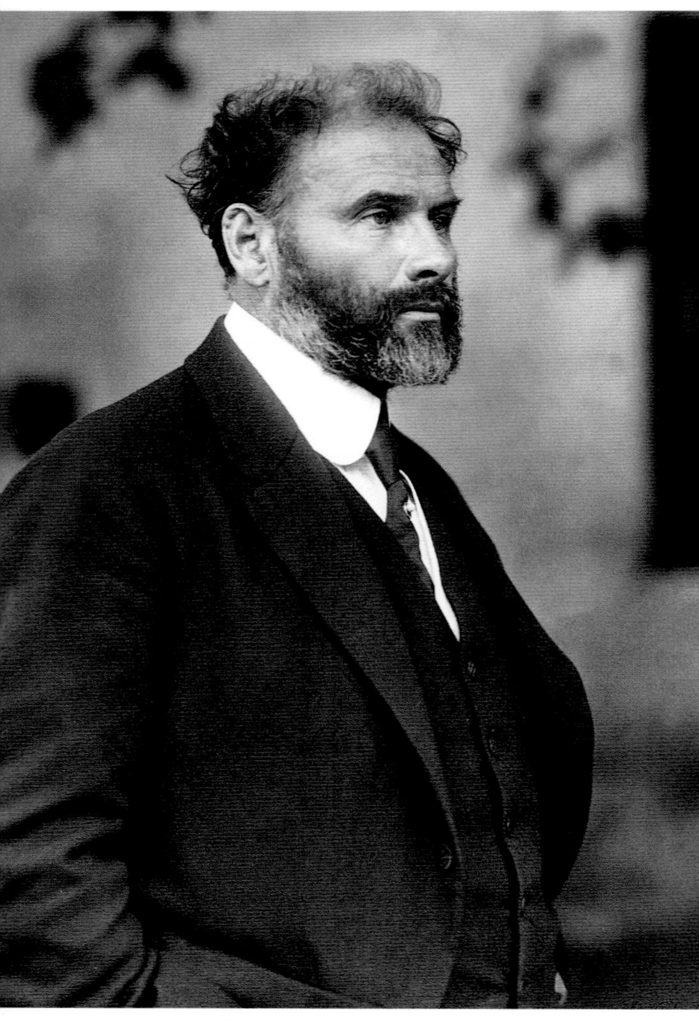

One of the lodestars of Viennese Modernism: Gustav Klimt

Borrowing from a role model

For his portraits, Schiele at first adopted design principles from the great Viennese portraitist Gustav Klimt. Klimt's depictions of beautiful women clad in shimmering robes were all the rage in the metropolis on the banks of the Danube.

Schiele approached his portraits much like the painter thirty years his senior, by constructing images out of contrasts: he situated the figure—rendered in a style ranging from realistic to idealized—against a background built up from pure ornament. He also adopted Klimt's use of brilliant colors and shiny gold, which can be seen in Schiele's painting of the classical figure of the king's daughter Danaë, asleep in front of an opulently designed background.

Soon, however, Schiele developed his own approach and turned to new themes for his images. He would quickly abandon the elaboration of the surface, and his color palette strayed at times from naturalistic tones. The pace of his development was unheard of. Thematically, he remained unbound to any time, and produced paintings and watercolors of landscapes, nudes, and allegorical depictions, in addition to countless portraits and self-portraits. Schiele's drawings, executed mostly in pencil and chalk, less often in charcoal or ink, were early evidence of his preference for bold contours. Rather than studies for paintings, they were for the most part independent works of art. This was immediately evident to collectors, who from a very early stage appreciated his works on paper, which, in addition to his portraiture, proved to be an important source of income for Schiele.

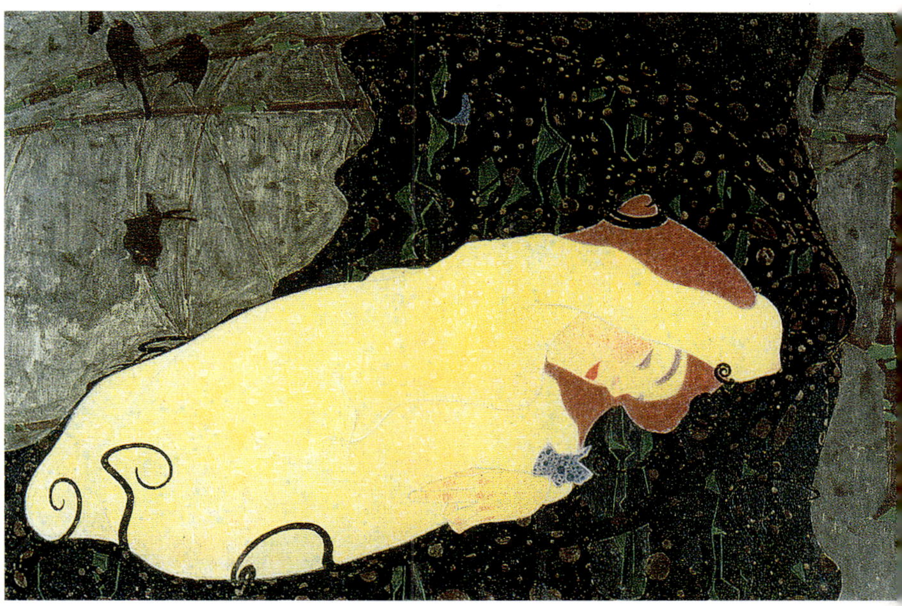

Shades of Klimt: Schiele's *Danaë* slumbers on glittering ornaments.

Stubbornly going his own way

Though many of his oil paintings were perceived as unsellable, Schiele clung to the notion that his patrons (and not only they) should unconditionally support him. When he began in 1912 to explore an allegorical depth in his paintings, the resulting works proved difficult for even Schiele's most faithful collectors. Even Schiele believed that his portrayals of biblical figures were of value only to him. Controversial motifs aside, the oftentimes monumental dimensions of his allegorical paintings hindered sales. The oil painting *Hermits,* for example, measures a mighty 180 x 180 cm —a space shared by two men dressed in black monks' habits. Gustav Klimt is one of the hermits, and leans with closed eyes against the shoulder of the younger one, bearing Schiele's own features. Though they couldn't sell, Schiele was undeterred from pursuing allegorical themes; in spite of being labor intensive and costly in terms of materials and models' fees, they took up an increasing amount of his creative energy. Of course, submitting to the tastes of his clients would hardly have been consistent with Schiele's firm principle of complete artistic freedom.

Uncommon perspectives

By painting landscapes, Schiele saved the money he normally spent on models. For a long time overshadowed by his scandalous nudes, landscapes represent approximately a third of his artistic output; between 1905 and 1907 alone he painted seventy-one separate works. Yet Schiele's faithful reproduction of what called his attention was short-lived: when he parted ways with the Jugendstil, he left the idyllic cityscapes behind him. The cities depicted by Schiele grew deserted; decay and loneliness found their way into the gloomy panoramas. The works depicting the Bohemian town Krumau (today Český Krumlov), the oft-visited birthplace of his mother, illustrate this stage in his development. Until the end of his life, Schiele would devotedly return to the motifs he developed there, often composing his paintings from sketches of previous years.

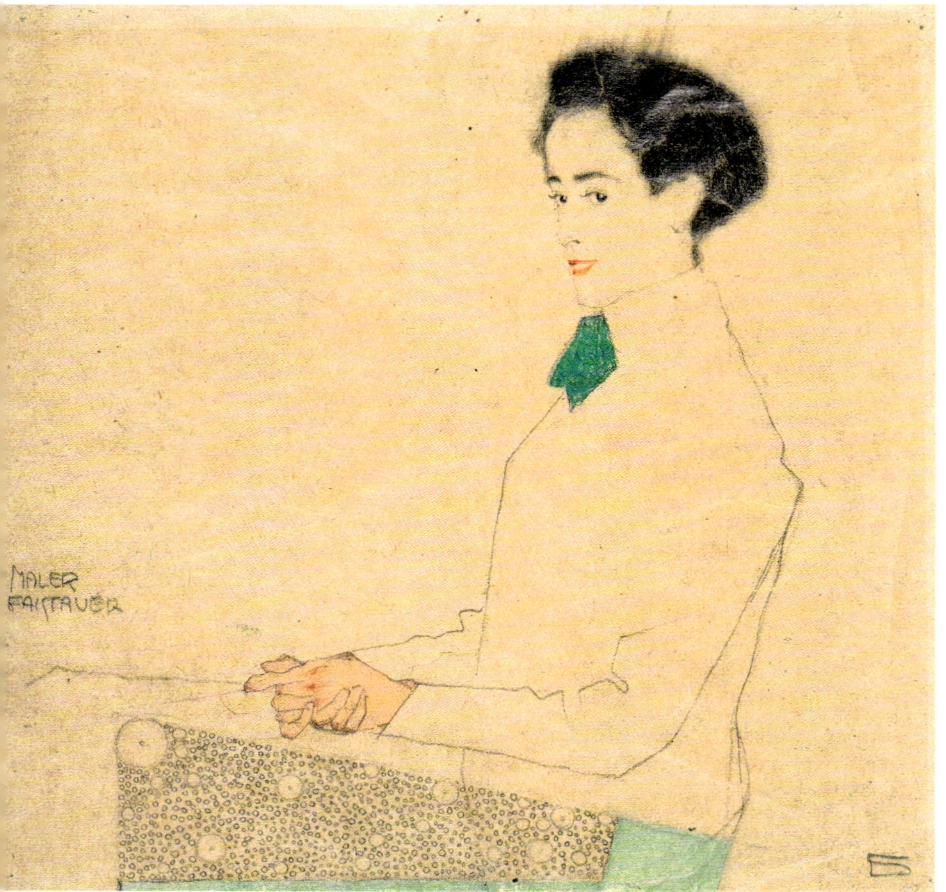

In 1909, Egon Schiele portrayed the members of the New Art Group. In contrast to Klimt's paintings, in this drawing of the painter Anton Faistauer Schiele left the background plain.

Schiele's land- and cityscapes grew increasingly reminiscent of his distorted figures. Hopelessness and emptiness dominated his works. Just as he let his figures "hang" on the surface (often scaling a ladder to find the right view of his studio models), Schiele seems to have obfuscated the source of spatial perception in his cityscapes. Sketching Krumau from the Schlossberg, he often combined different perspectives on one page that, even after careful observation, fail to reveal a precise spatial layout.

Poetry and painting

The eternal cycle of life, birth, and death were important themes in Schiele's work. Decline and illness held great significance for him, and not merely in his paintings. In his poems, Schiele, who lost his father in his youth, devoted a great deal of space to the themes of transience and death. "All is living dead," are the last lines of his 1910 poem "Tannenwald" (Fir Forest). Schiele's Expressionist lyricism was marked by an inventive use of language. The poem "Gewitteranzug" (Approaching Storm), for example, reveals Schiele's pleasure in neologisms: "Black mourning-weather-clouds rolled high over-everywhere—warning water-woods. Murmuring huts and humming-trees."

Schiele loved to tinker with such newly coined words. In the poem "Unter dem weissen Himmel" (Under the

An echo of the *Hermits* (see p. 51): *Two Men with Halos* is a postcard designed by Schiele for the Wiener Werkstätte but never printed.

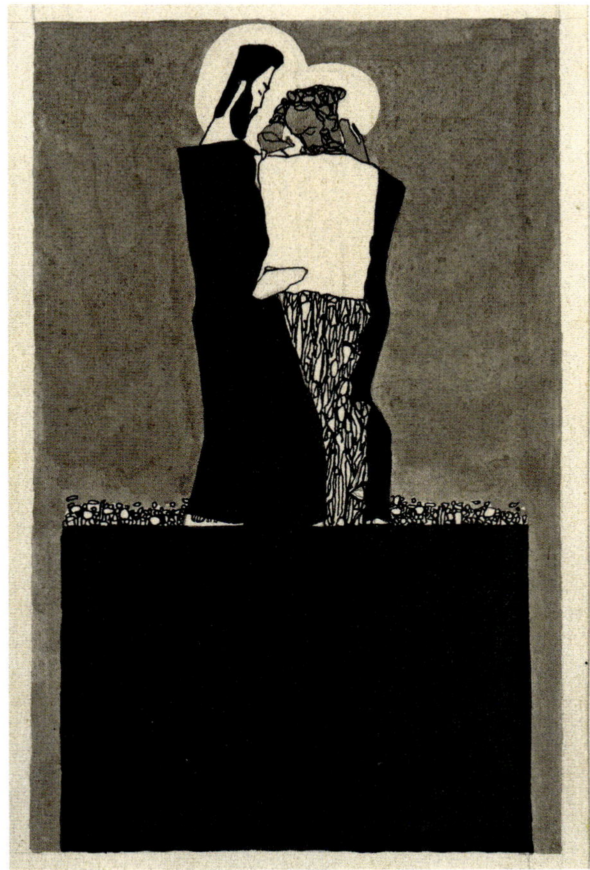

White Sky), Schiele describes a "wind-winter-land," where one finds the "black city, which has remained forever the same, where the stay-at-home peasants walk as always."

VISIONEN·

ALLES WAR MIR LIEB, ICH WOLLTE DIE
ZORNIGEN MENSCHEN LIEB ANSEHN DAMIT
IHRE AVGEN GEGENTVN MVSSEN VND
DIE NEIDIGEN WOLLT' ICH BESCHENKEN
VND IHNEN SAGEN DASS ICH WERTLOS BIN.
– ICH HÖRTE WEICHE WVLSTWINDE
DVRCH LINIEN VON LVFTEN STREICHEN; –
VND DAS MADCHEN DAS MIT KLAGENDER
STIMME VORLAS, VND DIE KINDER DIE
MICH GROSS ANSCHAVTEN VND MEINEN
GEGENBLICK DVRCH KOSEN ENTGEGNETEN,
VND DIE FERNEN WOLKEN SCHAVTEN MIT
GVTEN FALTENAVGEN AVF MICH. —
DIE WEISSEN BLEICHEN MADCHEN ZEIGTEN MIR
IHREN SCHWARZEN FVSS VND DAS ROTE
STRVMPFBAND VND SPRACHEN MIT DEN
SCHWARZEN FINGERN. – ICH ABER DACHTE
AN DIE WEITEN WELTEN, AN FINGERBLVMEN
VND NASSE MORGEN. OB ICH SELBST DA BIN
HATT' ICH KAVM GEWVSST. – ICH SAH DEN
PARK GELBGRÜN, BLAVGRÜN, ROTGRÜN,
ZITTERGRÜN, SONNIGGRÜN, VIOLETTGRÜN
VND HORCHTE DER BLÜHENDEN
ORANGEBLVMEN. – DANN BAND ICH MICH
AN DIE OVALE PARKMAVER VND HORCHTE
DER DÜNNFÜSSIGEN KINDER, DIE BLAVGETVPFT

"But I was thinking of the wide worlds, of fingerflowers and wet mornings"—Schiele got lyrical in his poem "Visionen" (Visions).

Schiele was equally innovative with sentence structure. Sentence snippets and loose sequences of words are punctuated by dashes. The desire to make visible his experiences took precedence over outer form. In this, Schiele was similar to the Expressionists, in both his poetry and his visual art. His prose poems succeed in conveying moods—mostly gloomy—in few words.

Arthur Roessler, Schiele's committed patron, sent the artist's poems to the Berlin magazine *Die Aktion*, the mouthpiece of Expressionist poetry and art. Until 1916, Schiele's work would appear repeatedly in the magazine, which even dedicated a special issue to him.

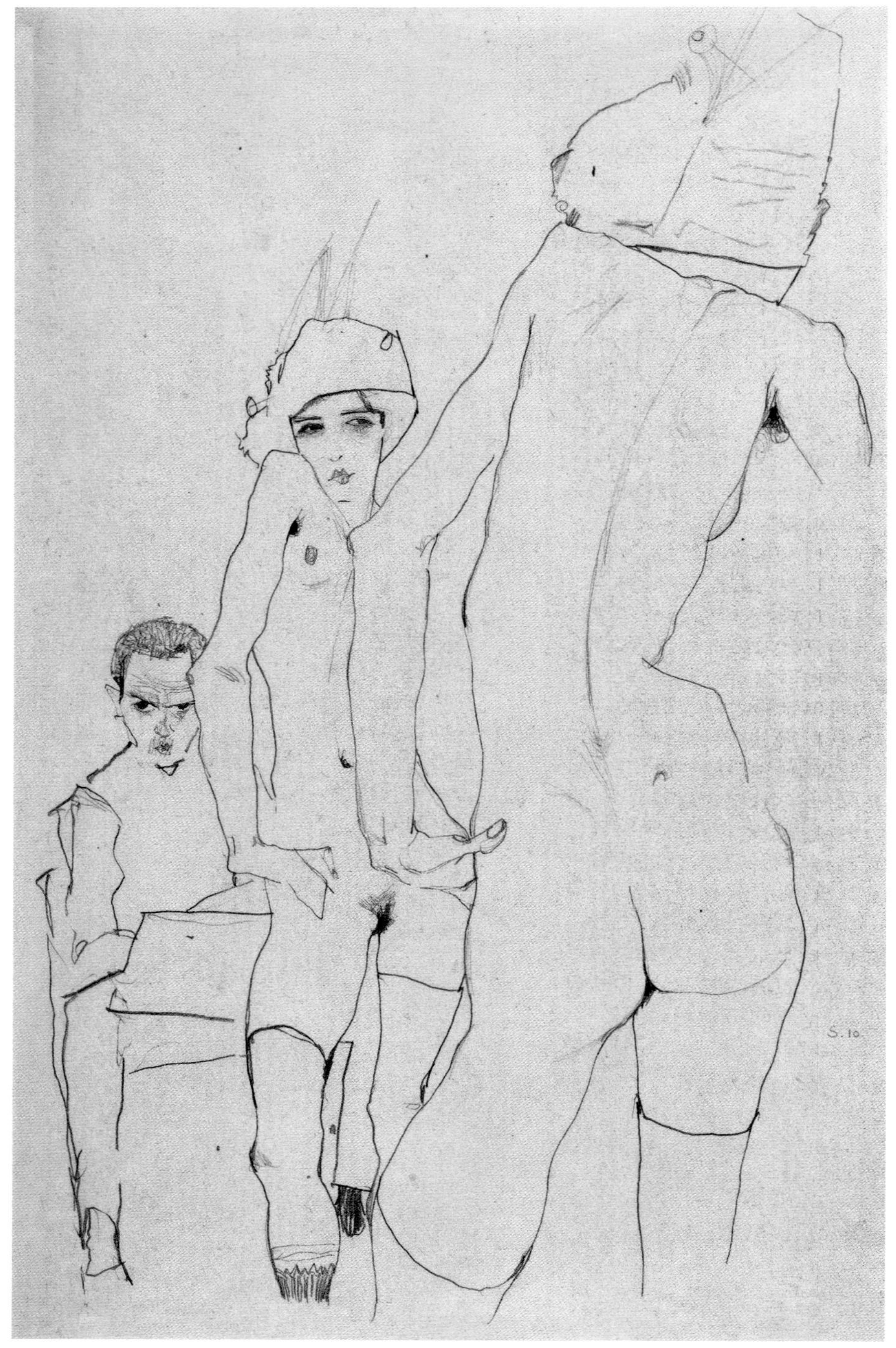

Reflection Egon Schiele often employed mirrors in his work. In this 1910 pencil drawing, Schiele sketches one of his nude models as he sits behind her.

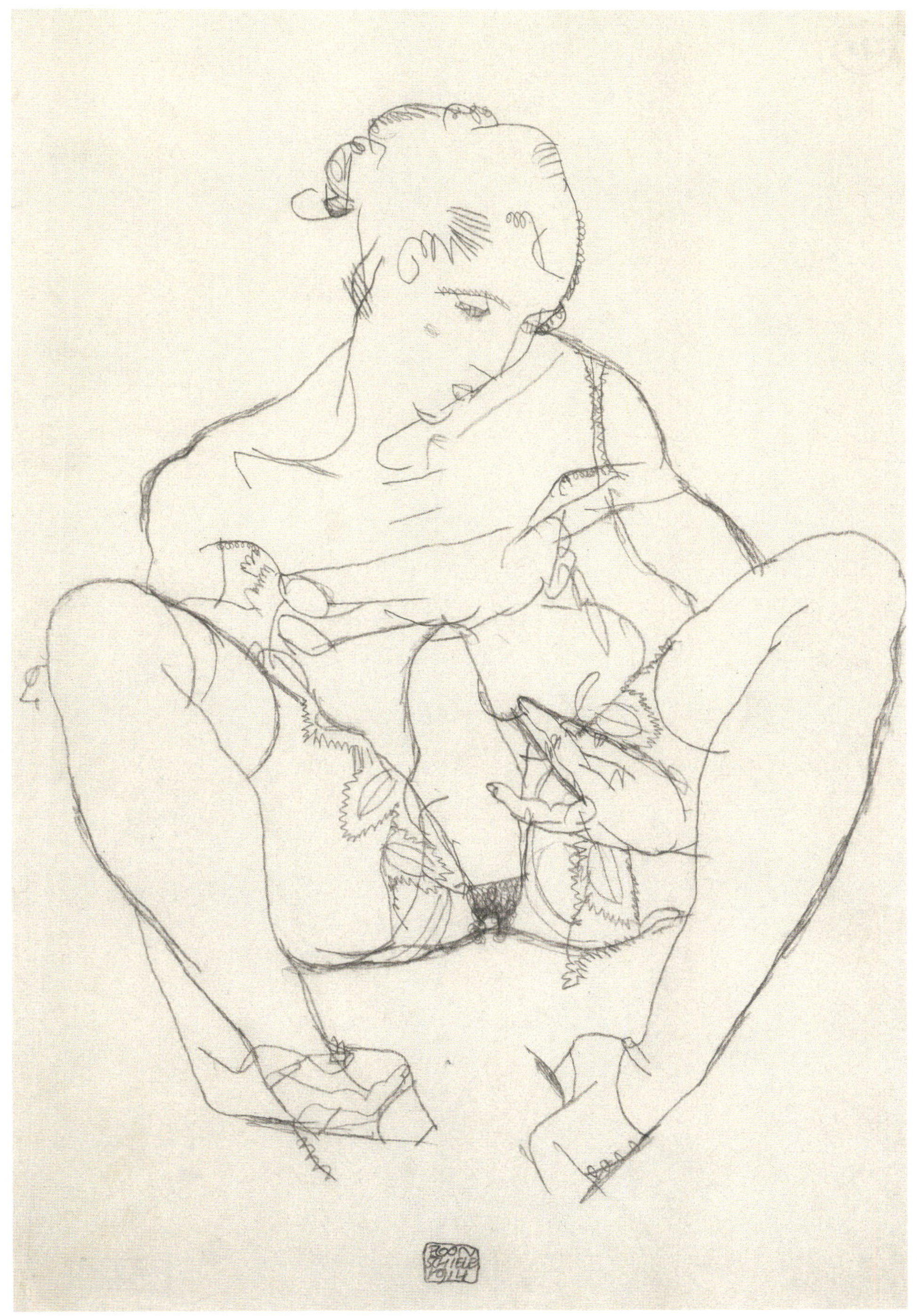

Subjective view Schiele depicted this young woman as if there were no more space on the page for the tips of her shoes. In fact, he showed only as much of a figure that interested him; everything else either falls away or is left unresolved.

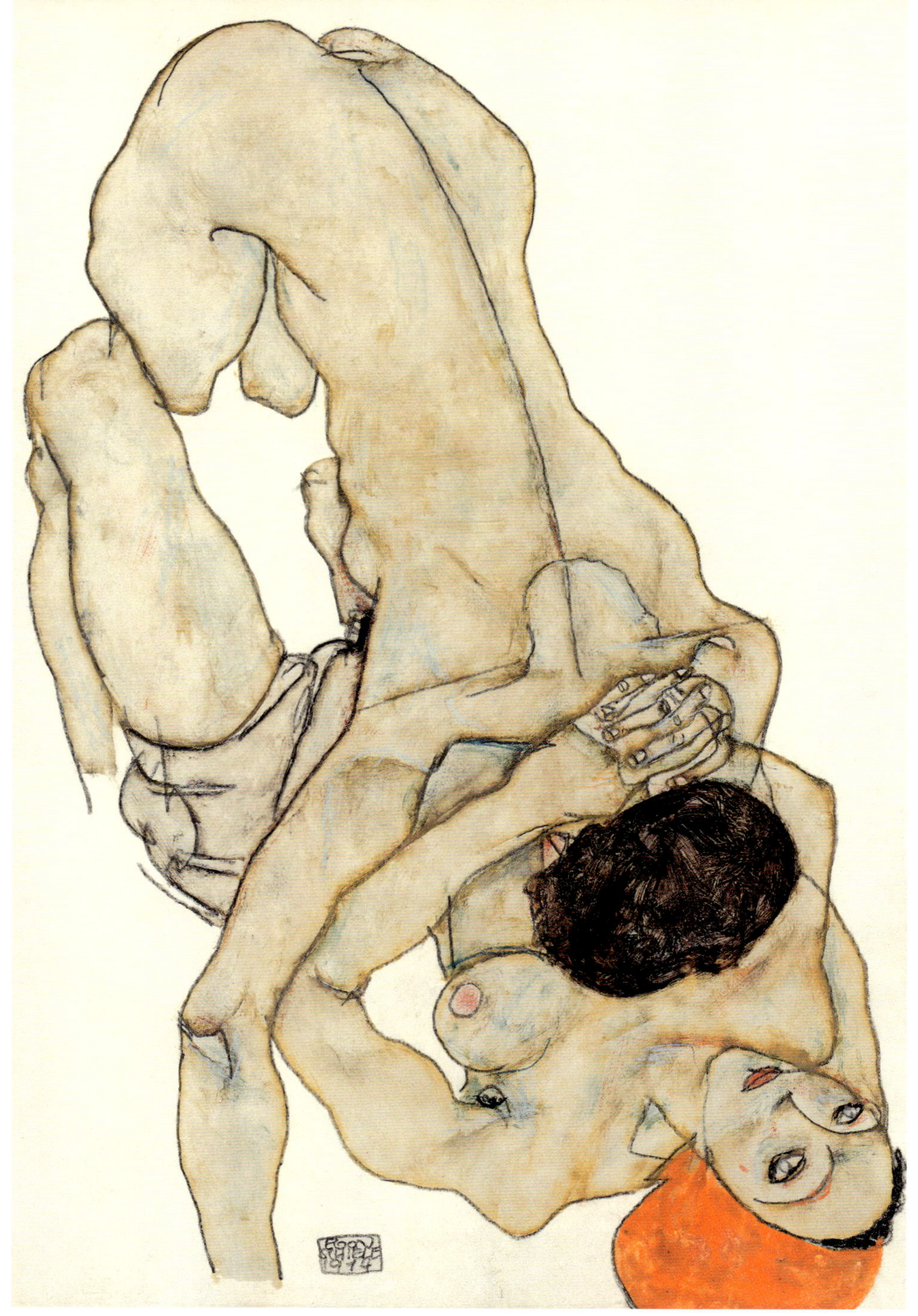

Scandal! Same-sex relationships were taboo in turn-of-the-century Vienna. Schiele didn't seem too worried. His *Lesbian Couple* was but one of many depictions of this theme. Again, Schiele included on the page only what was important to him, failing to even suggest the remaining body parts.

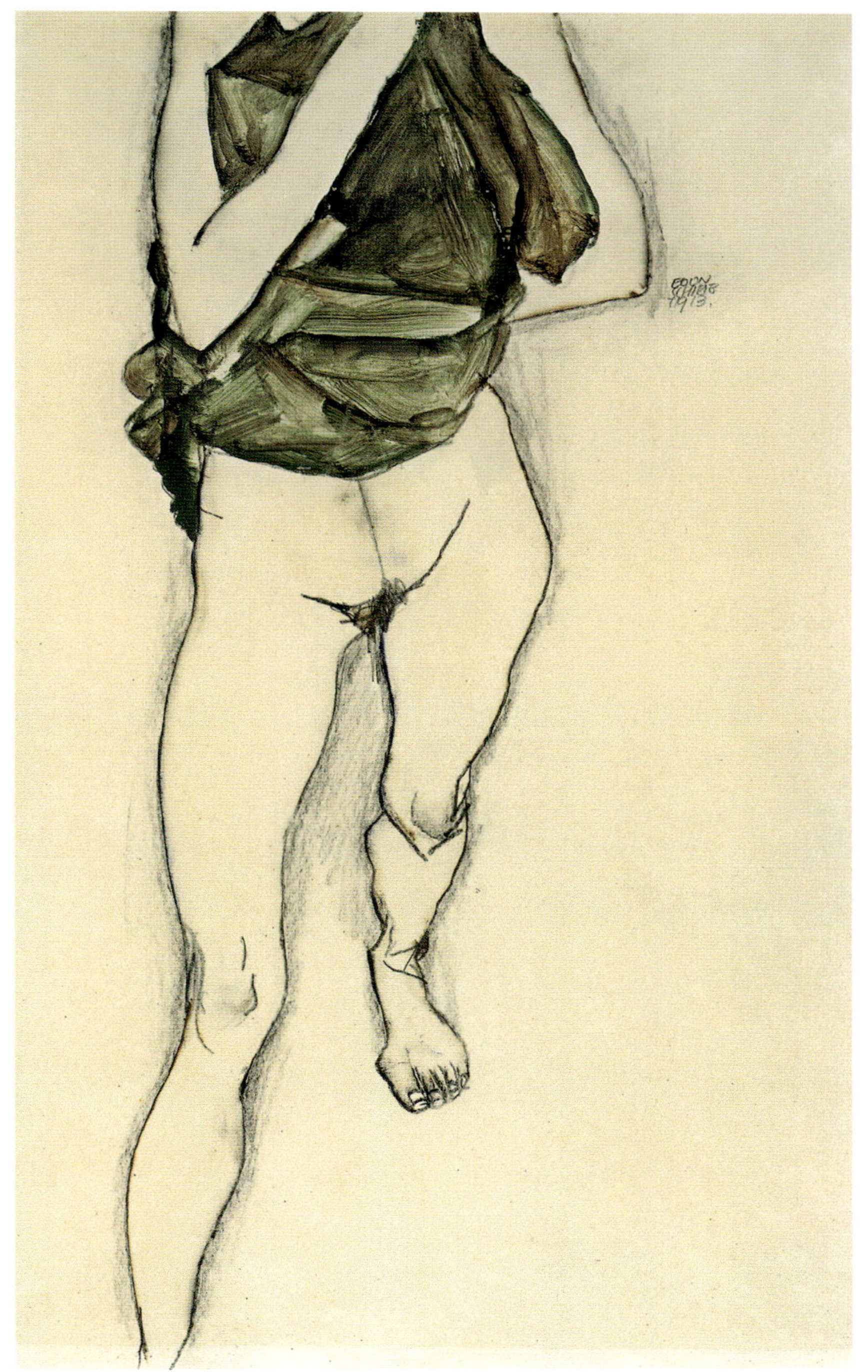

Unusual detail On this page, Schiele depicts only the legs, abdomen, and arms. Apart from the green of the raised shirt, Schiele used no color, sketching the body solely of lines in gouache.

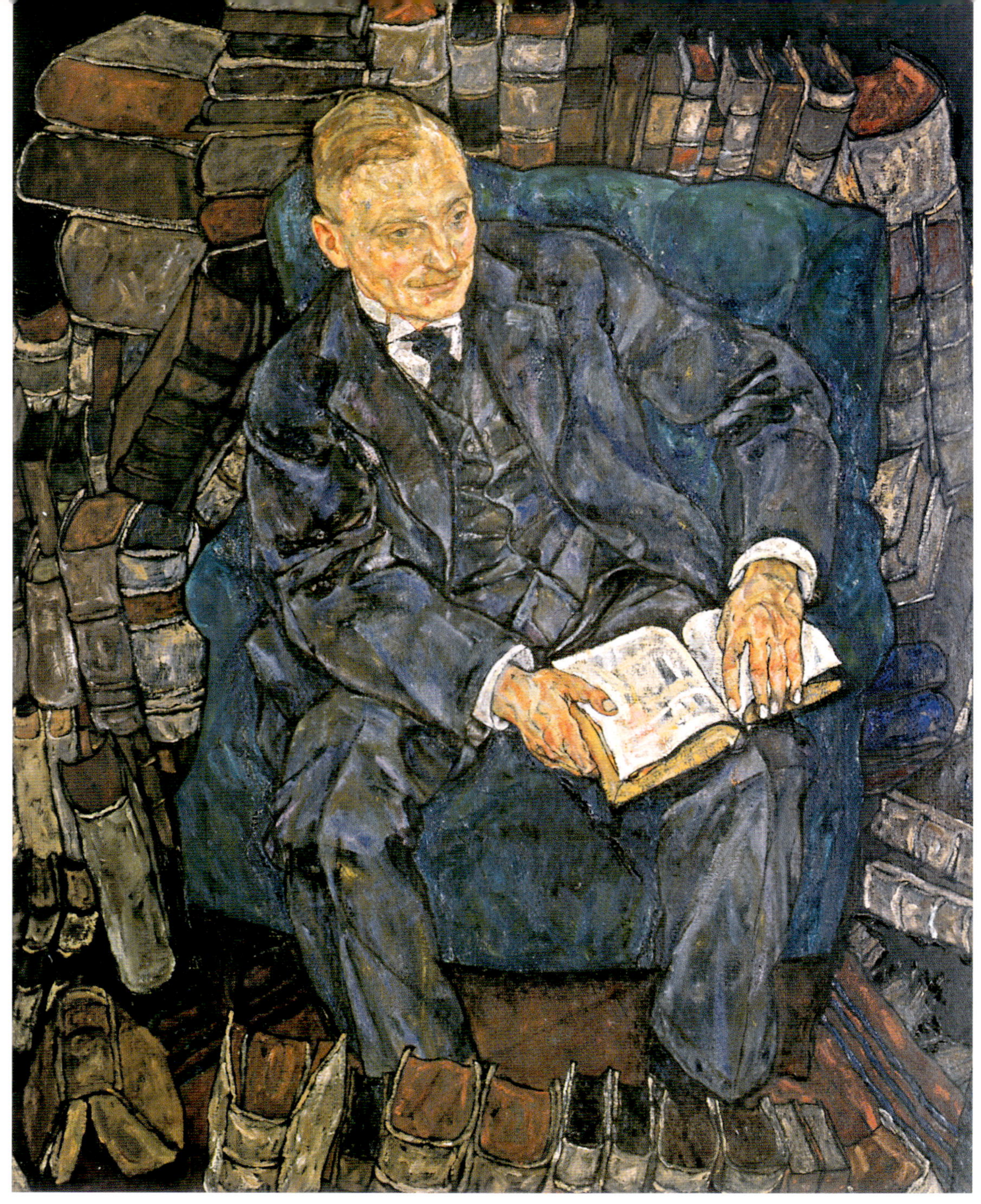

A confirmed collector Dr. Hugo Koller, sitting here between impressive stacks of books, was an art-loving businessman who owned an extensive library. Schiele thus depicted him among his literary treasures. Only seldom had the artist devoted so much attention to the rendering of the room as in this oil painting. It is one of Schiele's last portraits, executed only a few months before his premature death.

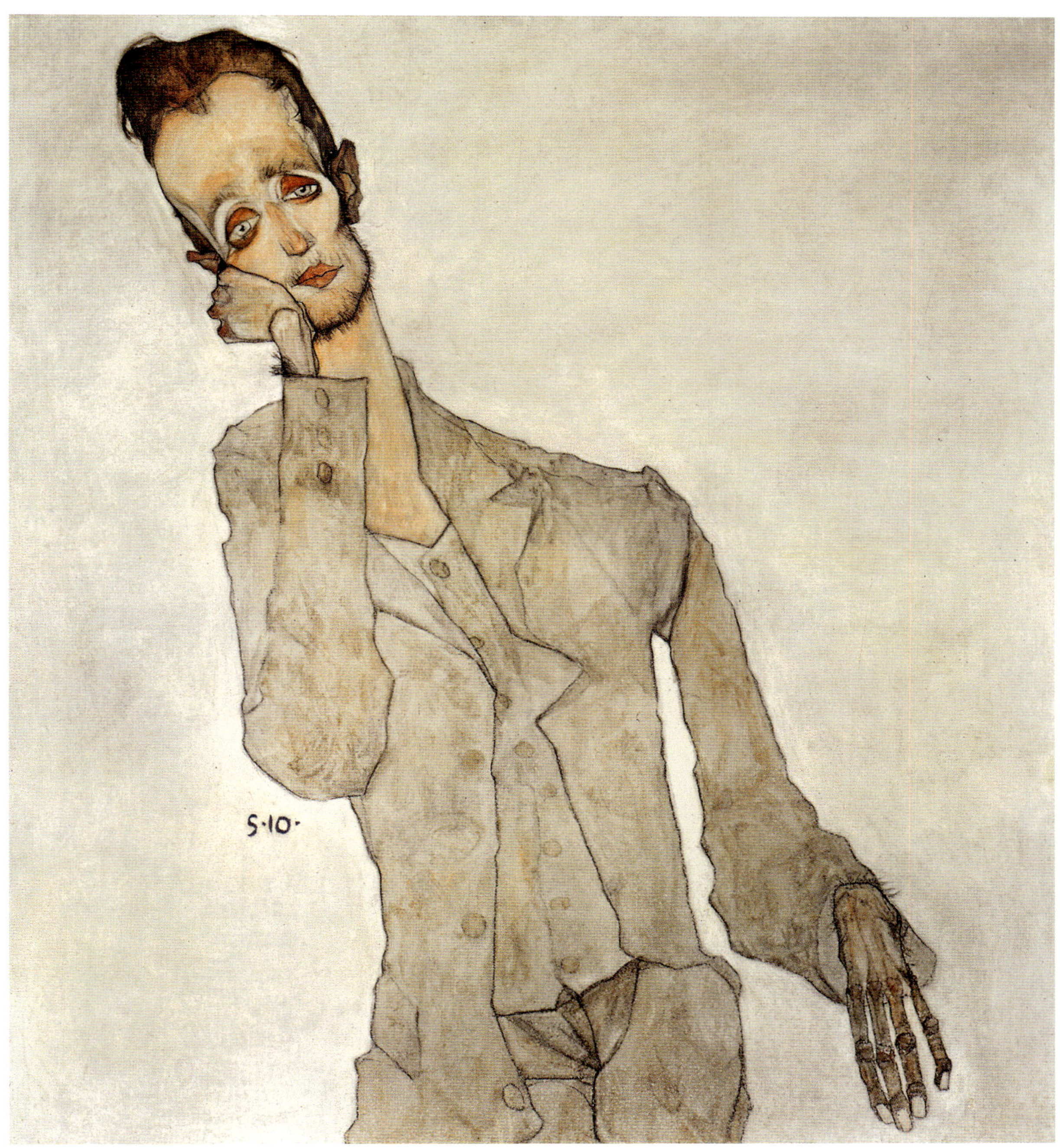

Gazing into space Karl Zakovsek, a fellow student of Schiele's at the Academy, was among the founding members of the New Art Group, and showed his work at the first exhibition at the Pisko Gallery. Unlucky in his art career, he was forced to earn a living as an art teacher. Schiele's portrait revealed the unembellished truth: an emaciated, unshaven fellow-artist without a shirt under his wrinkled suit.

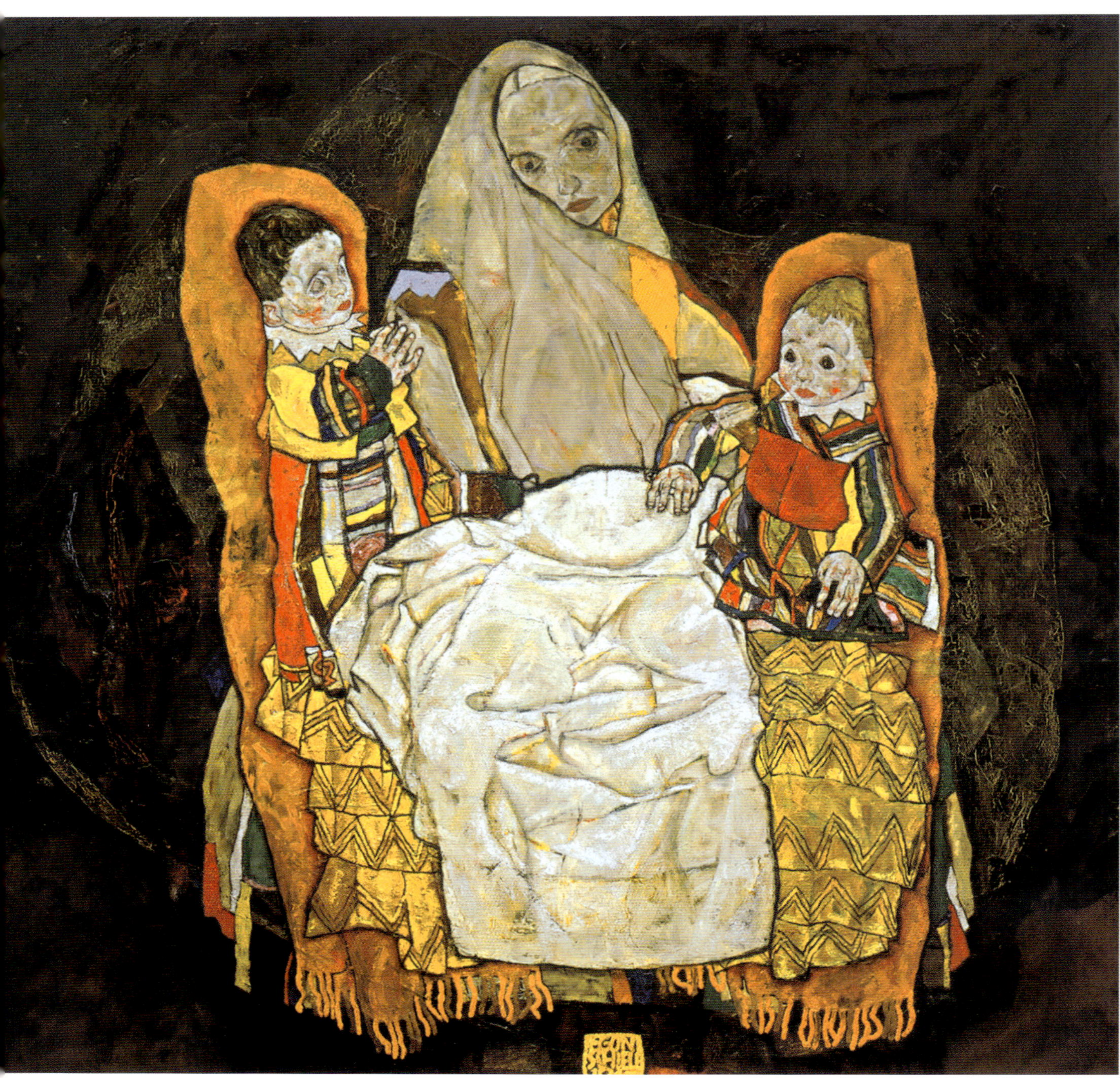

Life and death Both mother and children are deathly pale, an example of the proximity of life and death in Schiele's work. This is explained not only by the context of World War I, through which Schiele lived, but also by his family history: as a child and young man, Schiele experienced the deaths of a sister and his father, respectively.

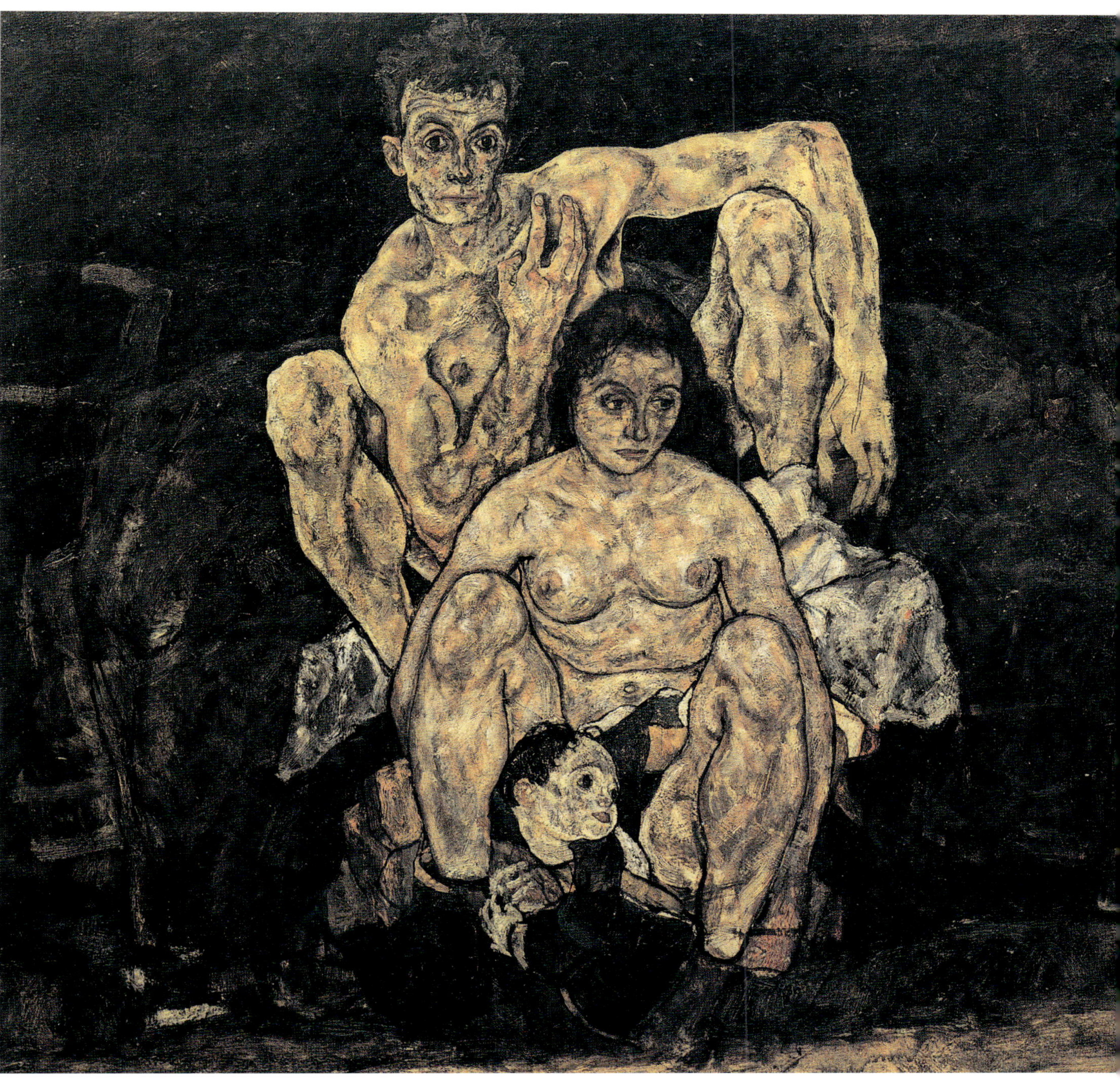

Family *Squatting Couple* was Schiele's title for this somber oil painting when he exhibited it in 1918. Only later was it renamed *The Family* and understood as a self-portrait. The man does in fact have Schiele's features. The woman depicted, however, is not his wife Edith, and the little boy between her legs was added later—a bouquet of flowers had previously occupied the space.

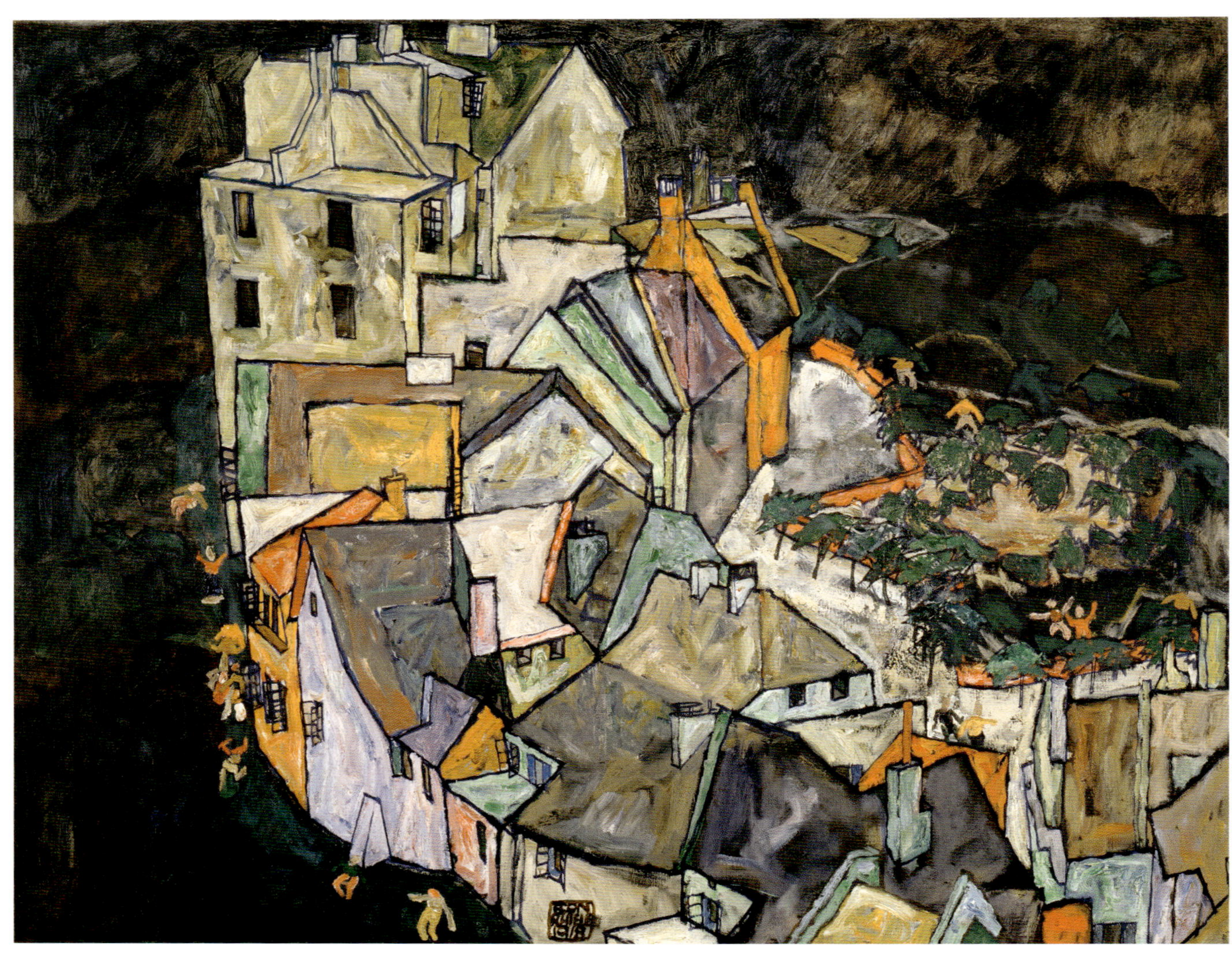

The outskirts of town *End of Town (Krumau Houses III)* is enlivened by small human figures. Nevertheless, the town and its colorful houses seems strangely deserted. The windows are dark; no lights are burning anywhere. The dark background contributes to the strange atmosphere.

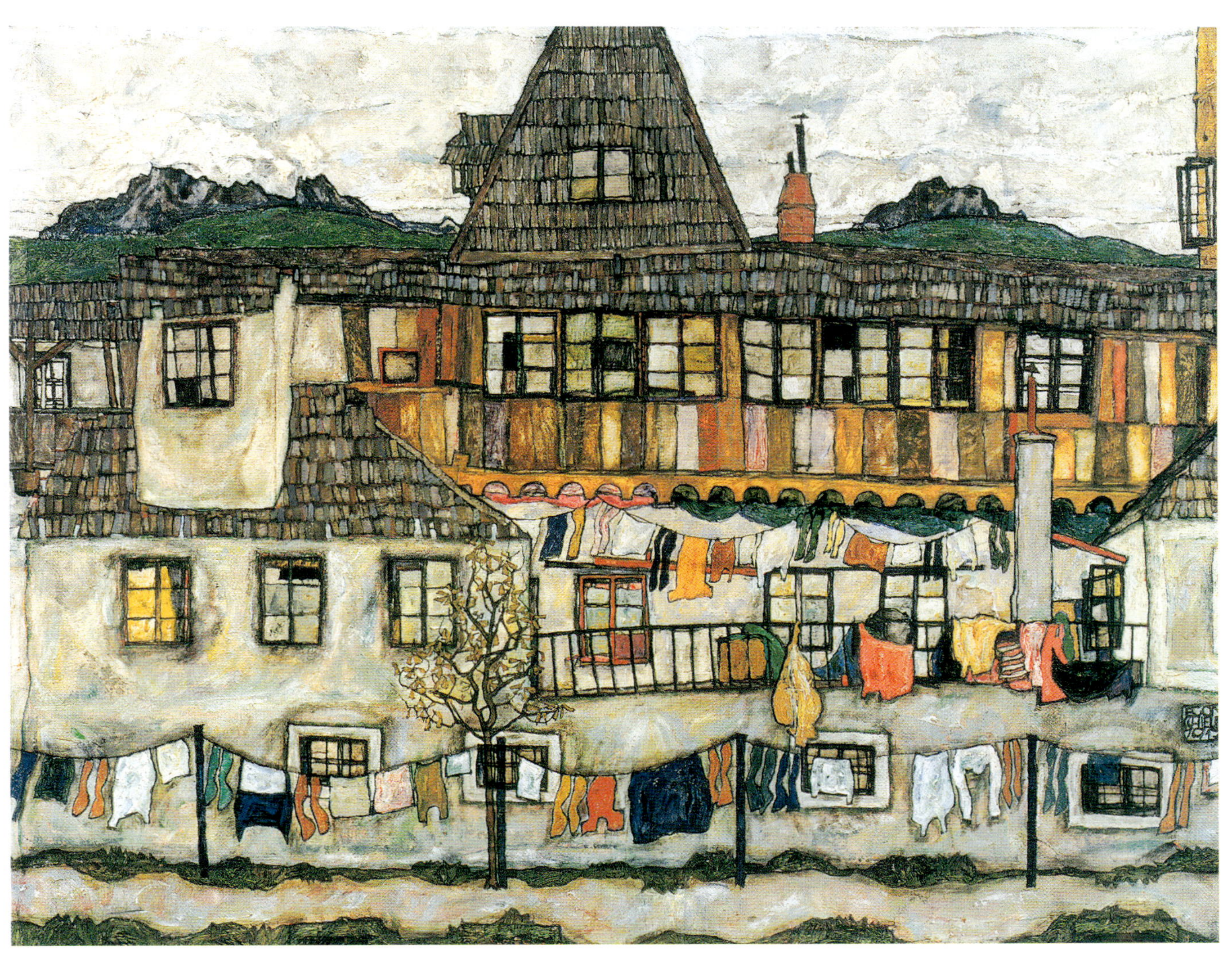

Play of colors A narrow path separates the observer from the *Suburban House with Washing.* The façade of the upper story and the laundry are rather powerful spots of color in front of the drab house wall.

The Life

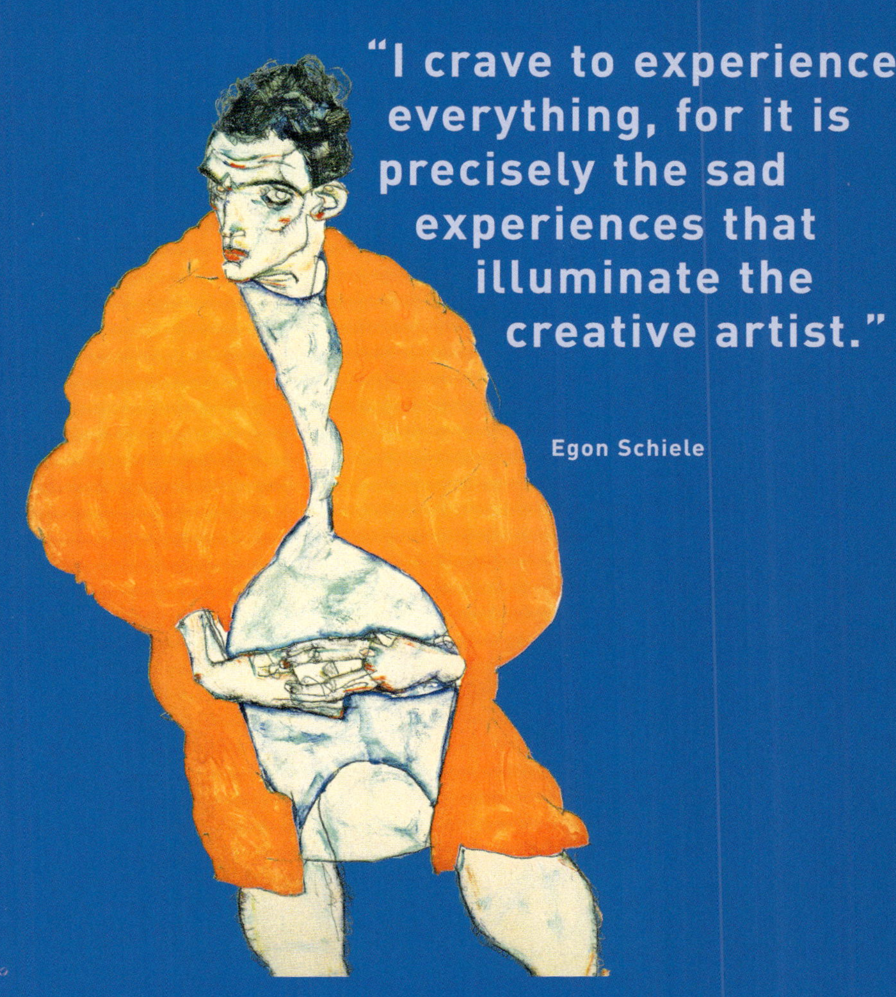

"I crave to experience everything, for it is precisely the sad experiences that illuminate the creative artist."

Egon Schiele

Short and tempestuous ...

... was Egon Schiele's life. His childhood in the quiet little town of Tulln would probably not have inspired most to reach for a sketchbook. But Schiele, who was as enthusiastic about the passing trains as for the Lower Austrian countryside, at times could hardly contain his hubris, only to retreat back into himself. "I am a human being. I love life and I love death," he declared at the age of twenty-one. One would be hard put to more succinctly and precisely summarize the scope of his passion.

Favorite sister

Egon Schiele had two sisters: the elder, Melanie, and Gerti, who was four years younger. Schiele took her with him on train journeys, she modeled for him, and he recommended her as a model to the fashion department of the Wiener Werkstätte. When the still-underage Gerti wished to marry Schiele's friend Anton Peschka, her brother at first resisted. He eventually backed down and gave his favorite sister the painting *Young Mother* as a wedding present. Afterwards, his little nephew would also model for him. Schiele drew and painted Gerti for the rest of his life. She would later recall her brother's "tough, often tyrannical manner": "He would come to my bed early in the morning with his watch in his hand to wake me. I had to sit as his model, in fact at his command."

Gerti Schiele not only frequently sat for her brother, but also worked as a fashion model for the Wiener Werkstätte.

"A master in the art of living"...

--> and "in the truest sense of the term," is how the collector Heinrich Benesch describes the artist.

--> Did Schiele see himself that way?

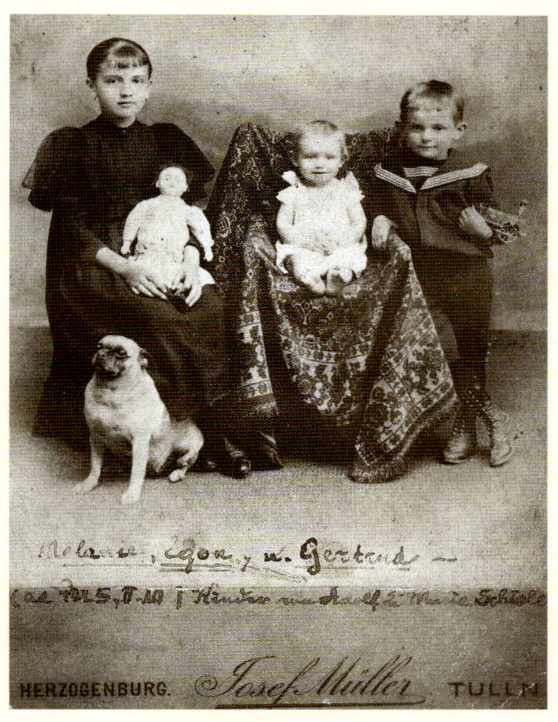

The eternal child

Among Schiele's estate after his death, were found not only the trains that had fascinated him as a child, but also a collection of folkloric and exotic objects, as well as toys. The collector Heinrich Benesch said of the collector Egon Schiele, "But he collected nothing of value, only small things, trifles, whose form and color appealed to his artistic sensibilities: small painted toys, peasant wood carvings, and reverse paintings on glass, colorful embroideries and headscarves, and the like." This photograph from his childhood, which shows Melanie, Gerti, and Egon Schiele, gives an idea of Egon's passion for toys (and trains).

Refuge

In 1912, Schiele moved into his studio at number 101 Hietzinger Strasse. He certainly was not the only one attracted to its quiet location on the western edge of town in Hietzing, Vienna's thirteenth district. The painters Gustav Klimt and Felix Albrecht Harta worked just around the corner on Feldmühlgasse. This elegant residential area around the castle of Schönbrunn, the summer residence of the Habsburgs, appealed to numerous artists and prosperous citizens.

The appearance of beauty

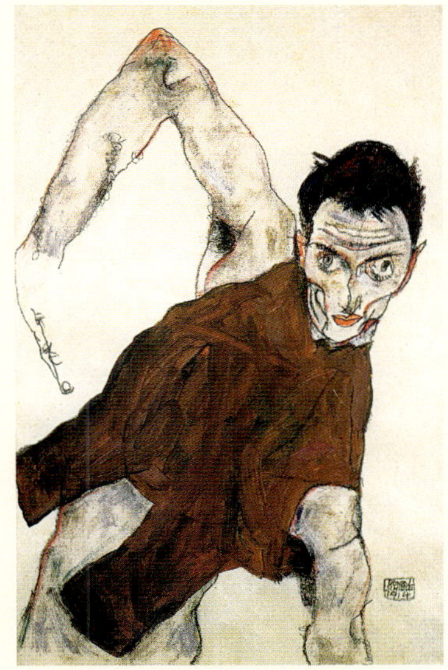

Actor and painter Albert Paris Gütersloh described Schiele after his death as exceptionally handsome. Schiele, he said, had nothing artistic about him, "No long hair, never even one day's growth of beard, never dirty fingernails, and even in his poorest days no scruffy jacket. He was—and it is not just the prettifying effect of memory speaking—an elegant young man whose good manners rarely, at least at that time and for that time, contrasted with his allegedly bad manner of painting." Schiele, on the other hand, continually stressed how bad things were for him as an independent artist: "I wore clothes, shoes, and hats handed down by my guardian, all of which were too big for me ... I was also long-haired and mostly unshaven." By his own account, he certainly did not give the impression of a "nice young man from a proper middle-class family of civil servants"—although (or because?) that is exactly what he was.

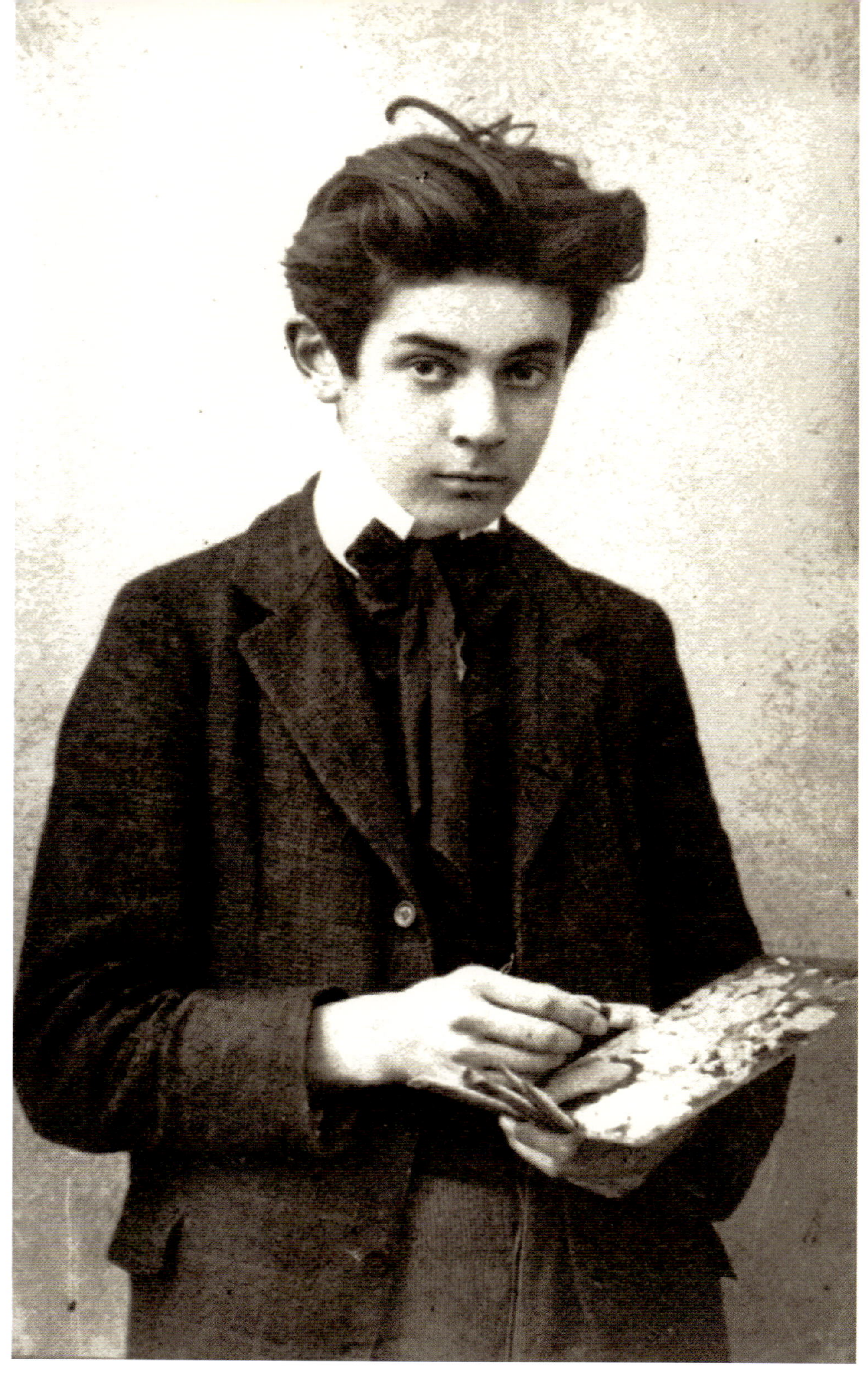

Equipped with brushes and palette, a fifteen-year-old Egon Schiele gazes, still somewhat cautiously, at the camera.

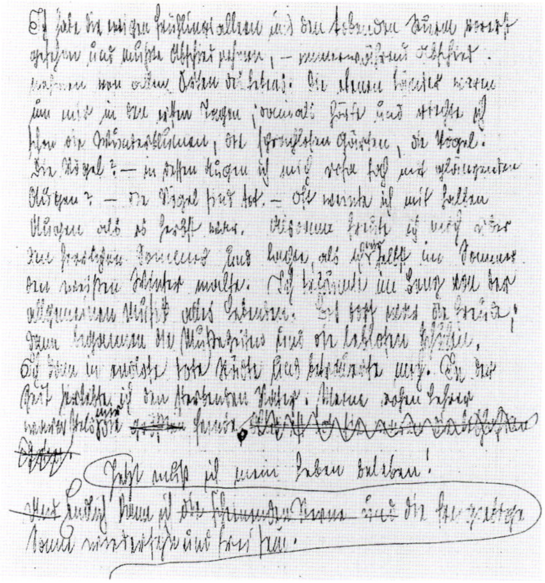

Schiele's handwritten version of his life in poetic form

A Child of the Railroad on an Artist's Track

As a child, Egon had learned how to get what he wanted, but often paid a very high price. He felt let down by his family as a young man, and after his conviction for the charge of exhibiting his racy nude studies, the painter had to finally face the consequences of society's lack of comprehension.

Childhood in Tulln

Egon Leo Adolf Schiele was born on June 12, 1890 in Tulln, Lower Austria. In this small town on the Danube, the family occupied a company apartment in the railroad station building. Egon's father, Adolf Eugen, worked for the Austrian railroad and was the stationmaster at Tulln. His mother Marie came from a well-off family of building contractors in Krumau, in southern Bohemia.

A true child of the railroad—his grandfather Karl Ludwig was an architect and railroad engineer—Egon took up

"Everything was pleasant to me, I wanted to look lovingly at the furious so that their eyes would meet mine, and I wanted to give gifts to the jealous and tell them that I'm worthless."

Egon Schiele, "Visionen" (Visions)

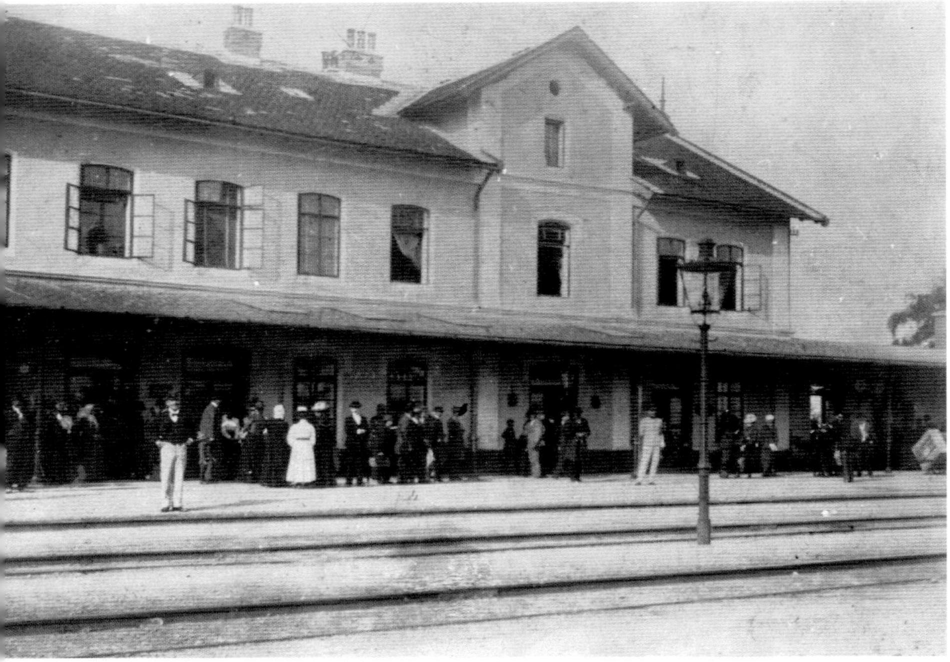

The Schiele family lived in a company apartment in the Tulln railroad station.

the pencil in his early youth and sketched all he saw from his window. His younger sister Gertrude (Gerti) told of the countless drawings made by her brother from the dining room window, of the trains pulling in and out, the platforms, crossing gates, and station buildings. In correspondence with Schiele's friend and collector Arthur Roessler, Gerti recalled her brother's masterful imitations of the noises made by the different trains: "For a good part of the day he would run in front of the station building, shuffling, hissing, snorting, and whistling." Roessler for his part, related a telling anecdote: he once found the twenty-three-year-old Schiele playing with the toy train set he had built for himself—his enthusiasm for trains clearly undiminished even in his adult years. Roessler was particularly impressed by the acoustic accompaniment to the event: "He could have appeared on any variety stage with it." Schiele refers to his years in Tulln as the happiest of his life, which ended rather abruptly when he began attending school.

To attend secondary school, the eleven-year-old Schiele was forced to move to Krems, where he lived with relatives and—when he couldn't avoid it—studied. In order to pursue engineering, which is what his parents had in mind for their only son, his scholastic success was not enough. So Schiele's father pursued every possible avenue, and beginning in 1902 Egon attended the Landesreal- und Obergymnasium, an academic high school in Klosterneuburg, which was closer to Tulln. But Egon remained far more interested in drawing than his other academic subjects; scatterbrained and not particularly attentive as a student, he ultimately had to repeat a year. Nor was Schiele's friendship with the later musician Arthur Löwenstein conducive to his academic career. The two students had worked out an elaborate method of producing "music" by building a "musical scale" out of pencils in the drawers of their wooden school desks. Probably the only thing truly impressive about their invention was its great volume.

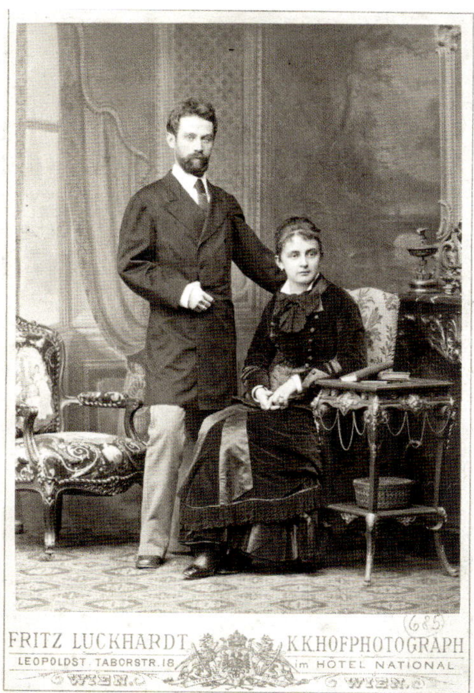

The artist's parents, Marie Soukup and Adolf Schiele, as fiancées

In 1904, the Schiele family moved to Klosterneuburg, north of Vienna. Egon would later use the town as a setting for a number of works.

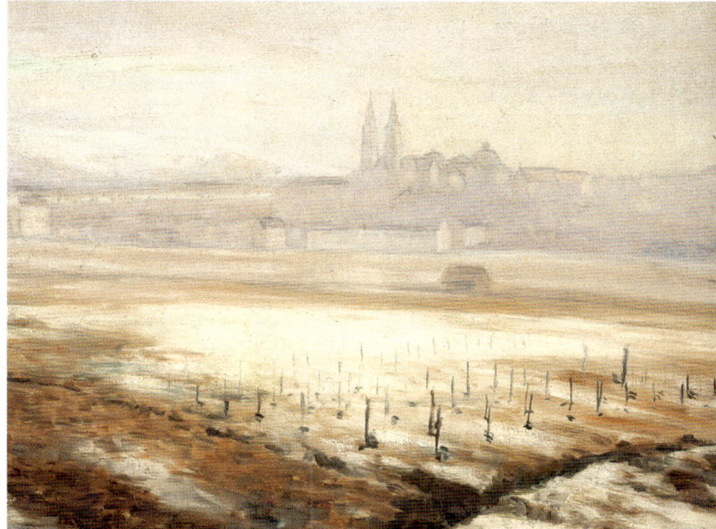

"Why do I paint graves?"

Presumably as the result of syphilis, Schiele's father suffered increasingly more frequent episodes of mental derangement. It is presumed that the same illness was also responsible for the two stillbirths experienced by Marie Schiele before giving birth to Egon. In 1903, Adolf lost his job due to his condition. The family was hardly able to live on his modest pension, especially because they had to move out of the company apartment in Tulln, and they looked for a new home in nearby Klosterneuburg. The family's economic situation deteriorated further when Adolf, in one of his attacks, burned his railroad stock certificates, the basis of their livelihood. Schiele's father died on New Year's Day, 1905. Years later he appeared to Egon in a dream, as he wrote to his sister Gerti, "As long as he was talking to me, I was tense and speechless." Schiele also discussed his relationship with his father with his friend and later brother-in-law Anton Peschka: "Even Gerti does not know; even if people believe that my life is happy, how many and what heavy emotional suffering I have to endure. I don't know if there is anyone who remembers my noble father with such sadness; I don't know who can understand why I seek out those places where my father used to be, where in my melancholic hours I deliberately allow myself to experience the pain inside me.—I believe in the immortality of all creatures, I believe that finery is simply superficial; I carry in me the more or less interwoven memory.... Why do I paint graves? And any number of similar pictures?—because this lives on intimately inside me."

No second father

After his father's death, a brother-in-law, the wealthy Leopold Czihaczek, was appointed guardian to Egon and his little sisters. Leopold was a music-lover,

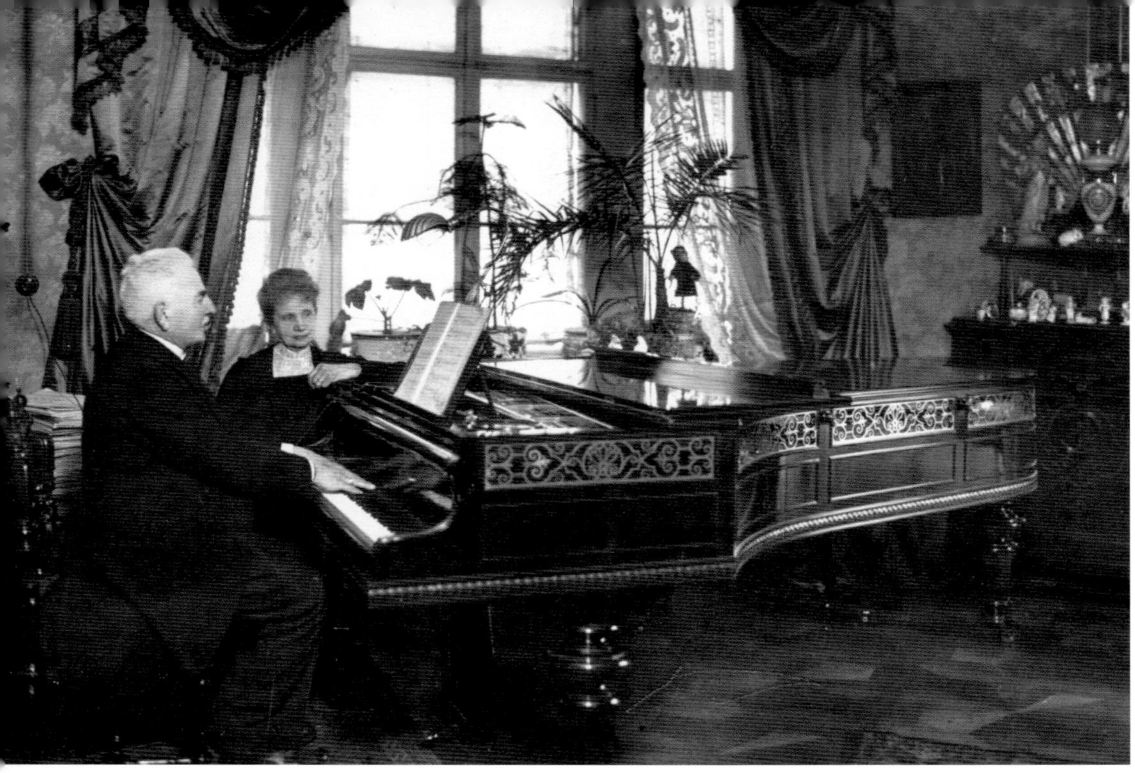

Egon's guardian Leopold Czihaczek at the piano as his wife Marie listens

had a box at the Viennese Burgtheater, and probably appreciated Egon's drawings—but not his grades at school!

He certainly did not sympathize with Egon's desire to become an artist. But Egon was resilient and convinced of his own talent; from the start he signed his drawings and paintings, and at times also dated them. His powers of perseverance, steeled by family arguments, were finally rewarded. Schiele applied to the progressive Vienna School of Arts and Crafts, but with his talent for drawing and painting was referred to the Academy of Fine Arts. He was not even sixteen years old when he passed the entrance examination in October 1906. Even Leopold was impressed, and sent a telegram home: "Egon in with flying colors."

During Schiele's years of studying in Vienna, his uncle allowed himself to be drawn or painted on a number of occasions. These portraits were a welcome opportunity for the art student to test his talent outside the rigid rules of the Academy. But when Egon prematurely left the Academy after only three years, Leopold's patience ran out. It became clear to Egon that he couldn't rely on the complicity of his uncle, who ultimately decided that the best thing for him was military education! On Egon's twentieth birthday, his uncle renounced his guardianship, the prelude to which was a particularly heated correspondence. On one occasion, Egon explained to him his egocentric "approach to life" in the most emphatic terms: "Self-confidence is the foundation of courage, danger holds a certain attraction for the self-confident; people with imagination are more adventurous ... Courage is the frame of mind in which one deliberately confronts danger ... Independence is great luck, doubly so for people of intellect who likes to be self-reliant [*sic*] ... Life is said to be a battle against the attacks of enemies, through floods and afflictions. Each individual must battle against themselves and enjoy what he is born to by nature ... But nothing is more shameful than dependence, nothing is more pernicious and shameful for the strong disposition ... It is nature that must bear all the blame."

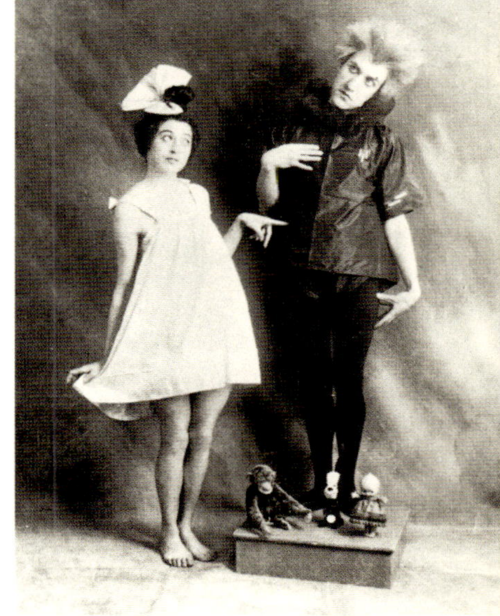

Schiele's friend Erwin Domenik Osen with the dancer Moa during a mime performance

And yet a defiant and provocative Schiele later had no problem with asking his guardian for money. His uncle's reply was predictable: "I am not a cash cow, remember that."

Estranged from the family

Schiele, by then with his own studio in Vienna's ninth district, expected no help from his mother, who herself managed on a small pension. The two repeatedly squabbled, their sporadic correspondence often marked by bitterness. In January 1913, Egon wrote on the envelope of a letter, "Letters pointless, as I myself am doing much worse." And he would later write, "What I do is my business, I am master enough of myself and I refuse to tolerate interference from wherever it comes ... and I believe that your situation is truly not as uncertain as mine often was; if worst comes to worst Peschka is still there ... So there is not and never will be a question of starving." He told his mother that occasionally her letters went directly onto the fire (where his mother allegedly consigned the boy's drawings to punish him). Schiele's arrogance often jumps off the page of his letters, like in March 1913: "Undoubtedly I will be the largest, finest, most costly, purest, and most valuable fruit—through my own free will all fine and noble forces have united in me."

His mother struck back and said she felt neglected and thought her children should care for her. Schiele once described the support he received from his family in these terms: "From my mother, every time I saw her, I received reproaches and nothing else; from my guardian I received five kronen every Monday. And from this I bought first of all twenty Sport cigarettes, which not surprisingly didn't last me seven days, so

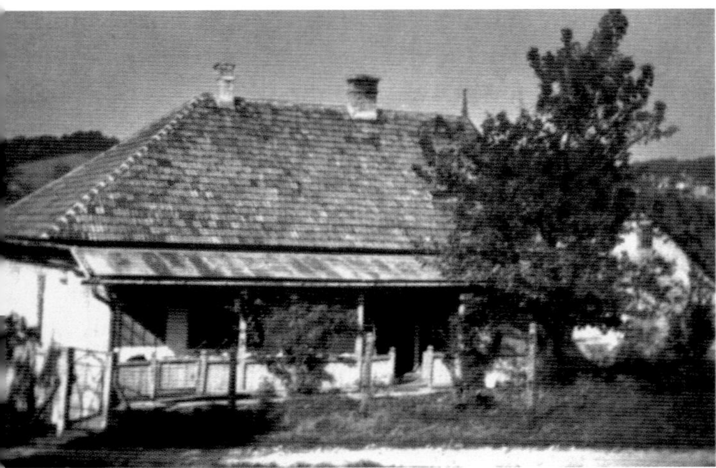

Egon Schiele's house at number 48 Austrasse in Neulengbach

Painters together: Egon Schiele with the New Artist Group member (and his future brother-in-law) Anton Peschka in Krumau

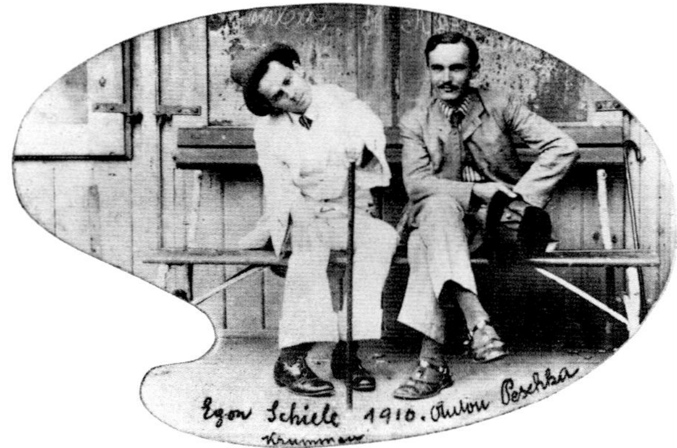

that by the weekend I was forced to pick the butts out of the garbage and smoke them, freshly recycled."

Tired of Vienna

The portrait commissions that came in hardly relieved his financial woes. Nor did his largesse and extravagance make it any easier. Work that Klimt arranged for him at the Wiener Werkstätte was a mere drop in the bucket. All told, Schiele had tired of Vienna; he felt the art scene was mired in envy and competition, and wrote to Anton Peschka of his feelings: "There is a shadow over Vienna, the city is black ... I must see new things and investigate them. I want to taste dark waters and see crackling trees and wild winds. I want to gaze in astonishment at moldy garden fences."

Freethinkers take in the country air

And so the twenty-one-year-old took off. Together with Valerie (Wally) Neuzil, his favorite model and mistress, he traveled to Krumau, his mother's hometown on the Vltava. The little town fascinated the painter, and throughout his life he consistently returned to it as a motif in his artwork. But the love was not reciprocal. As if the unmarried couple living in sin were not enough, or Schiele's oftentimes-extravagant outfits of his own design, two of the artist's friends showed up. The painter Anton Peschka and the mime artist and former theater painter Erwin Domenik Osen, or Mime von Osen, as he called himself (p. 65), appeared to get a whiff of the Krumau country air. Portraits of these months show Schiele and Osen with wild grimaces on their faces. After three months, the people of Krumau had had enough. Schiele's work with nude models, and especially his drawing of children, who went in

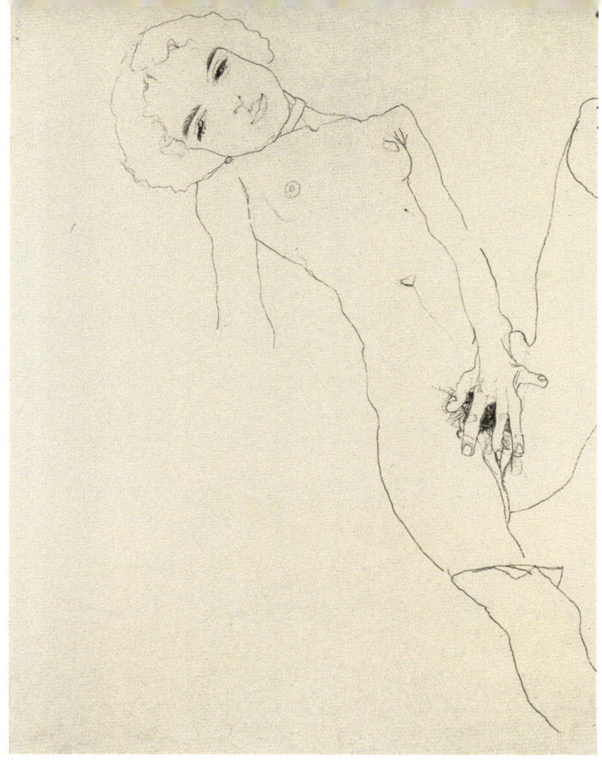

Potential for controversy: nudes like these attracted more attention than Schiele wanted

and out of his house, was looked on with disfavor. In July, Schiele packed his bags and left Krumau to its philistine dreams. He was disappointed, and he told Roessler, "You know how much I enjoy being in Krumau; and now it has been made impossible for me: the people simply boycott us, because we are Reds. Of course I could confront them, even all seven thousand of them, but I don't have the time."

Calm before the storm

Returning to Vienna was not an option. Egon and Wally moved on to the little town of Neulengbach, west of Vienna, where Schiele rented out a garden studio for his work. But this period was only the calm before the storm that was to break out the following winter. The inhabitants of Neulengbach also disapproved of an unmarried couple living together, but above all Schiele's choice of models—he preferred drawing children—was viewed with more than simple mistrust. The situation escalated, and in April 1912 formal complaints were levied against the artist.

Schiele on trial

"For the charge of indecency and the seduction of a minor," Schiele was first held in custody awaiting trial at the Neulengbach district court, and was then moved to nearby St. Pölten. On April 13, 1912, the twenty-one-year-old stood in front of the examining magistrate. While Schiele was able to refute the more serious charge of child abuse during the ninety-minute hearing, he was ultimately convicted for displaying an erotic nude study on a studio wall that was visible to children. The many other, no-less objectionable nude drawings Schiele had stored away and that were also confiscated, were not the object of the complaint, just the one drawing. And this one drawing was burned in front of Schiele's eyes.

It was not only the countryside where this attitude toward nude drawings prevailed; Gustav Klimt himself had been censured in Vienna a decade earlier. An edition of the Secession magazine *Ver Sacrum* containing his nude drawings was seized and the copies destroyed. Though the trial that followed ended in

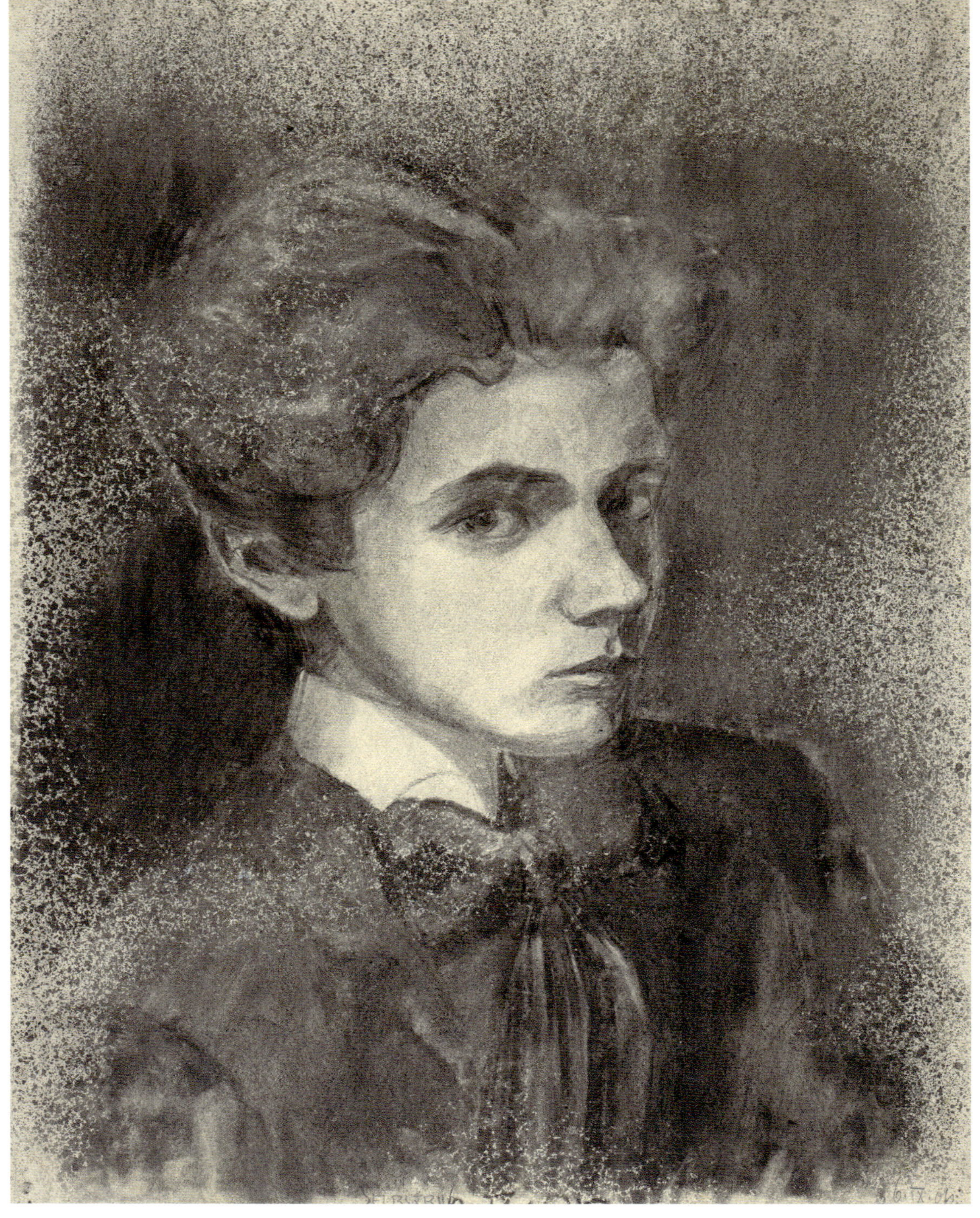

Future student Egon Schiele drew this self-portrait a few weeks before beginning his studies at the Vienna Academy of Fine Arts. He was sixteen years old. Apart from drawing in charcoal, he used scumbling and spattering techniques, the latter being particularly popular with the Secession artists.

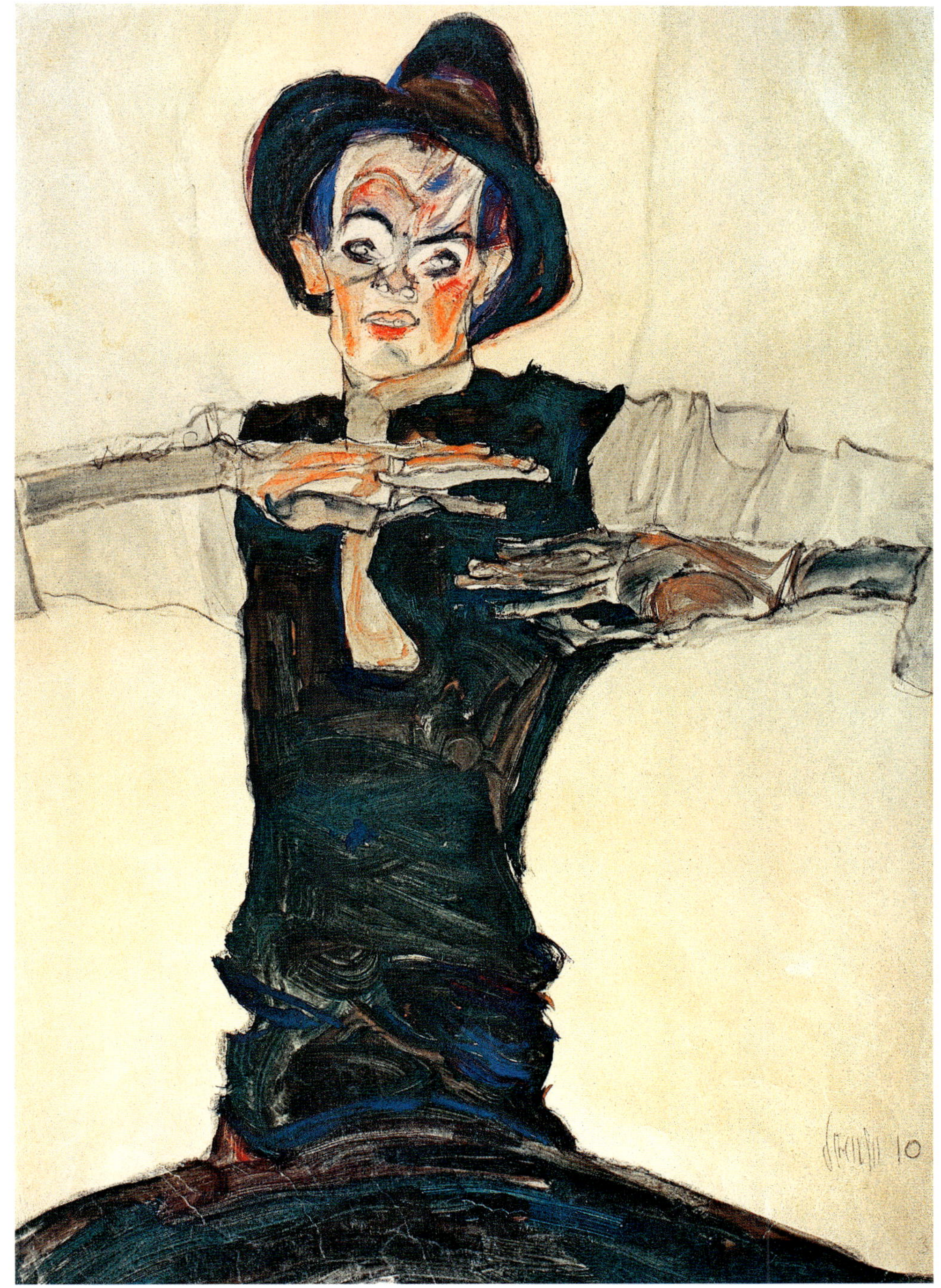

Self-portrait "I know that I have developed immensely as an artist, I have seen and experienced, and struggled incessantly against the 'business' of art." But the situation was not always as crystal clear as Schiele formulated it in September 1911. In this *Self-Portrait with Brown Hat* that Schiele had completed the previous year, he seems rather torn. Between bourgeois appearances and artistic freedom perhaps?

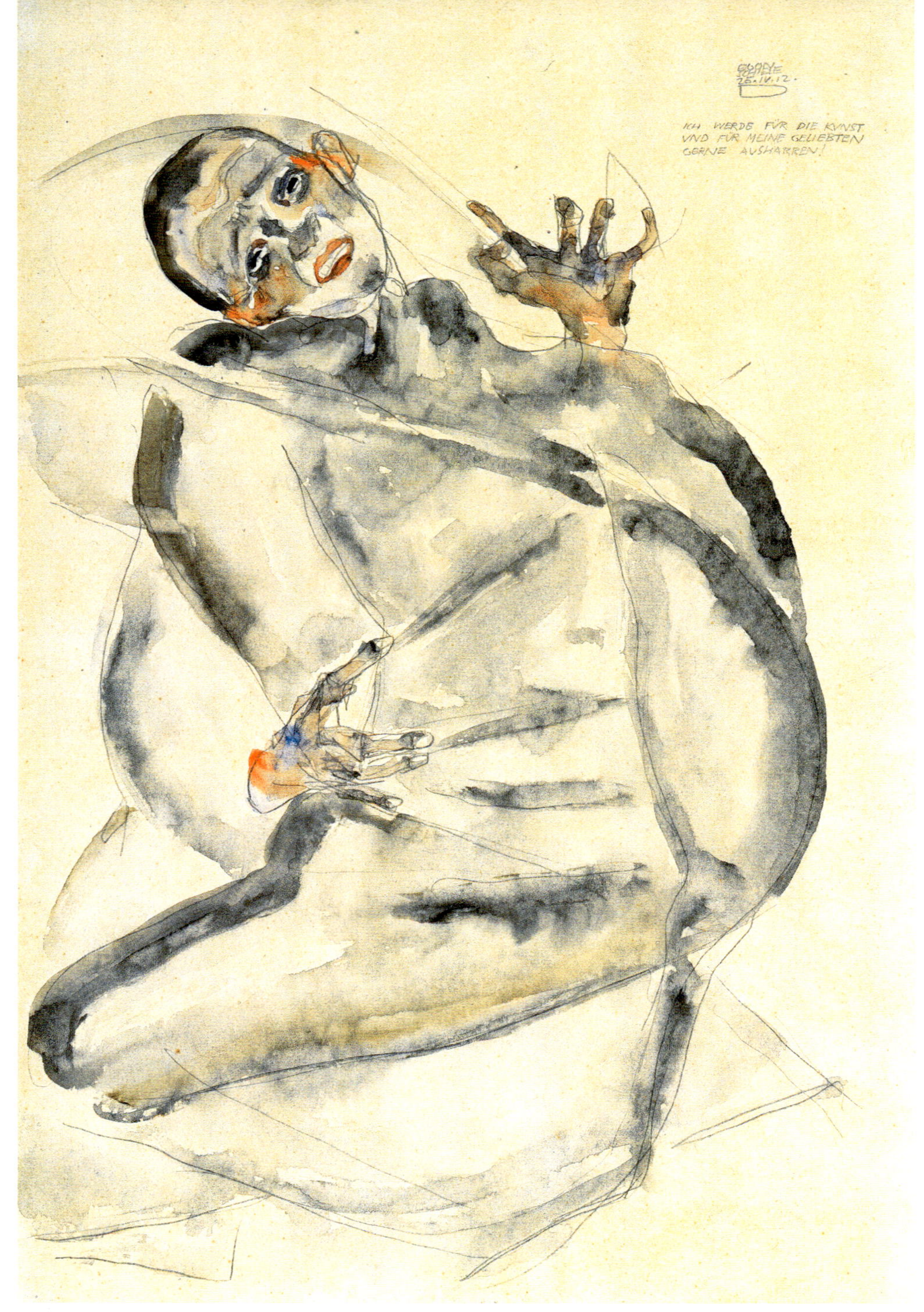

Misunderstood "I will gladly endure for art and my loved ones!" The *Self-Portrait as Prisoner* bearing this inscription was executed during Schiele's imprisonment in 1912. The depressed painter not only represented himself in this portrait as a tortured soul, but later on also stressed his own martyr-like characteristics, often seeing himself as a victim of society's incomprehension.

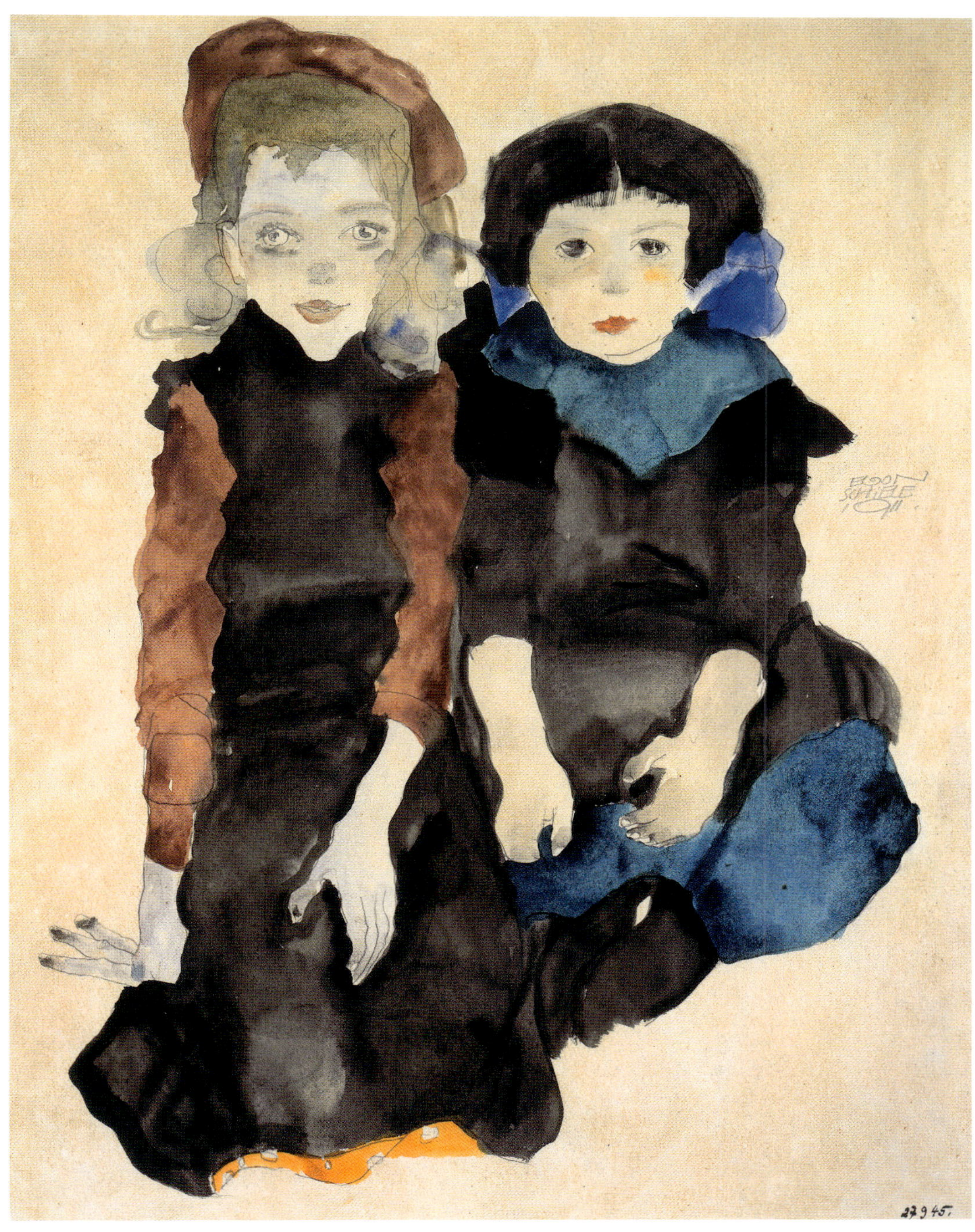

Two crouching girls Though Egon Schiele was using watercolors, he barely allowed the separate color fields to blend. As he so often did, Schiele failed to anchor the figures in space. The two very different girls look straight into the observer's eyes.

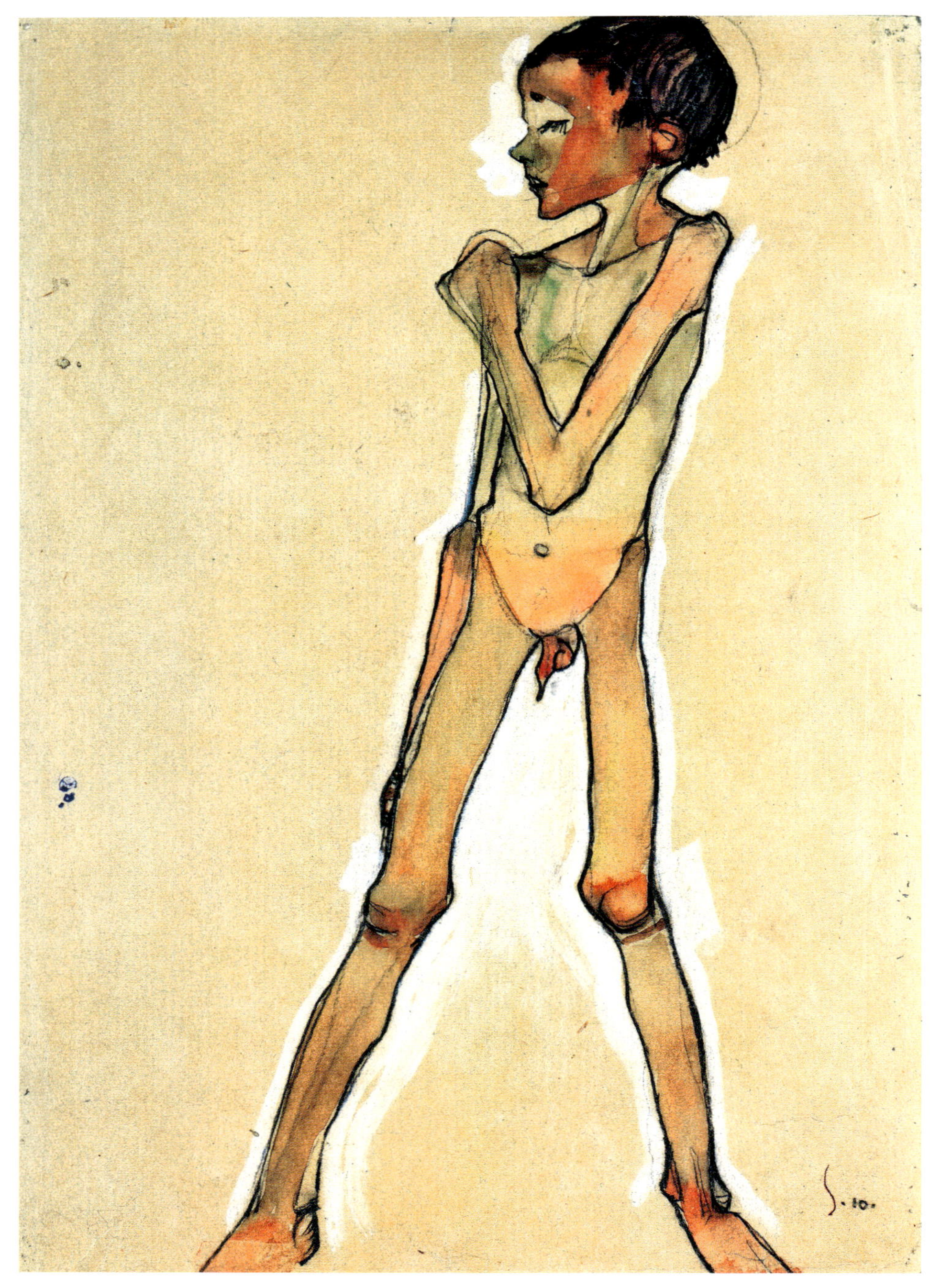

Emphasizing the silhouette Schiele used black chalk and watercolors for this depiction of a naked boy. The body is outlined in black, and the outlines in turn are surrounded with opaque white, making the boy appear even bonier.

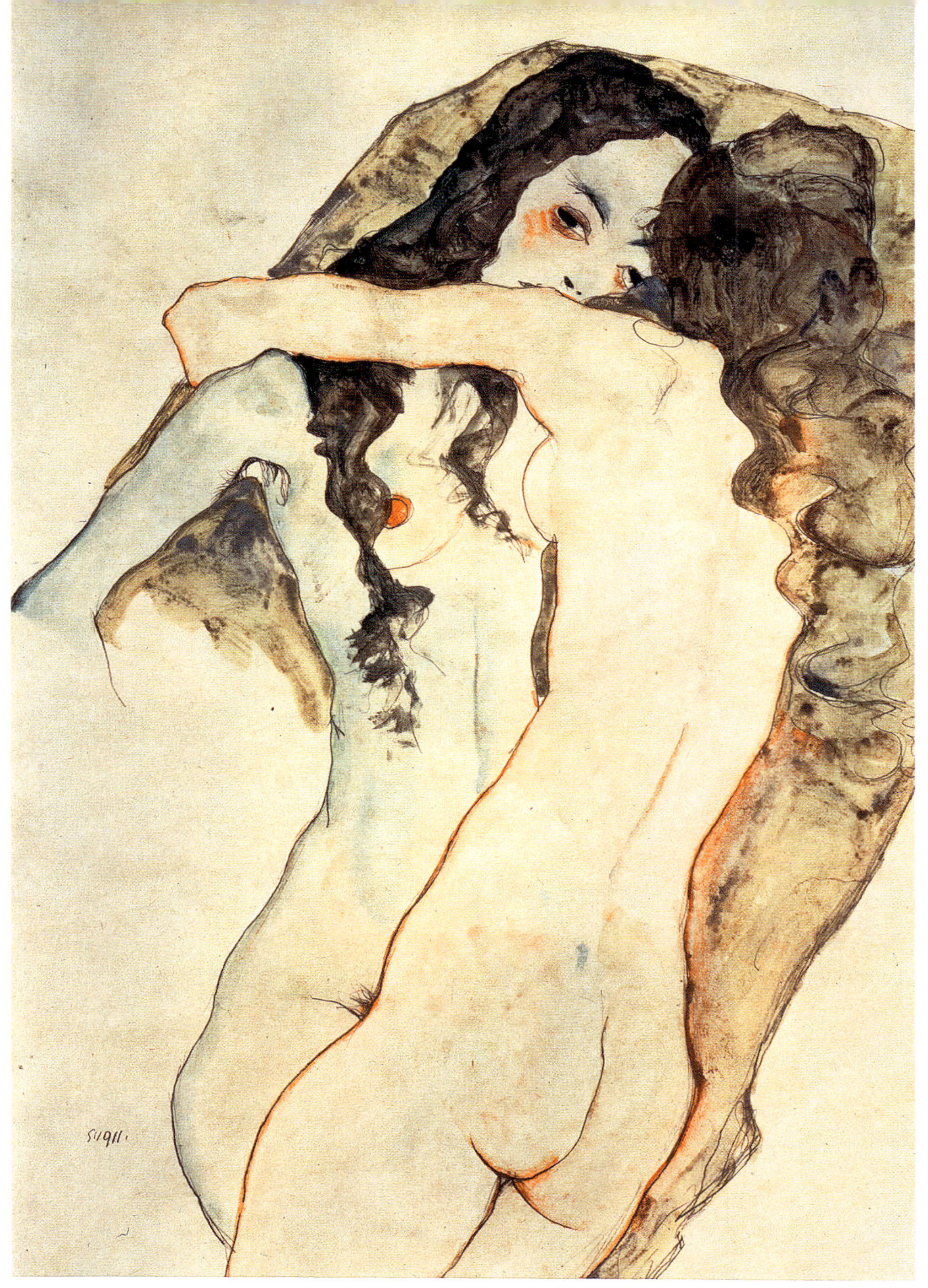

Fine line Egon Schiele presumably painted pictures such as this on commission. He surely realized that he was walking a fine line with such motifs—homosexuality was seen as unnatural.

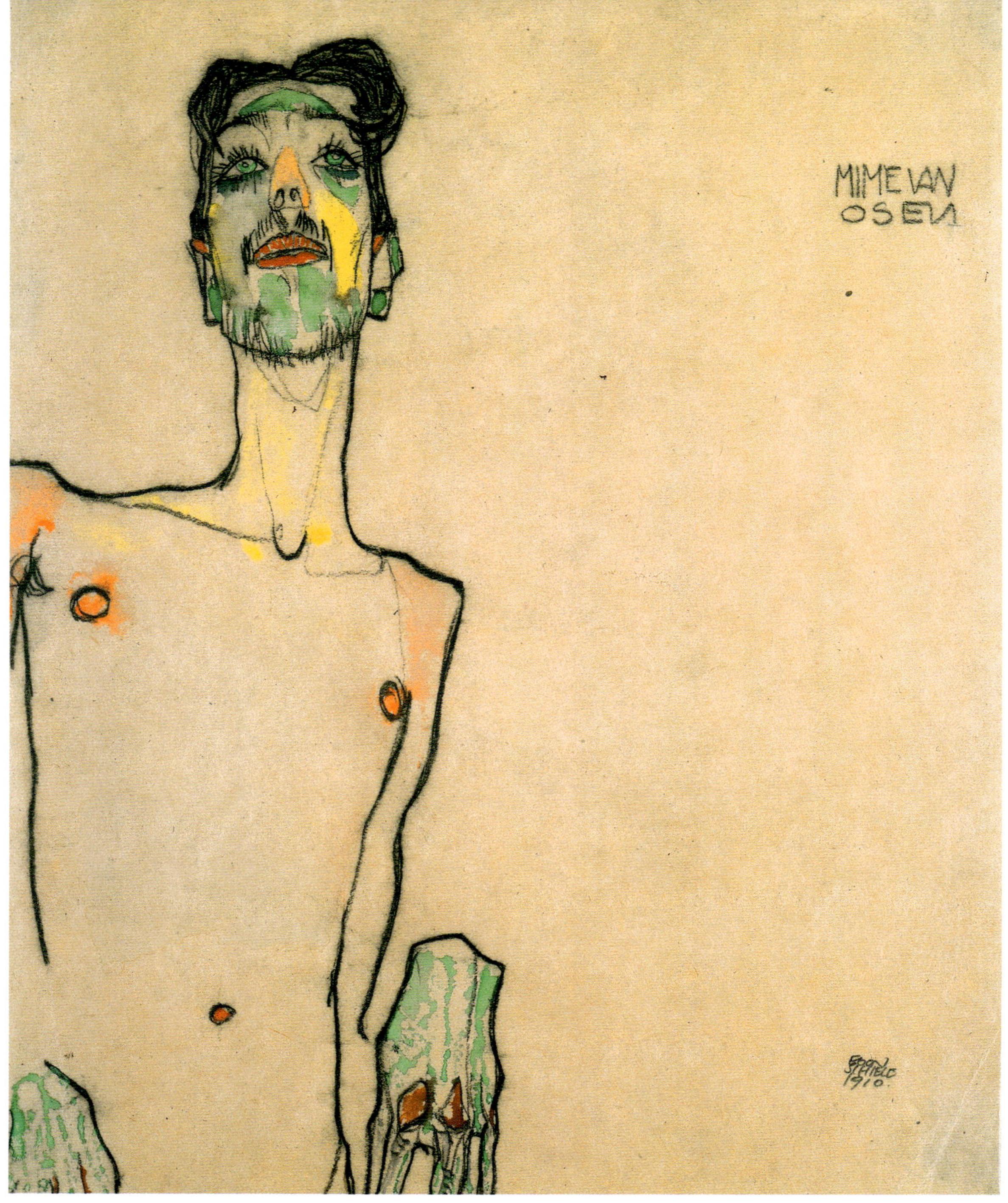

Image of a traveling companion Egon Schiele portrayed his friend Erwin Domenik Osen, who called himself Mime van Osen, on numerous occasions. A trained dancer, Osen visited the artist in Krumau where this semi-nude was painted. Schiele used the same green for both face and hands, and cut off Osen's body by extending the drawing to the very edge of the page.

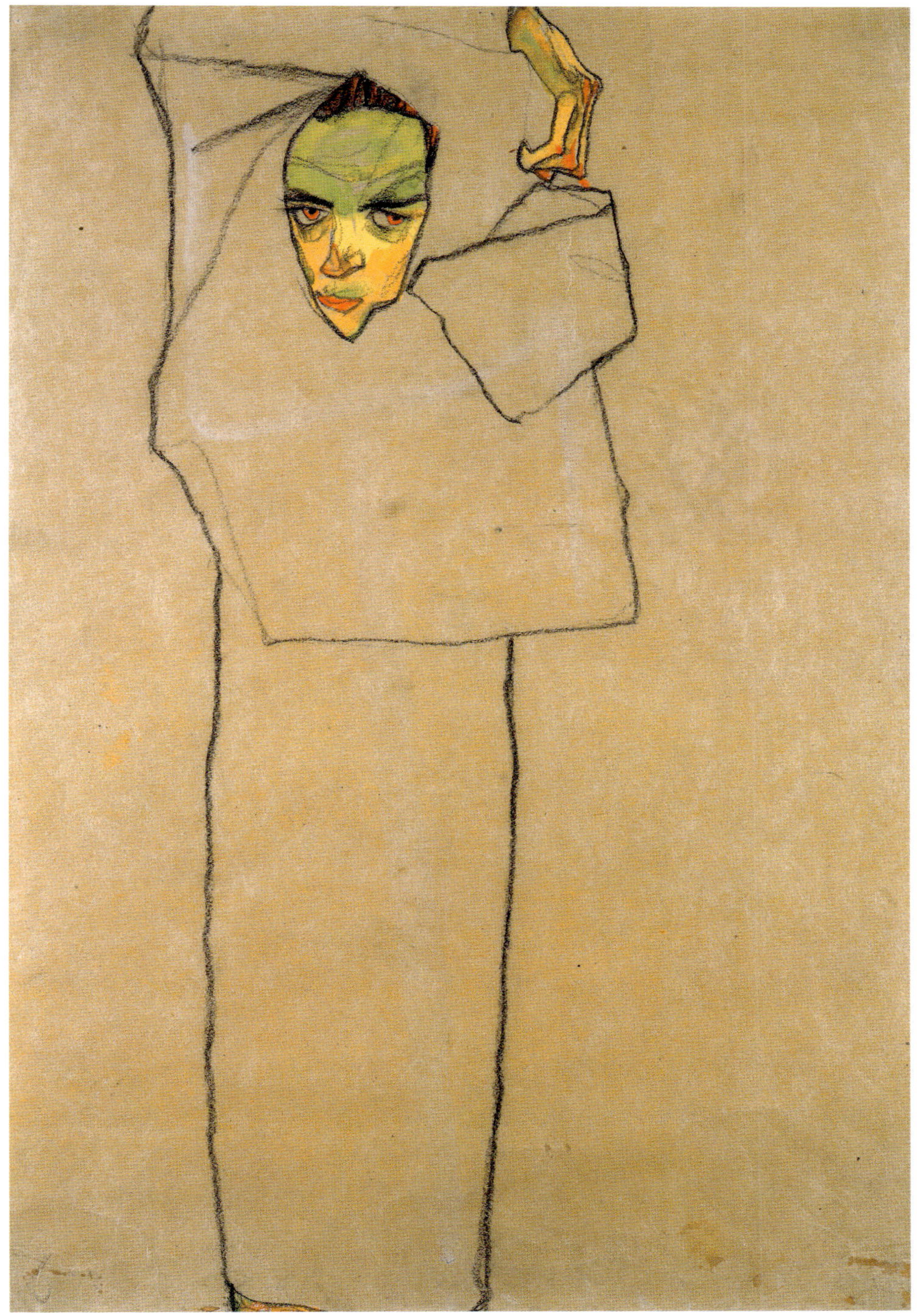

Fellow-artist Alongside his portraits of artist friends, in 1910 Schiele painted a number of self-portraits, including this one originally titled "Portrait of a Man Pulling his Shirt Over his Head." He hardly bothered to give it dimension. Schiele's preference for incongruous colors is also evident: his face and hand are rendered in yellow, green, orange, and a touch of brown.

acquittal, the outcome could not disguise how thin the ice was on which the artists tread with their erotic motifs. In 1910, drawings by Schiele for a Prague exhibition of the New Artist Group were taken off the walls—before the show opened—because of their "obscene character."

Arrested

During the twenty-four days of his arrest, Schiele painted twelve watercolors that reflected his fear and sadness. In his *Self-Portrait as Prisoner,* he depicted himself with wide eyes and clenched teeth (p. 70). On another page, Schiele wrote the line, "To obstruct the artist is a crime; it means the murder of budding life." Schiele's self-image was evident: all creative artists must be supported, so that they can fulfill their creative mission. In 1915, he depicted himself as St. Sebastian, pierced with arrows like the Roman martyr (p. 82).

A number of Schiele's friends and patrons turned against him as a result of the criminal conviction. Arthur Roessler, however, stood by him, as a friend and as a collector. Heinrich Benesch also remained loyal, visiting Schiele in prison and accompanying the depressed artist back to Vienna. A postcard from Oskar Reichel to Roessler reveals that the collectors were in contact with one another about their concern for Schiele's well being.

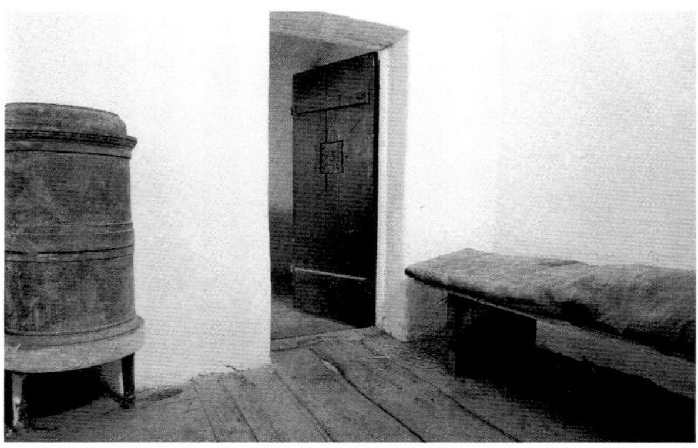
The prison in Neulengbach where Egon Schiele was held in custody awaiting trial

Return to Vienna

Schiele's economic situation was precarious; the trial and imprisonment had cost him both time and energy,

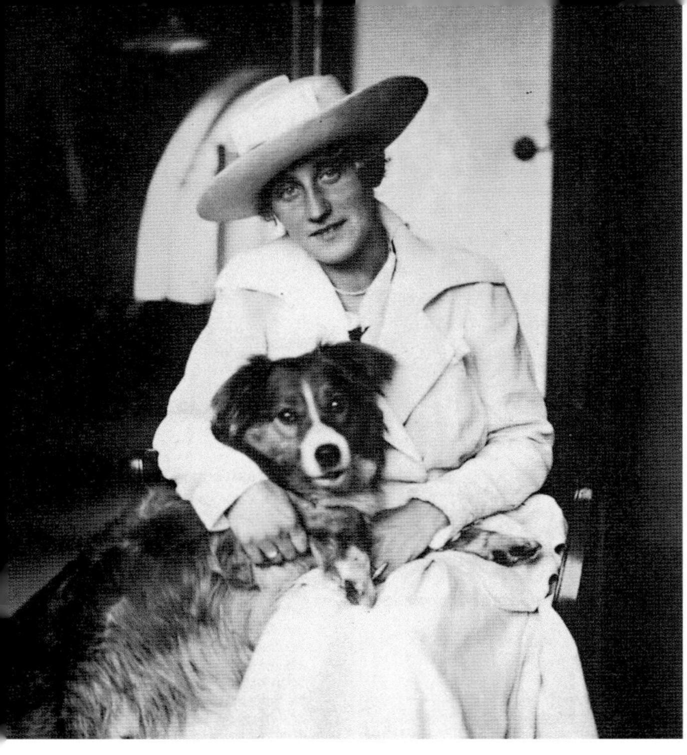

Schiele's wife Edith with her dog Lord

and he was forced to pay the costs of the trial. He also needed to pay for his new studio apartment in Vienna's thirteenth district where he was to live. At any rate, the scandal had no long-term effects on his career. Invitations to exhibit kept streaming in, and, thanks to Roessler's efforts, Munich gallery owner Hans Goltz organized a one-man show for Schiele. It was a huge success for the young artist, but unfortunately—yet again—not for his wallet. Goltz informed him, "In Germany, your paintings, in your current stage of artistic development, are not sellable." While such comments might have piqued Schiele's self-confidence, they did not leave any lasting impression. At the end of 1916, a planned exhibition at the Galerie Arnot in Vienna actually fell through as a result of his excessive financial demands. The gallery owner Guido Arnot spoke bluntly: "The Galerie Arnot cannot exist merely from the honor bestowed on it by one Herr Egon Schiele exhibiting his works." Schiele was not yet prepared to back down, but soon after he did. Schiele was unable to afford his studio rent and accumulated debts in the amount of twenty-five hundred kronen, a substantial sum that could have supported an entire family for several months! Schiele even considered looking for a job to bring in some money.

In the midst of this financial crisis, during which Schiele deliberated taking a position as a cartographer, two young ladies in the neighborhood caught his eye. In the winter of 1914–15, Schiele went out with Edith and Adele Harms, at first accompanied by his girlfriend Wally. With the outbreak of World War I, Schiele originally avoided conscription into military service due to his slender stature and a congenitally weak heart. Nevertheless, he perceived the war as a watershed, and wrote to his sister Gerti only a few weeks after its outbreak, in November 1914, "We live in the most phenomenal times that the world has ever seen.—We have become used to all sorts of hardships—hundreds of thousands of people are perishing miserably—everyone must bear his fate living or dying—we have become hard and fearless.—What was before 1914 belongs to another world ..."

Egon Schiele (center) in 1916
with comrades from the prisoner
of war camp for Russian officers

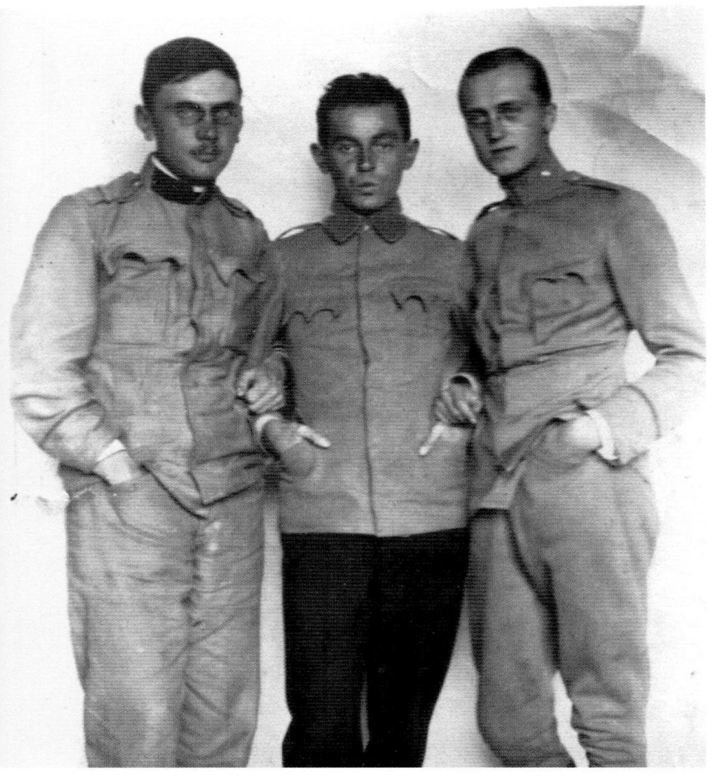

Conscription

In the spring of 1915, Schiele made a decision: his heart belonged to the younger of the Harms sisters, Edith. At her request, he separated from his long-term girlfriend Wally, and the young couple quickly married in June 1915. But just four days after the simple wedding, Schiele was finally called up to perform his military service in Bohemia. In June 1915, the artist arrived in Prague, accompanied by his wife. What a honeymoon! Schiele had served for exactly two weeks before he wrote his mother about his aversion to the army: "Dear Mother,—I have now been a soldier for 14 days—things are going pretty badly for me, as you can imagine ... I have not yet gone for a walk in Neuhaus for the uniforms disgust me. What are you doing?—how much longer will this wretched war go on—it is the worst time that human beings have ever gone through—just why are we actually on this Earth?" And in the midst of the letter, he slipped in a reproach: "My comrades are constantly receiving cakes and pastries and letters from home, and I have not yet had anything from anywhere."

After his period of training, Schiele was excused from service at the front on the grounds of limited fitness. He was assigned to guard duty and was originally able to serve in the environs of Vienna. Later, however, he was moved to areas further away from the capital, and, whenever possible, Edith moved with him. In Mühling, Lower Austria, where he was stationed in the summer of 1916, in addition to his clerical duties, Schiele was given the chance to practice his art. He portrayed Austrian and Russian soldiers and depicted his superiors. He also kept a war journal.

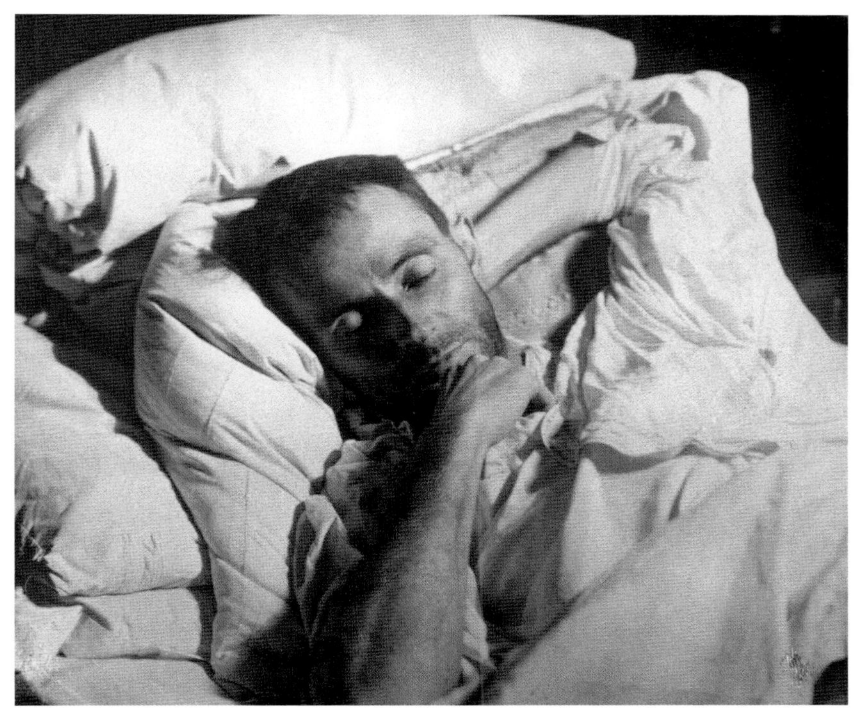
Egon Schiele on his deathbed

In April 1918, Schiele succeeded in being transferred to the army museum in Vienna, where he was responsible for the organization of exhibitions, and was permitted to live in his studio. Schiele owed his privileged position less to his influential patrons than to his success at the Secession exhibition in March of that year. In spite of these special concessions, the artist felt drained by his military service. His lack of discipline and difficulties with the military authorities were only part of his problems. Schiele was not nearly as patriotic as was expected in those days: "I don't care where I live, that is, what nation I belong to." Against orders, he sometimes wore civilian clothes rather than his uniform on the street to avoid having to salute the officers he encountered.

Early death

At the very least, Schiele's financial situation had improved. In July 1918, the Schieles moved into a spacious studio apartment in the Hietzing district of Vienna, and Edith was expecting a baby. While the young family was doing better, the Austrian-Hungarian Empire was on its knees. The end of the World War I was imminent. The starving and exhausted population was an easy target for the Spanish influenza epidemic that raged throughout Europe. Within a few months, more people succumbed than had died during four years of war. In her sixth month of pregnancy, Edith fell ill, and died in October of that year. Only three days later, on October 31, 1918, Egon Schiele died at the age of twenty-eight.

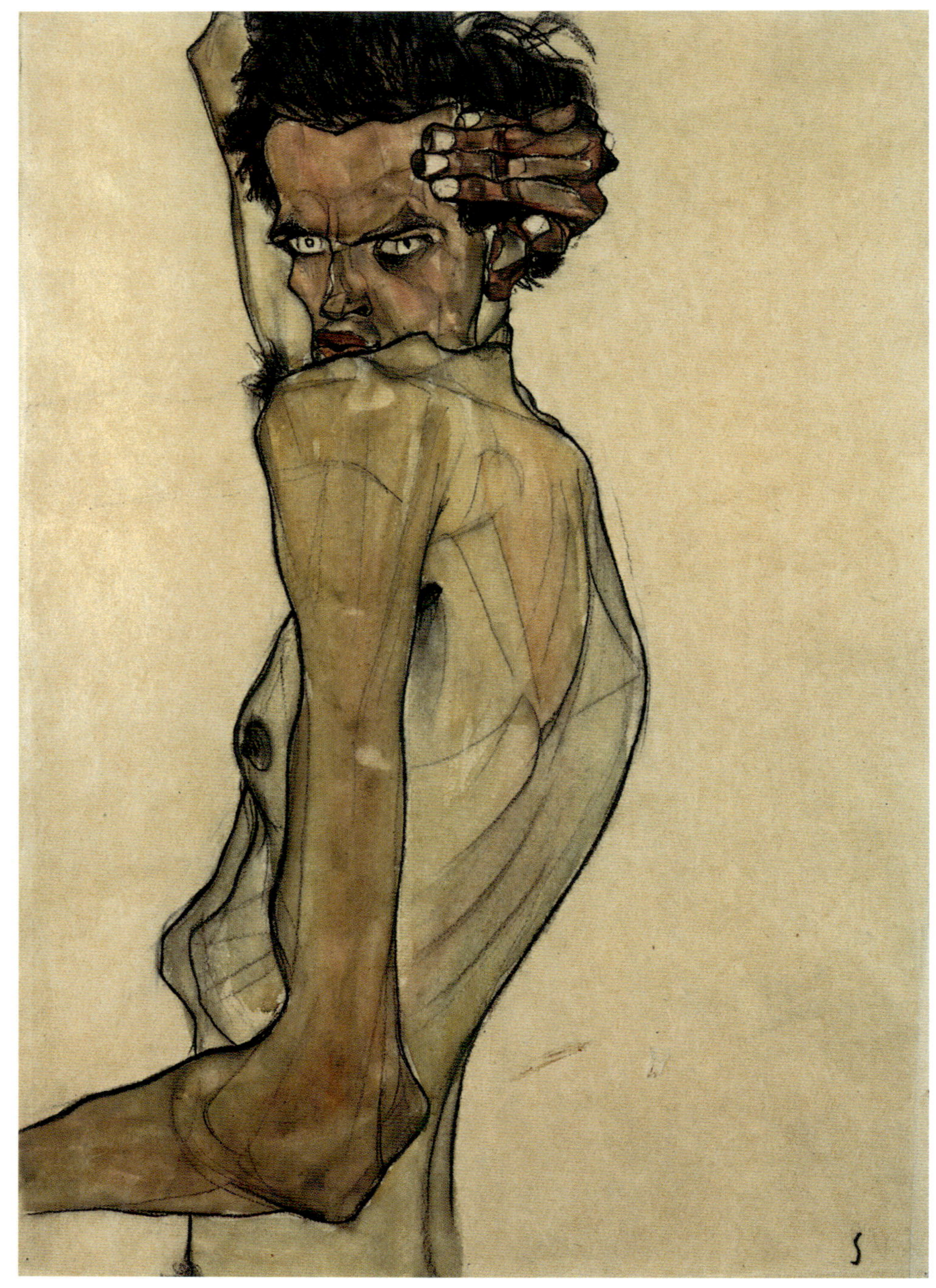

About things "Schiele was unusual not only as an artist, but also as a human being.... Everyday matters could not affect him. He always looked beyond them towards the elevated goal of his ambition." Heinrich Benesch on Egon Schiele

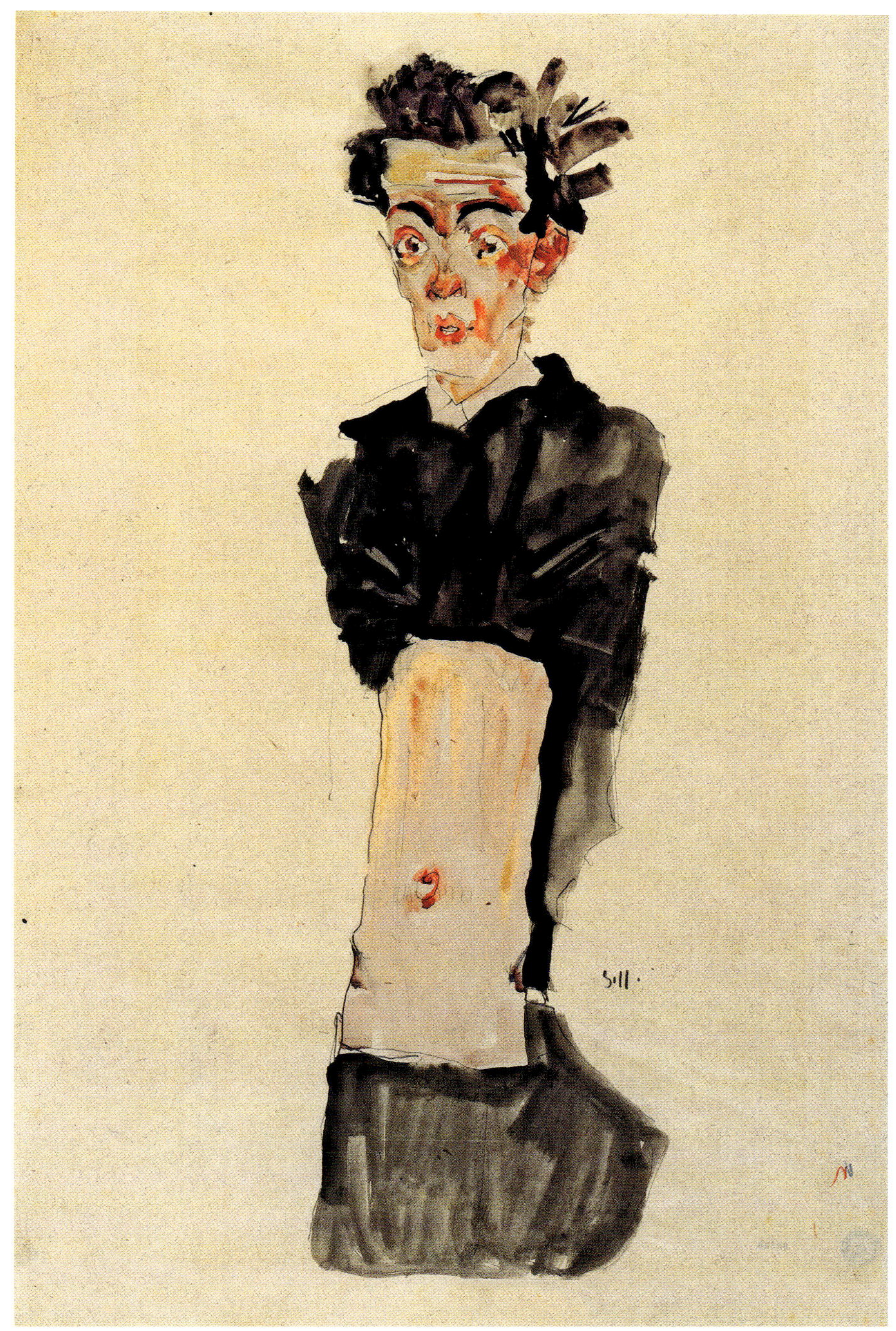

Exposed His hair stands on end, his eyes are wide open, his mouth gapes in shock—here Schiele seems to freeze in front of his own mirror image. His exposed belly and distorted face contrast with the artist's black clothing.

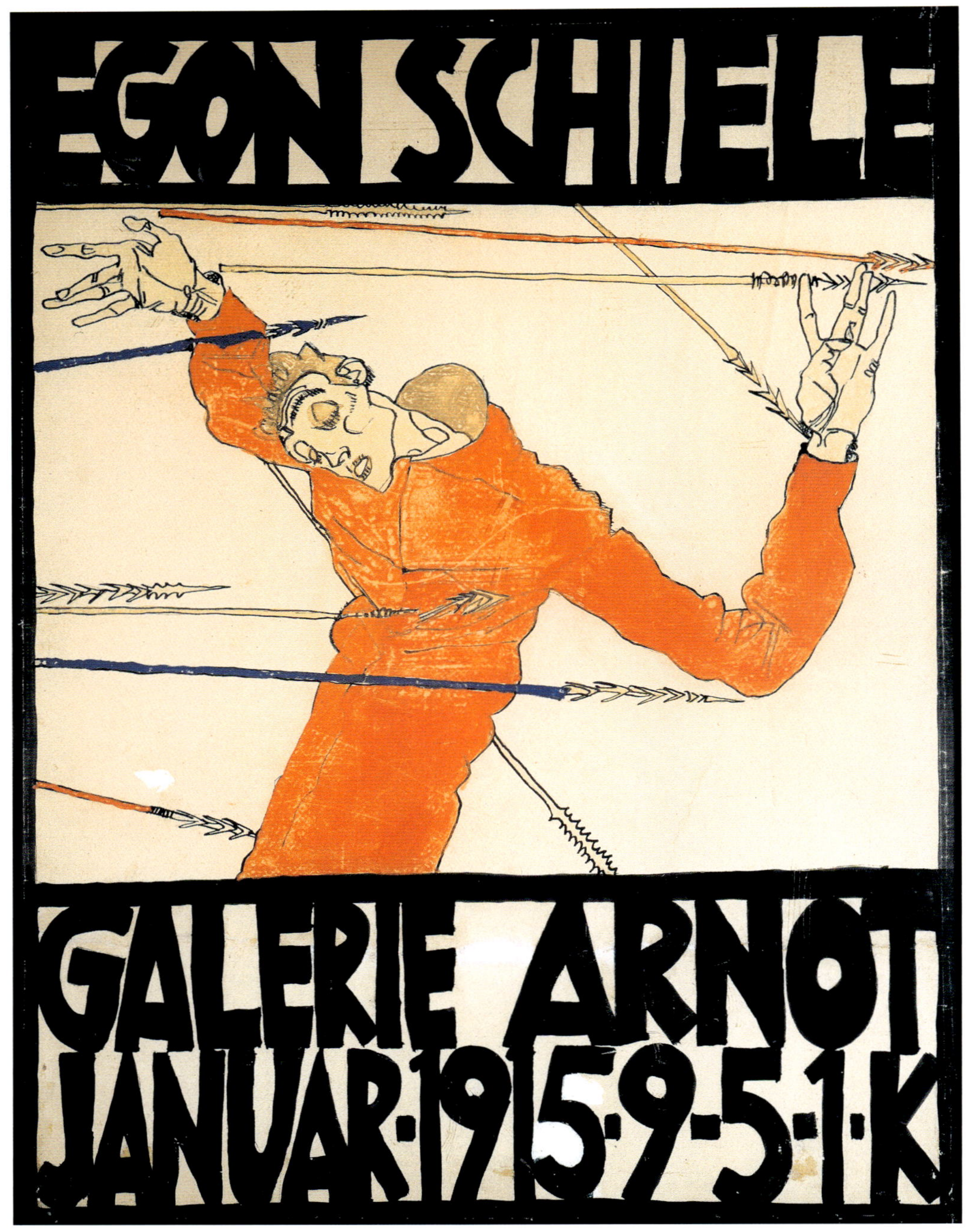

Martyr In a poster design for an exhibition at the Galerie Arnot in Vienna, Schiele depicted himself as St. Sebastian, pierced by arrows. His conviction and imprisonment left scars. But not only for Schiele; even his Expressionist colleague, the painter Oskar Kokoschka, depicted himself a number of times with this motif.

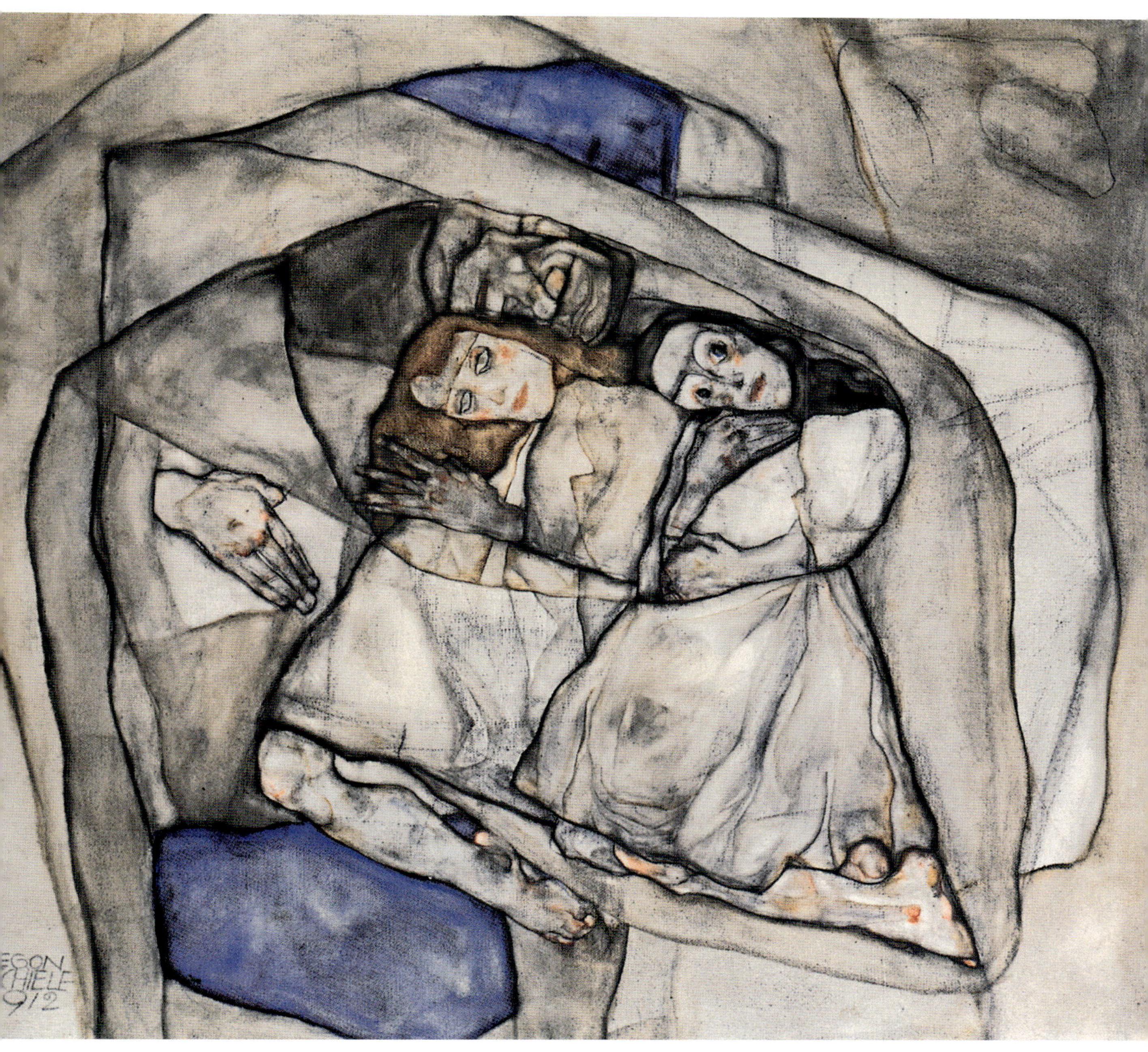

Conversion Two women kneel before a man in a monk's habit, presumably a self-portrait of Schiele. The three figures seem to cling together in a sort of capsule. Shortly after his 1912 imprisonment, Schiele depicted himself in several works as a monk or saint.

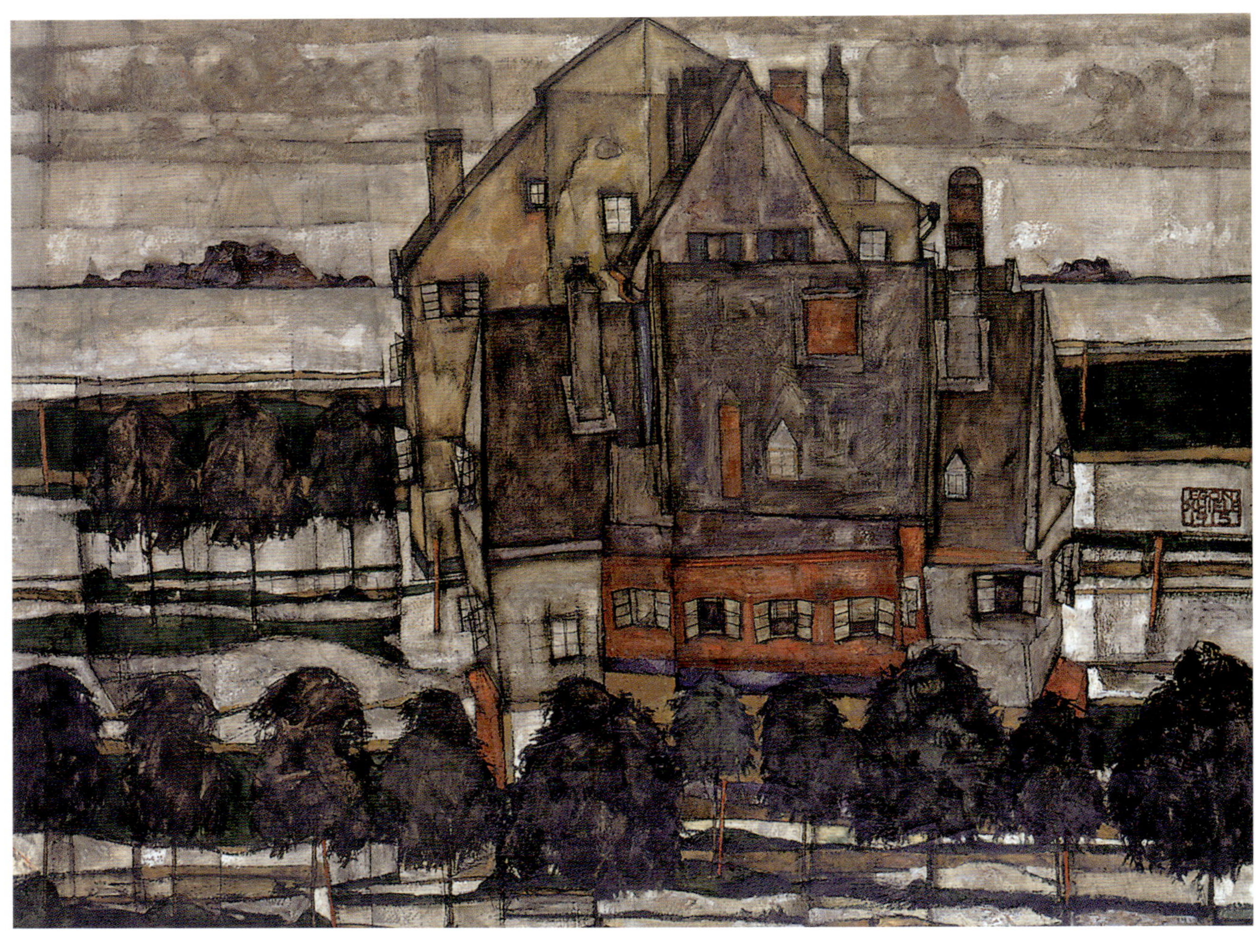

Place of retreat and source of inspiration Krumau is not recorded as the motif of this painting, but Schiele's affection for the birthplace of his mother, Marie Soukup, increases the likelihood that he saw these *Individual Houses* on one of his many journeys there.

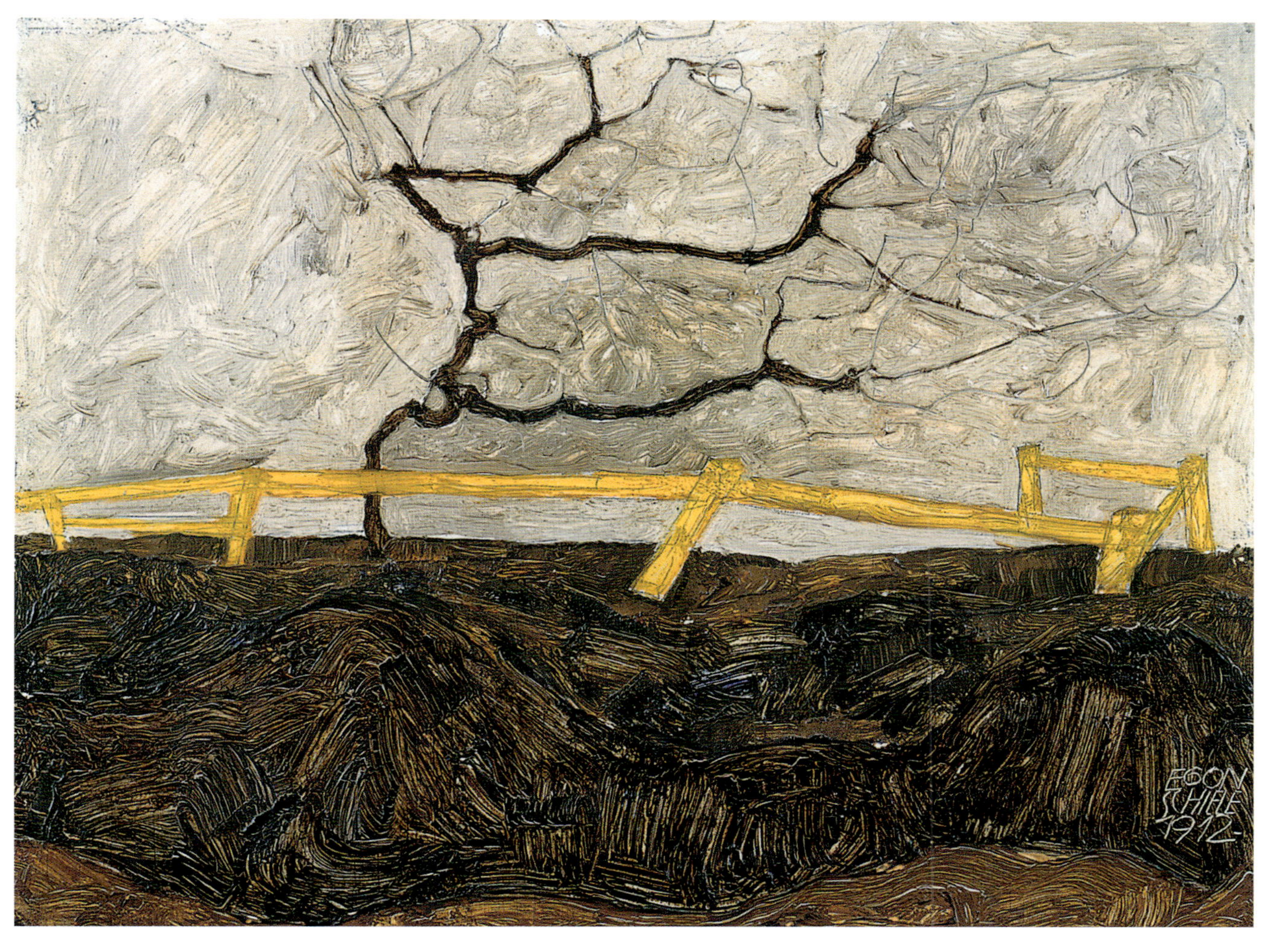

Late fall Decline, illness, and death were all popular motifs in the works of Expressionist artists. Schiele's *Bare Tree Behind a Fence* stands alone in the wind, with not a sign of life remaining.

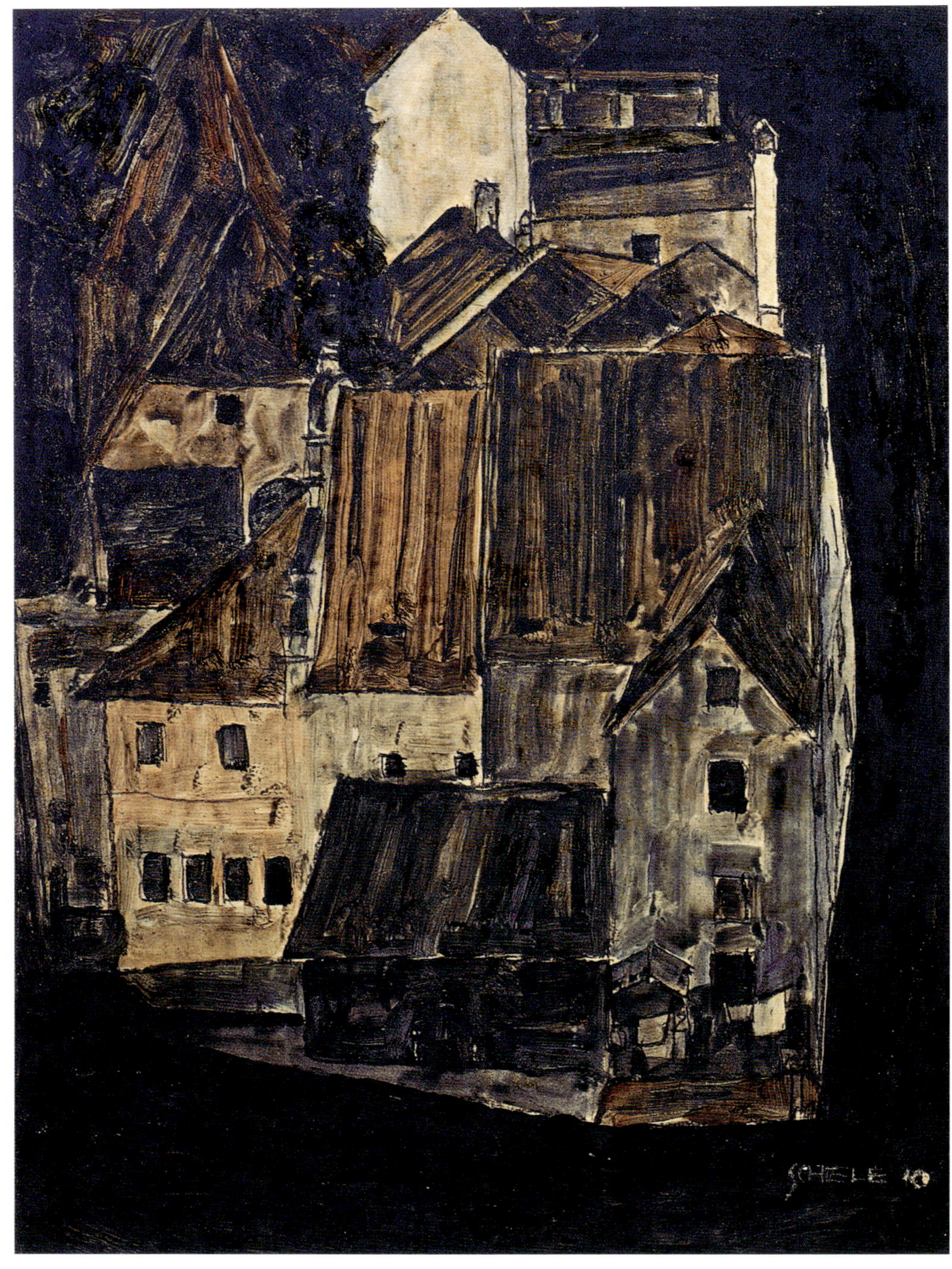

Morbid atmosphere From 1910 to 1911, Schiele dedicated himself to more somber colors and motifs. Vienna, which had been the cause of so much hardship, was, for the time being, left behind. Yet this hardly seems to have lightened his mood. Death remained an important motif for Schiele during his entire creative life; his 1910 poem "Tannenwald" (Fir Forest) closes with the line, "All is living dead."

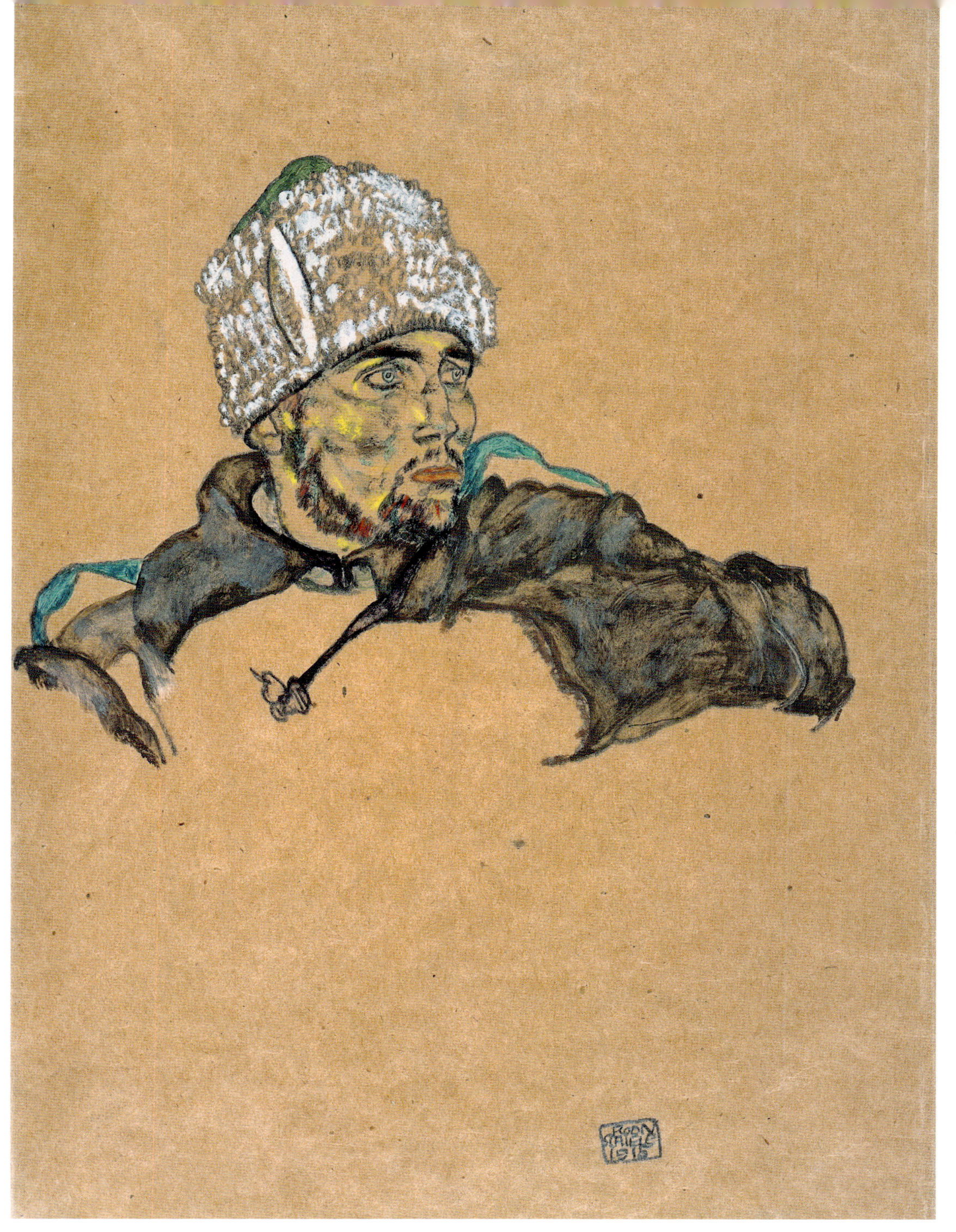

Image of war Schiele received a number of special favors during his time in the army. It was not least due to his talent that he was given the opportunity, along with his clerical duties, to practice his art. In 1915, he drafted this *Russian Prisoner of War with Fur Hat.*

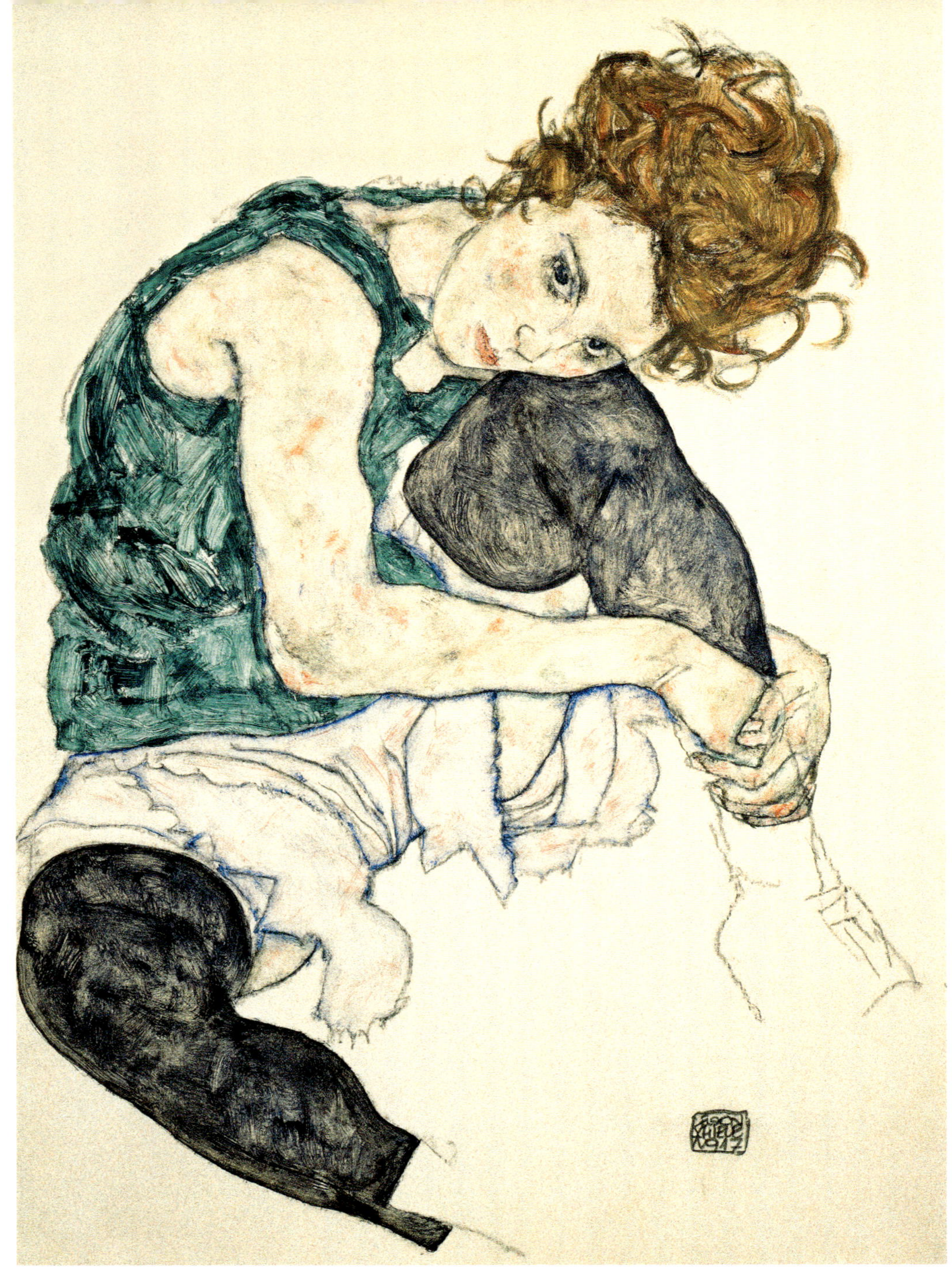

Family ties The model for this *Seated Woman with Bent Knee* was presumably Adele Harms, the sister of Egon's wife Edith. Schiele seems to have valued her highly as a model—and perhaps Edith had to keep her jealousy in check when she sat for him.

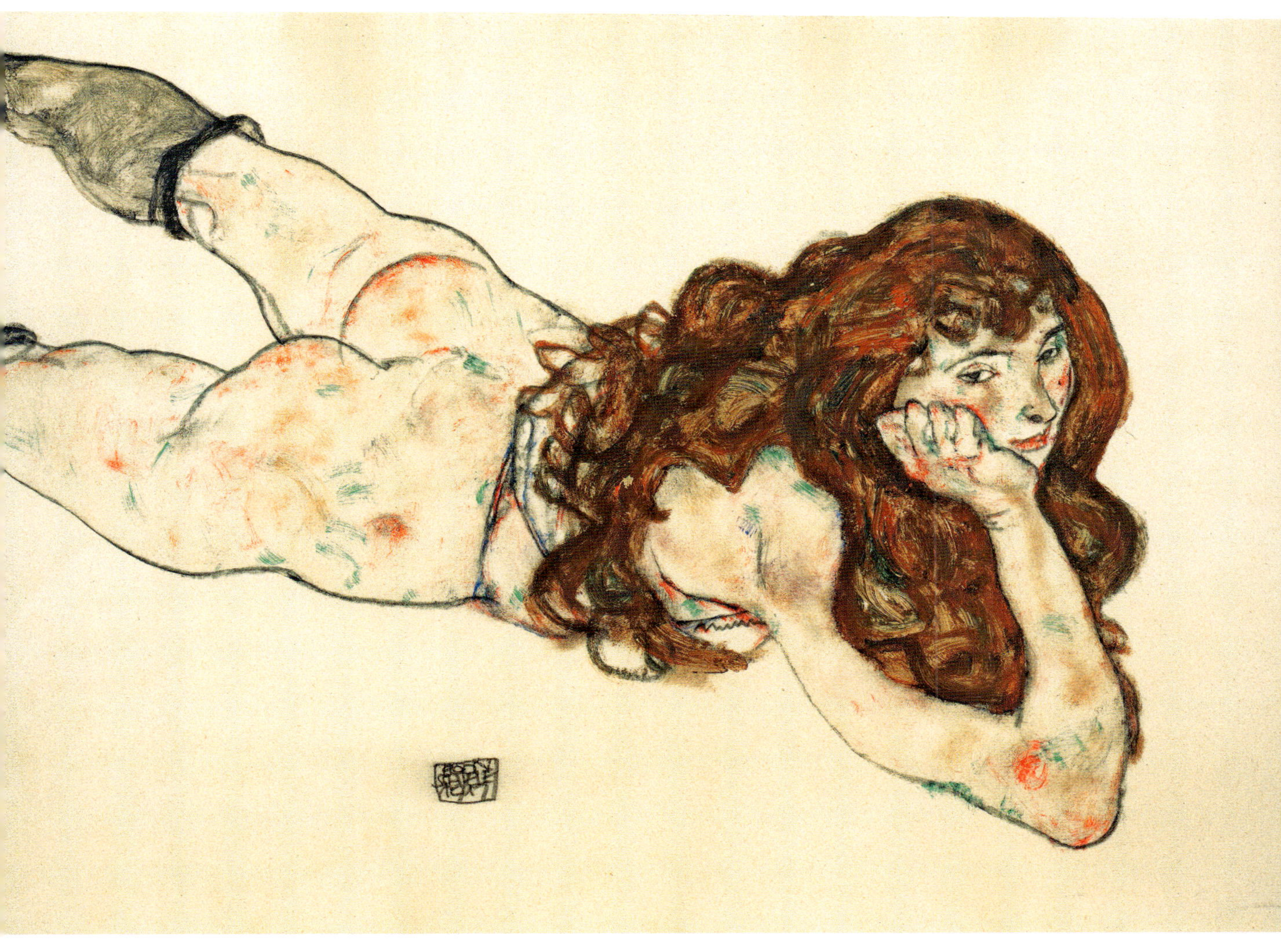

Magnificent hair Lying on her stomach, this woman gazes in seeming boredom at the observer as she supports her head, framed by a mane of red hair, with her right arm. In contrast to his earlier nude studies, here Schiele abandoned his deformation of the body; the empty background remains.

The Loves

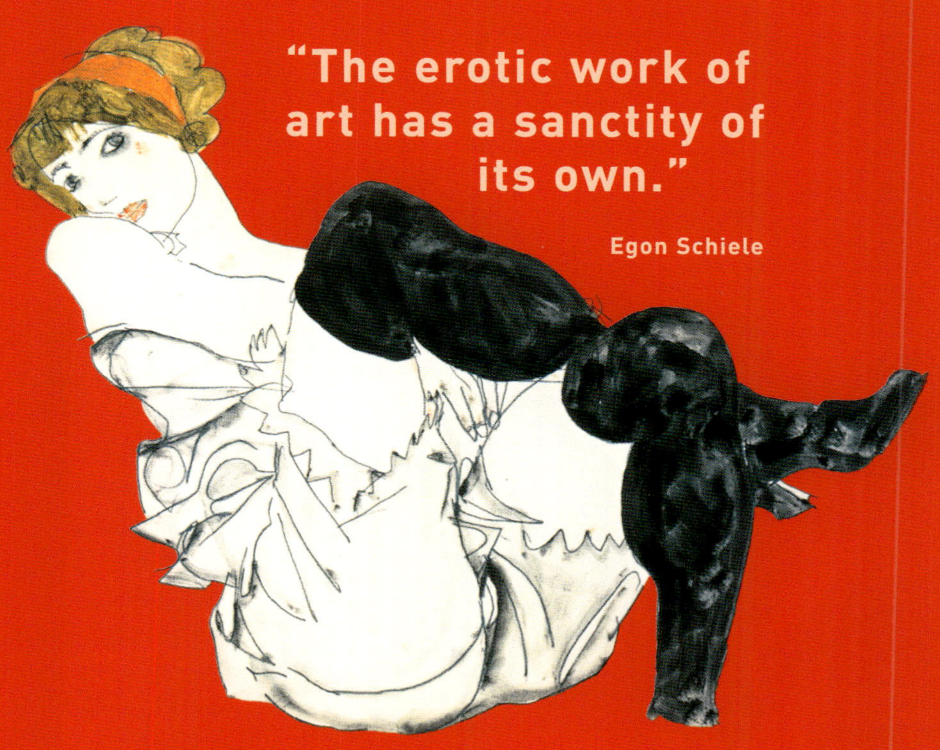

"The erotic work of art has a sanctity of its own."

Egon Schiele

A Twittering Lark versus the "Good Match"

Schiele's uninhibited nude studies and his unconventional lifestyle scandalized some of his contemporaries. For years the artist shared a home with Wally, his favorite model—and this in turn-of-the-century Vienna, where the reputation of artists' models was little better than that of prostitutes! Yet when the question of marriage arose, the painter ultimately took a middle-class bride.

Schiele's muses

In Schiele's day, artists' models almost always came from the lower classes, and were often prostitutes. For his candid and, for their time, daring erotic nudes, some even depicting pregnant women, Schiele found models among the patients of a gynecologist friend. His wife Edith did not wait long: immediately after marrying she forbid her husband from using any female models apart from herself. And her jealousy was certainly not unfounded. Schiele, however, paid little heed to her request; his notebook for 1918 includes notes about 117 different models.

A gynecologist friend put Schiele in contact with the pregnant women who sat for him.

Journeys ...

--> are immensely enjoyable for Schiele—preferably in the company of a female.

--> with his little sister Gerti were made by train to Italy, and his mistress Wally accompanied Schiele to take in the country air.

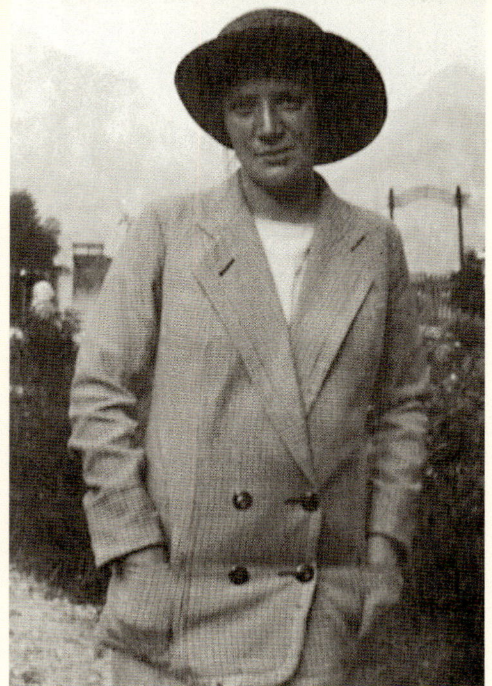

Model and mistress: Wally Neuzil

Egon called Wally his "twittering lark" because of her constant chattering. Valerie Neuzil modeled for Schiele, and for years was also his life partner, mistress, and confidante—but in the end he married someone else. Wherever Egon and Wally went, they immediately caused a scandal by "living in sin," behavior which of course conflicted with the bourgeois values of the time.

> **"What is tragic is only what one takes tragically, and Schiele took nothing tragically ..."**
>
> **Heinrich Benesch**

From a good family

"I plan to get married, advantageously, perhaps not to Wally." This was Egon Schiele's "romantic" announcement to his collector and patron Roessler in February 1915 about his possible marriage plans. Edith Harms was his chosen one, a girl from a good family, in stark contrast to his long-term mistress Wally. Her parents at first were not at all enthusiastic about their little daughter's liaison with a flighty artist. Her mother was especially concerned with guarding the reputation of her well-protected child, and thus a planned two-day Easter journey with Egon turned into a day trip. And with a warning: "I have all the authority I need to lodge a veto if necessary," she informed her would-be son-in-law.

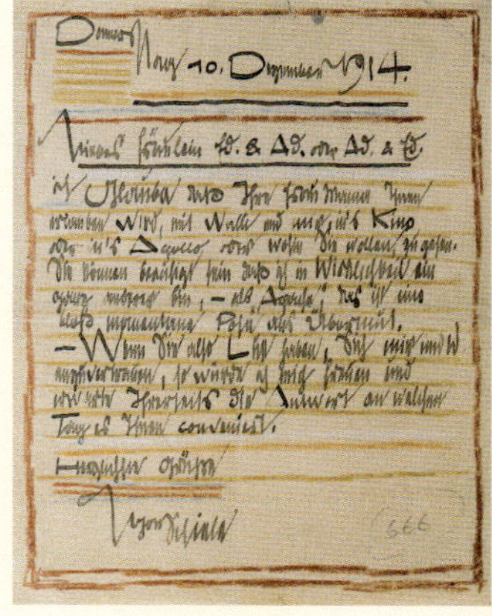

10. Dezember 1914.

Schiele addressed this letter to the sisters Edith and Adele Harms—he had not decided to which of the two his heart belonged.

Freud and bourgeois sexual morality

The treatment of sexuality and eroticism at the turn of the century was fraught with hypocrisy. Sigmund Freud confronted this moral double standard—sexuality, even the visiting of prostitutes, was accepted so long as it took place in secret. The Viennese neurologist's research into the human psyche and the effects of a repressed sex drive inspired countless artists of the time. With his nude studies, Schiele also railed against the repressive morality criticized by Freud.

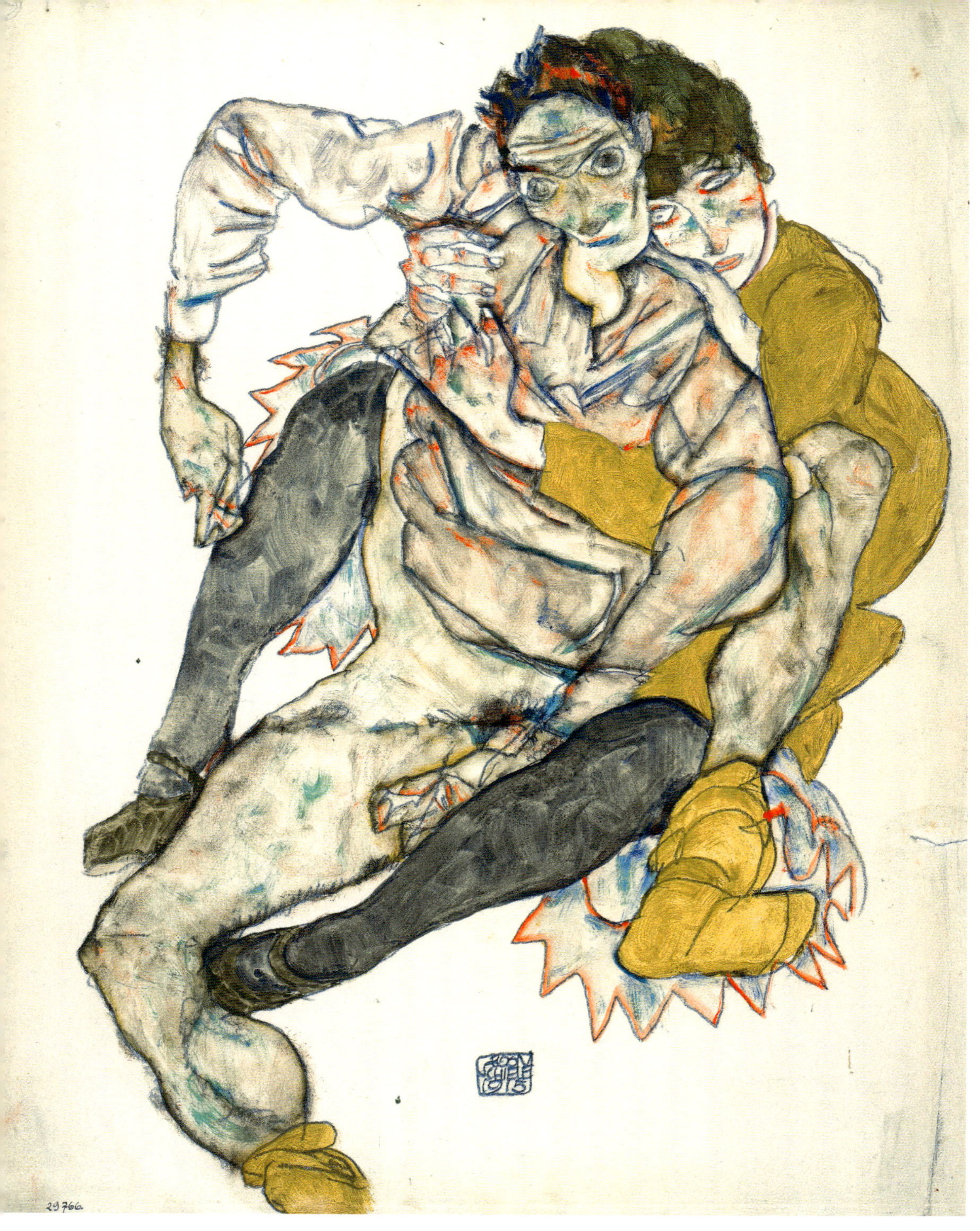

The young couple Egon and Edith Schiele in a close embrace.

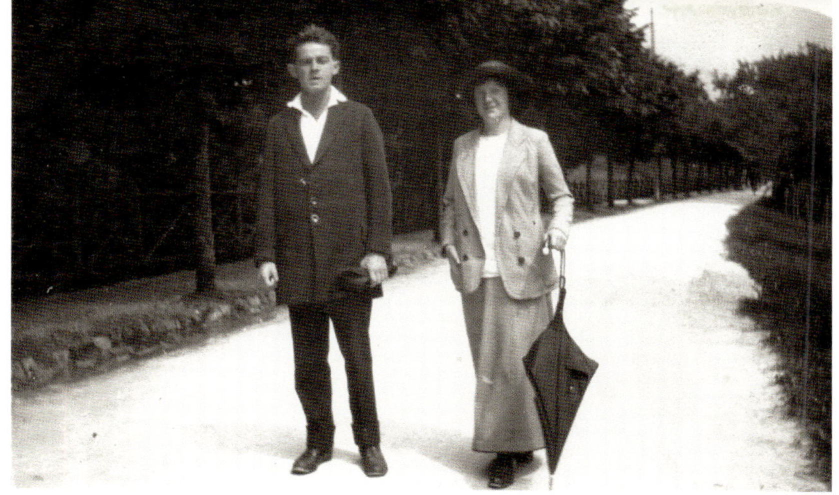

Egon Schiele and Wally Neuzil going for a walk.

Two Is One Too Many

After years of shacking up with his model Wally, Egon Schiele opted for a more bourgeois lifestyle—and requested the hand of Edith Harms. The newlyweds' bliss, however, was short-lived ...

A scandalous lifestyle

The seventeen-year-old Wally Neuzil represented a real ray of hope for Schiele. In the spring of 1911—still only twenty—he was living through a major creative crisis. Vienna and its traditional art scene were sapping his energy. In the meantime, Schiele acquired his own studio, and with it concerns over money. This cheerful strawberry-blonde girl who had previously modeled for Klimt, came along at just the right time. Wally Neuzil kneels in the painting *Cardinal and Nun,* is presumably also the *Mourning Woman,* and sat for *Wally in a Red Blouse with Raised Knees,* along with countless other depictions. But that was not all. Soon Wally and Egon were living together. In the glittery world of turn-of-the-century Vienna, this was certainly ripe for scandal.

Those who see in Schiele's artwork nothing but the naked, the obscenely naked and nothing else, are beyond help ..."

Arthur Roessler in an essay on Egon Schiele, 1911

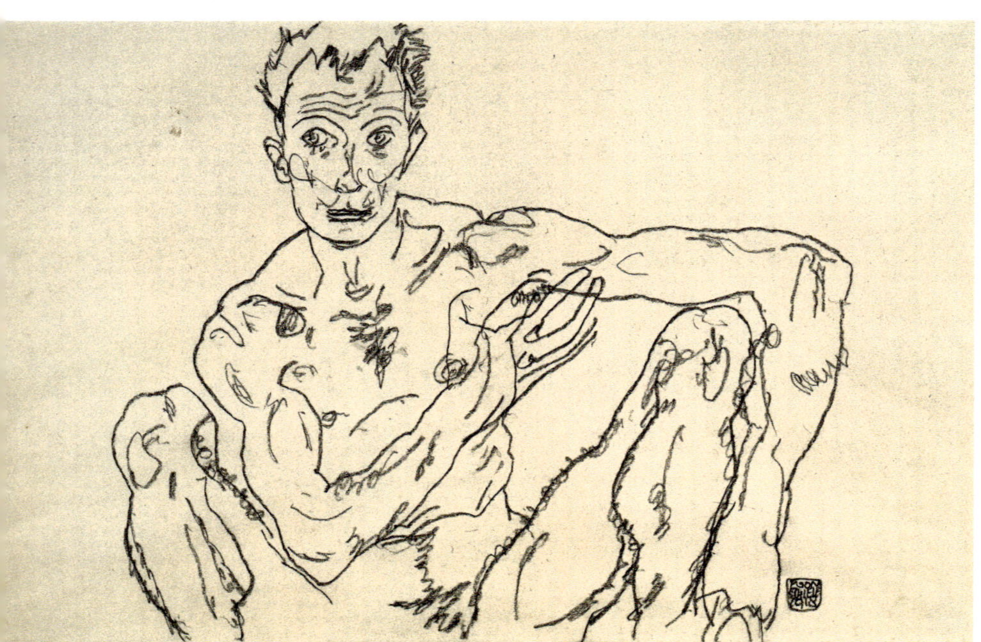

Egon Schiele depicted himself in 1918 in a nude self-portrait.

Vienna's underbelly

Discreet visits to prostitutes (and the reputation of artists' models were hardly any better) were socially acceptable, but shacking up with an underage model? Hardly. Especially since Schiele didn't even bother to hide the relationship.

In order to give the appearance of conforming to the strict social norms, many of Schiele's contemporaries were drawn into the shadow world of secret relationships. Stefan Zweig described the delicate situation in his autobiography *The World of Yesterday:* "I cannot recall a single comrade of my youth who did not come to me with pale and troubled mien, one because he was ill or feared illness, another because he was being blackmailed because of an abortion, a third because he lacked the money to be cured without the knowledge of his family, the fourth because he did not know how to pay hush money to a waitress who claimed to have had a child by him, the fifth because his wallet had been stolen in a brothel and he did not dare to go to the police."

Provocative nudes

Wally accompanied Egon to the small village of Krumau, where the two spent the summer of 1911. They were quickly unable to defend themselves from the animosity of the villagers. A move to Neulengbach changed nothing: living out of wedlock was not yet acceptable, and clashed particularly with the traditional values of country folk. Not to mention, of course, that the underage Wally was posing naked for the artist. The resulting images can only be understood as pure provocation, going far beyond what until then was the representation of the (female or male) nude. Even though the nude figure had been a common artistic motif for centuries, many of Schiele's pages still shocked and disturbed his contemporaries, and continue to shock today. Even Oskar Kokoschka, who was also vilified as a young artist for his pictorial language, did not hold his tongue in 1964 on the occasion of the Schiele retrospective in London, describing the artist as a "pornographer."

The Harms family gathered in the living room. From left to right: father Johannes Harms, Edith, mother Josefine, Adele, Fritz Erdmann (a son from a first marriage), and son Adolf.

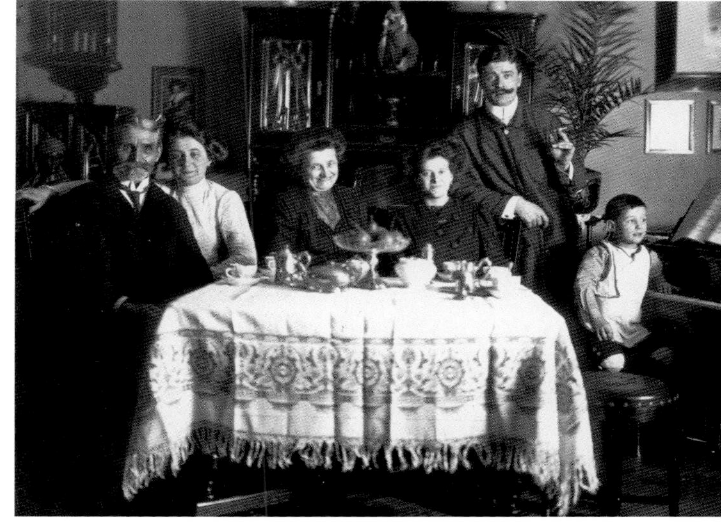

Even before Schiele met Wally, he was drawing from female models. His two sisters, Melanie and above all Gerti, four years younger, diligently posed for him, as did professional models and street girls.

The nude inspired in classical antiquity was in vogue at the time, and idealized poses, both male and female, were in demand. But Schiele's nudes were far removed from classical poses, from their graceful beauty. They were uncontrolled and ecstatic in their passion, yet the figures made direct eye contact with the observer—there was no furtiveness here. Schiele did not concern himself with realistic depictions: he smothered the reduced forms of his female models' bodies in yellow, green, red. Schiele depicted lovers and even same-sex couples of both genders—this at a time when homosexuality was forbidden. And his depictions of masturbating men and women were scandalous in view of the time's pathologization of onanism. While Schiele did not aestheticize, he did not approach the pornography of which many contemporary critics accused him. Rather, his nudes disturb because of their perspective, the direct view of the genitalia, the distortion of the depicted figures.

Noble Wally

One of Schiele's nude drawings turned out to be disastrous for him—or rather the fact that Schiele hung it in his studio where it was visible to children. A trial was followed by more than three weeks in the prison at Neulengbach. During his weeks of imprisonment, Wally was once again Schiele's only ray of hope. And the young girl must have been just as shocked by the situation as Schiele himself. At first Wally was not allowed to go near him, but she refused to be put off and visited Egon daily. Communication was at first

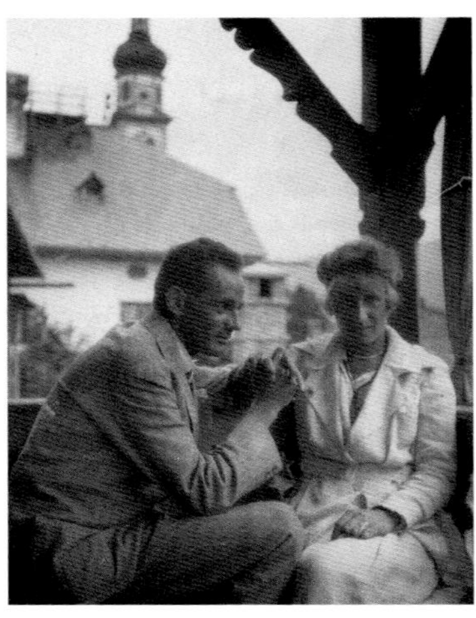

The Schieles in the summer of 1918

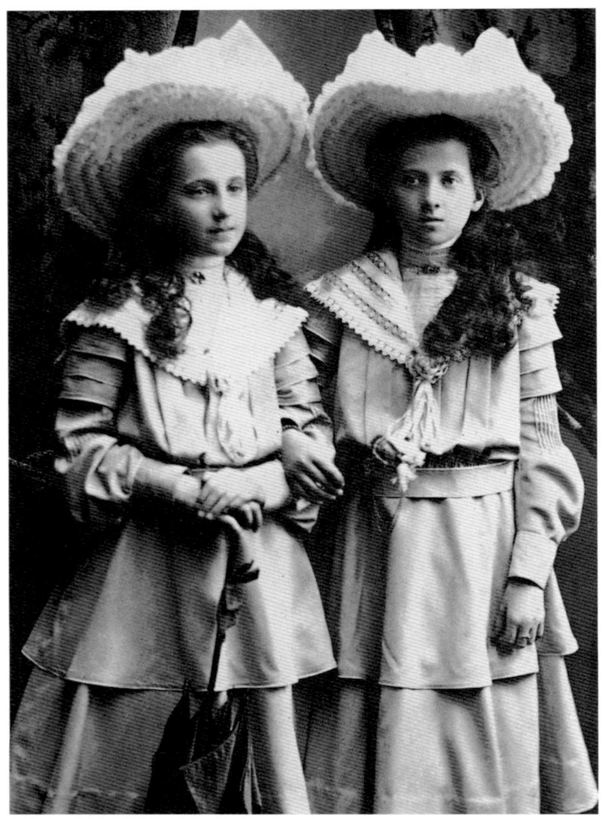

Ultra-fashionable: sisters Adele and Edith as children

possible only through a barred window. Schiele was greatly appreciative of Wally's support. He would later comment about her loyalty during this major crisis, saying that she had behaved "nobly."

In the summer of the following year, Egon and Wally traveled to the Traunsee at Arthur Roessler's invitation. This summer holiday is the source of some of the few photographs of the couple.

A partner for life

Schiele, however, apparently had a very different idea about who would be the woman of his life. He had other plans for himself other than that of a societal troublemaker. He aspired to more than a bohemian life à la Klimt and children out of wedlock.

In December 1914 Schiele began to flirt with two young ladies at once, nearby his studio on Hietzinger Hauptstrasse. The Harms sisters, Edith and Adele, received a beautifully designed letter in which Egon asks whether they might be allowed to go to the cinema with him (and Wally!). What qualified Wally of all people to chaperone must remain an open question. What is also unclear is which of the sisters had captured his heart. For safety's sake, he included both in his salutation—in an original way: "Dear Fräulein Ed. & Ad. or Ad. & Ed."

This letter was not the end. Egon appeared in person at the Harms house. His choice fell upon the younger of the two sisters, Edith. The family was not immediately enthusiastic about the choice of suitor. And Edith also had her doubts about the reputation that preceded the artist. But she finally decided in favor of Schiele, as she informed her intended in the spring of 1915: "Let them all talk (my people, I mean), my opinions are not theirs, so I can entirely lose myself in your ideas and opinions ... I don't want to, and will not,

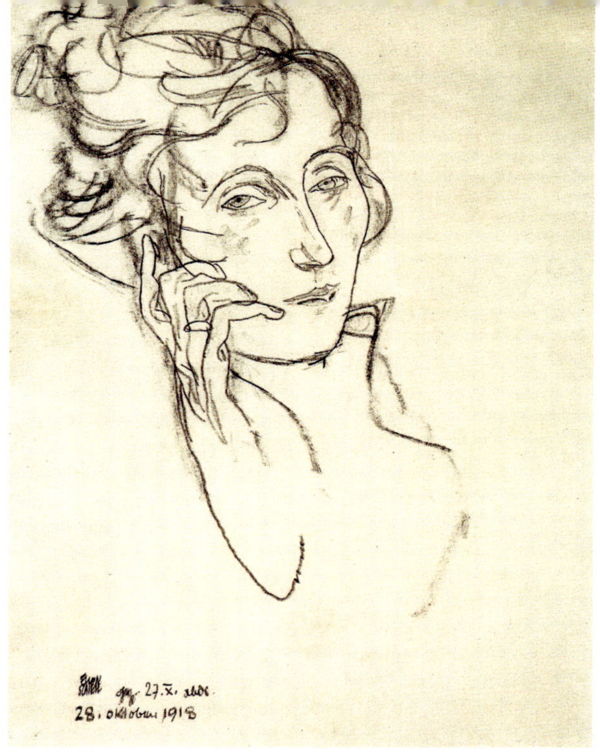

Schiele's last work is this drawing of his wife on her deathbed.

make any rules for you, but now you can understand the business with your lady friend, I demand ... nothing impossible. I am fond of you, but I don't think that I am blindly in love, and my jealousy demands the step with W... You are more to me—than my family, don't underestimate that ... I love my people very much. You are everything to me, and I will obey you ..."

Farewell to Wally

This declaration of love had the desired effect on Schiele. But Edith also took action with Wally. According to Roessler, she explained both expansively and triumphantly to her weeping rival why she should renounce Egon. Schiele met Wally once more at his regular haunt, the Café Eichberger, and put to her an extravagant proposal: Wally could still be his "former lover" for a yearly summer holiday ... she said goodbye. She ended all contact with Schiele, but stayed in touch with his patron Roessler. She joined the Red Cross during WWI to serve as a nurse at the front. In December 1917, Wally died in Split of a scarlet fever infection.

Egon obviously had no time to lose. He took advantage of his chance at a bourgeois life and married Edith in June 1915. He even learned to appreciate his father-in-law, Johannes. Yet whether the young couple were realistic concerning their financial situation is questionable. At any rate, Edith was not as well off as Schiele had probably hoped. The newlyweds, however, were not given much time to settle their debts. Four days after the wedding, Schiele began his military service in Prague.

Brief happiness

The two were not destined to have a long life together. After Schiele's erratic army career, during which he was forced to relocate several times, they finally set up an apartment in Vienna together in 1918; Edith was expecting her first child. A short time later the pregnant girl contracted Spanish influenza, from which she eventually died. Only three days later, Egon followed his wife in death.

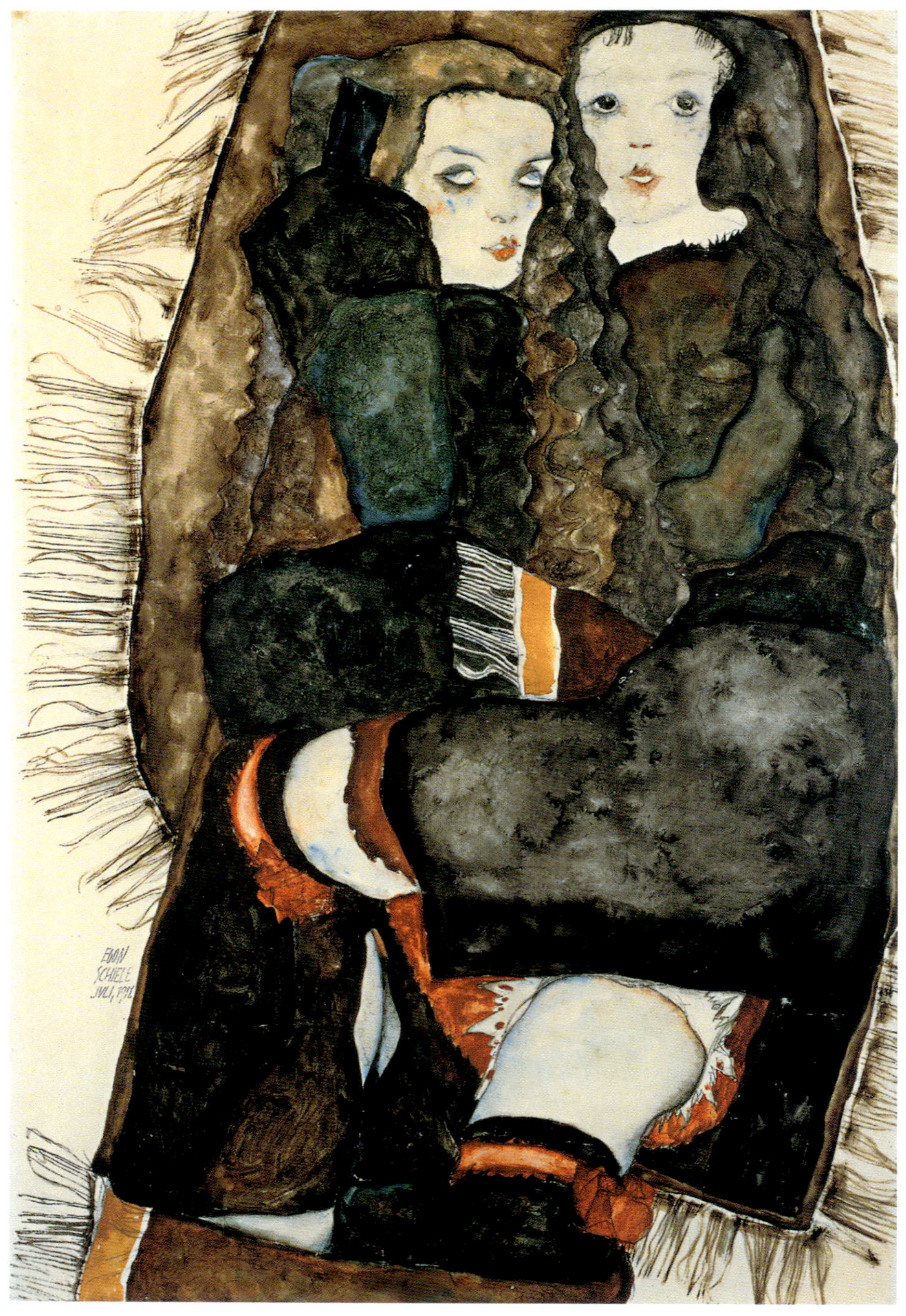

View from above Schiele's favorite perspective for landscapes as well as nude studies was a bird's-eye view. In *Two Girls on a Fringed Blanket* from 1911, he contemplated the girls from above. He hardly allows an impression of space to develop; even the brown blanket is extended to fill much of the frame.

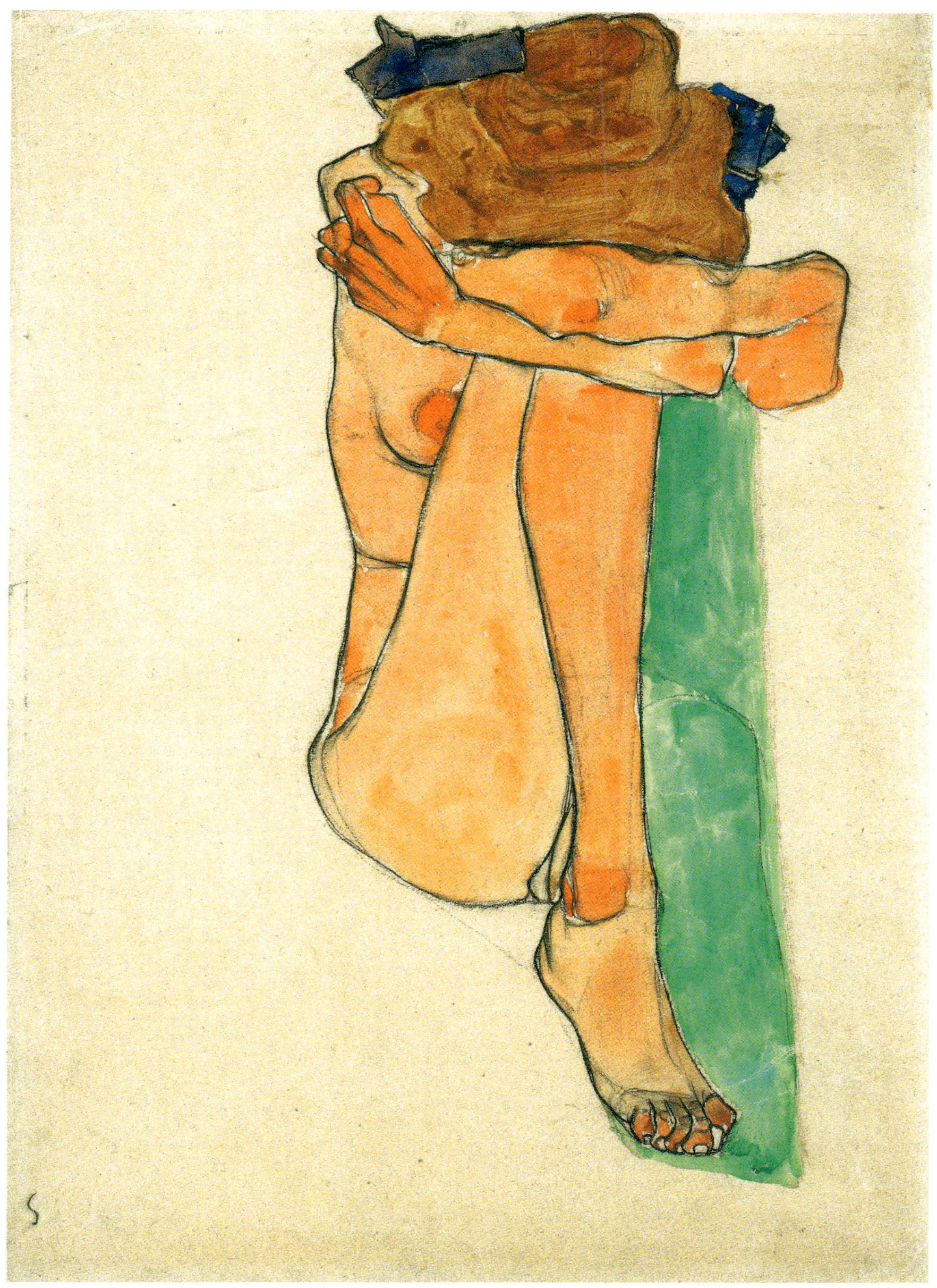

Naked bodies Schiele was twenty years old when he began using the nude as a motif in his works. He produced an entire series in 1910, including this *Female Nude with Green Cushion.* The contours of the woman's body are soft, and the skin tone is to a large extent naturally rendered. The Jugendstil preference for softly curving lines still shines through.

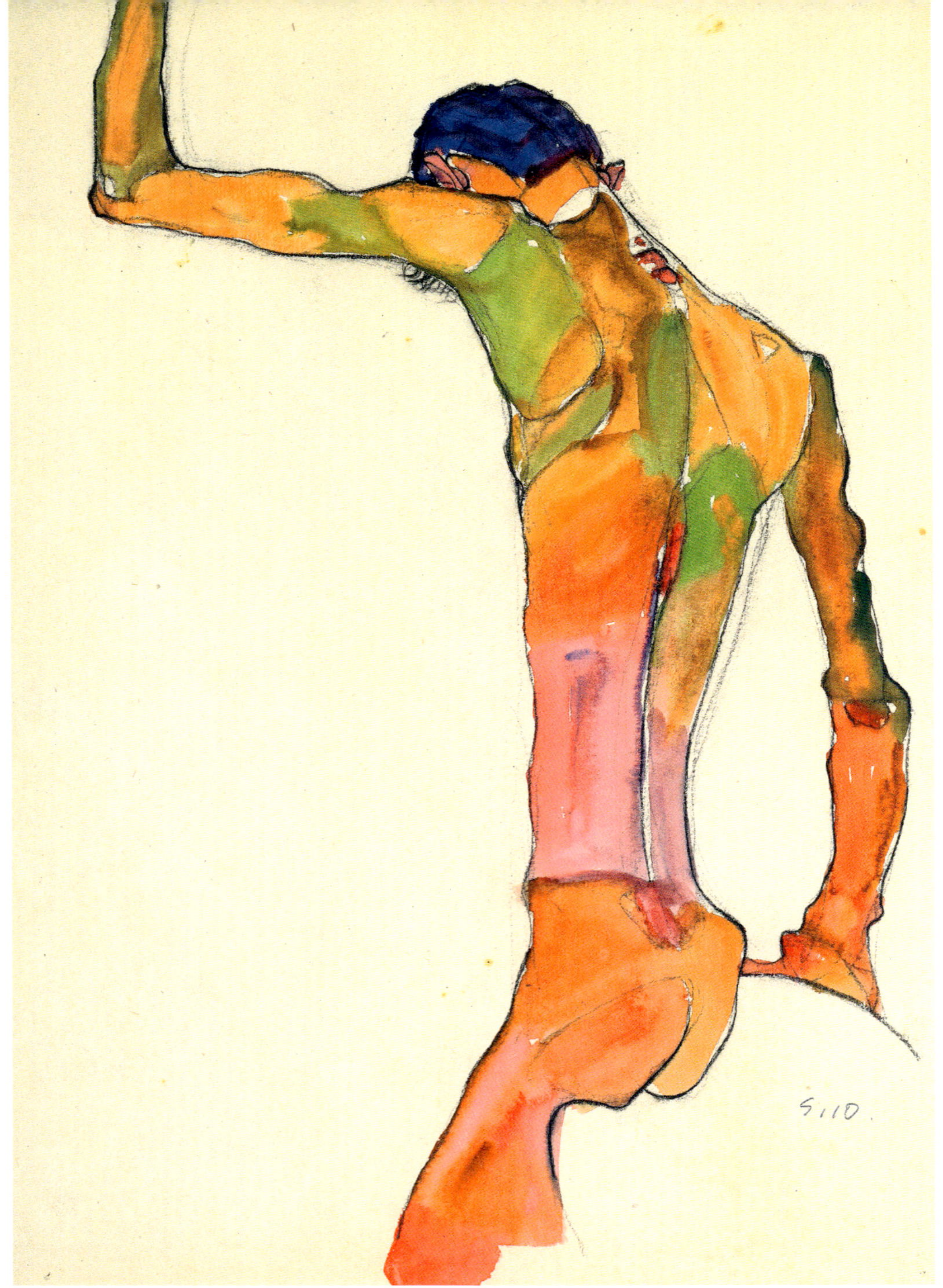

Colorful shimmer Pink and grass-green with orange are the colors Schiele chose for this nude seen from the back. The shock of hair is bluish-violet, and the length of the back and the limbs are unnaturally extended—one could hardly imagine a less realistic rendering.

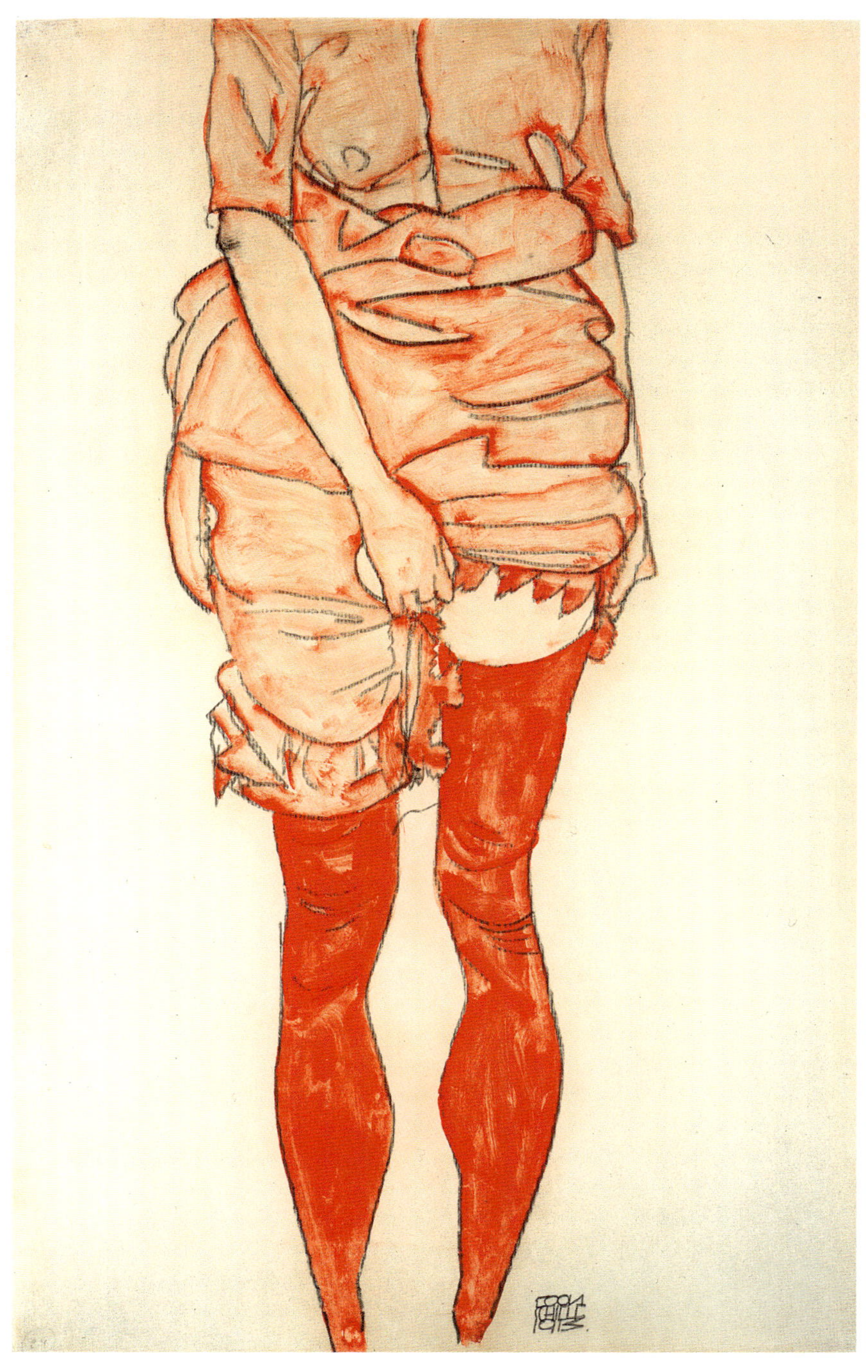

Headless Many of Schiele's female figures of 1913 are depicted without heads. This model had to do not only without her head, but also without her feet. The red-stockinged legs occupy the lower half of the page; the red of the gathered-up dress is somewhat paler.

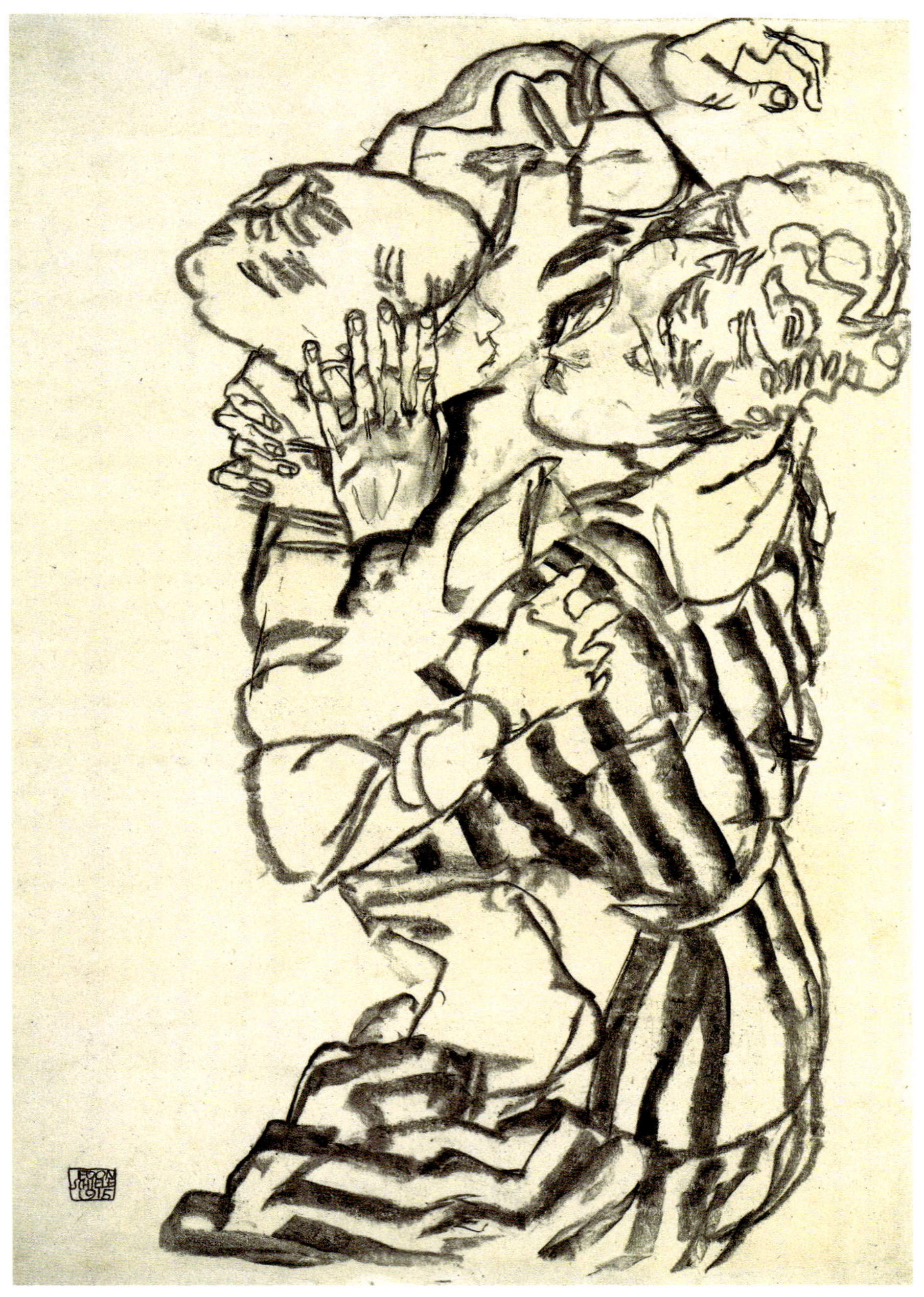

Private happiness In 1915 Schiele drew his wife with her nephew in her arms. At the time he produced a great many portraits of Schiele family members, above all his sister Gerti and her son Anton. Dedicating himself to nudes was impossible given Schiele's work conditions: his artistic activities took place only in the context of his military service.

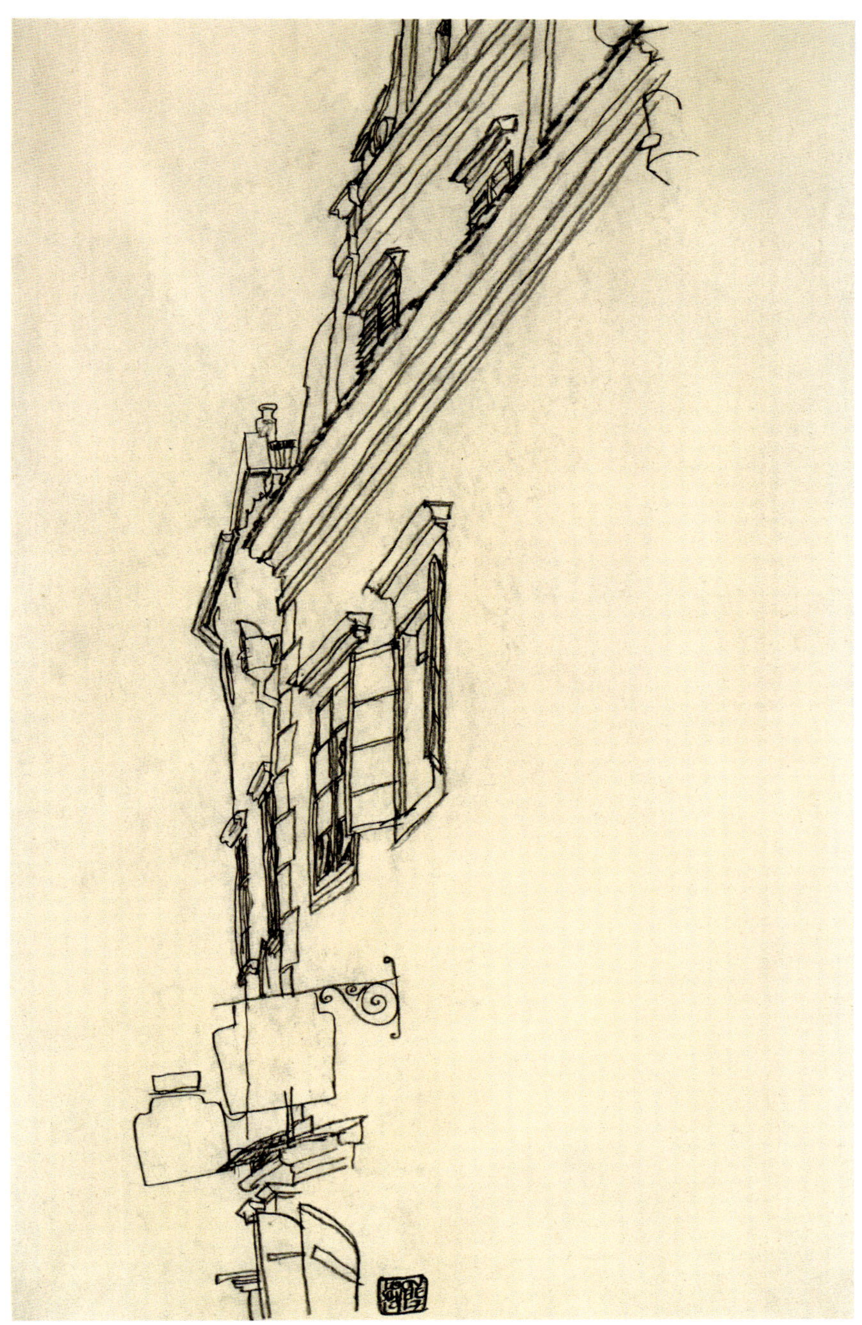

Family roots In 1917 Egon Schiele recorded these two houses with Renaissance pediments at an oblique angle. The buildings stand on Latrongasse in Krumau. Schiele's mother Marie came from this small Bohemian town, which for years provided motifs for his townscapes.

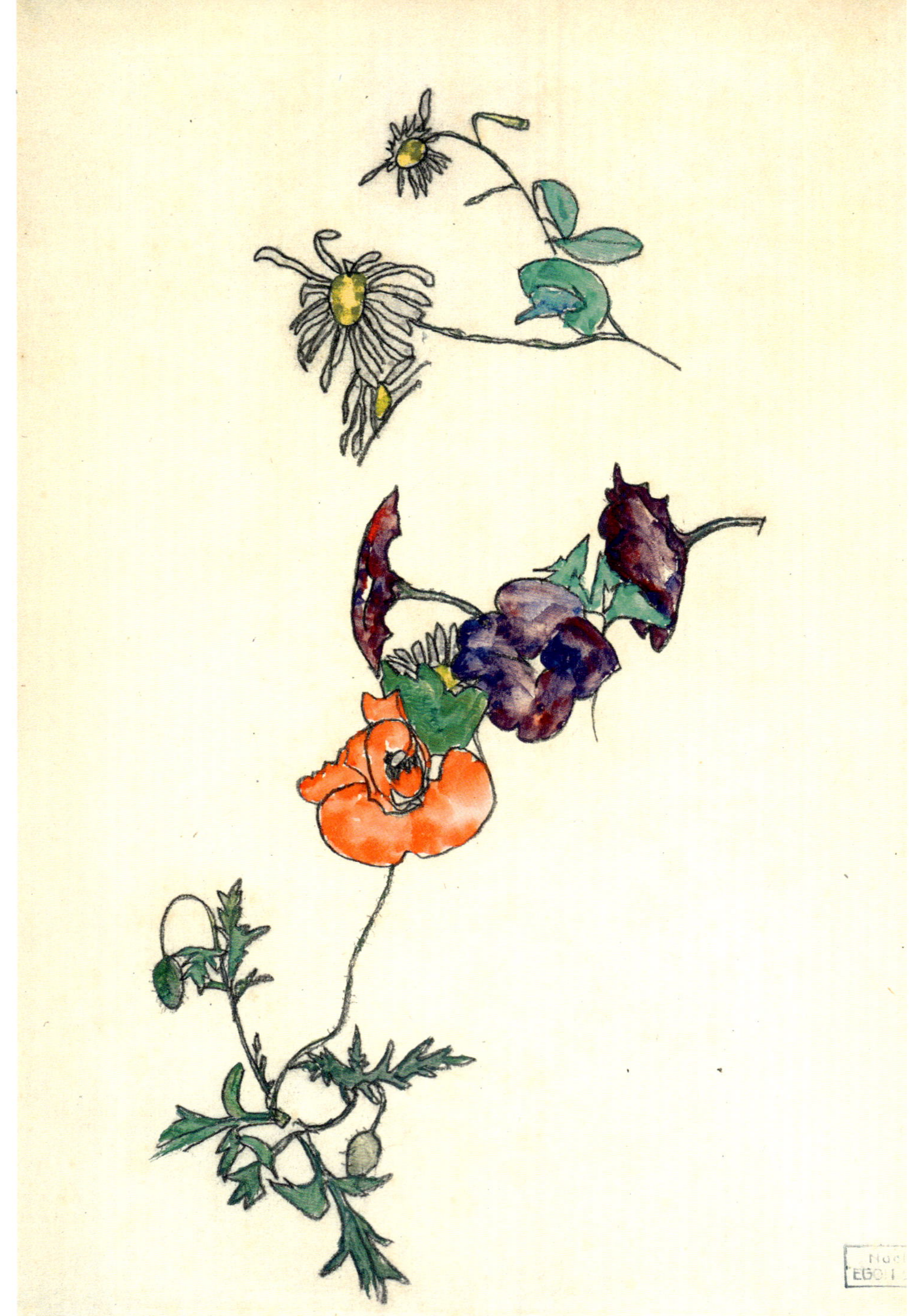

Glorious blooms Marguerites, morning glories, and a red poppy float on the paper; the delicate pencil outlines are filled in with watercolors. In contrast to his earlier drawings, in the last three years of his career Schiele depicted both people and objects in a naturalistic fashion. Anchoring them in the space was still not his style.

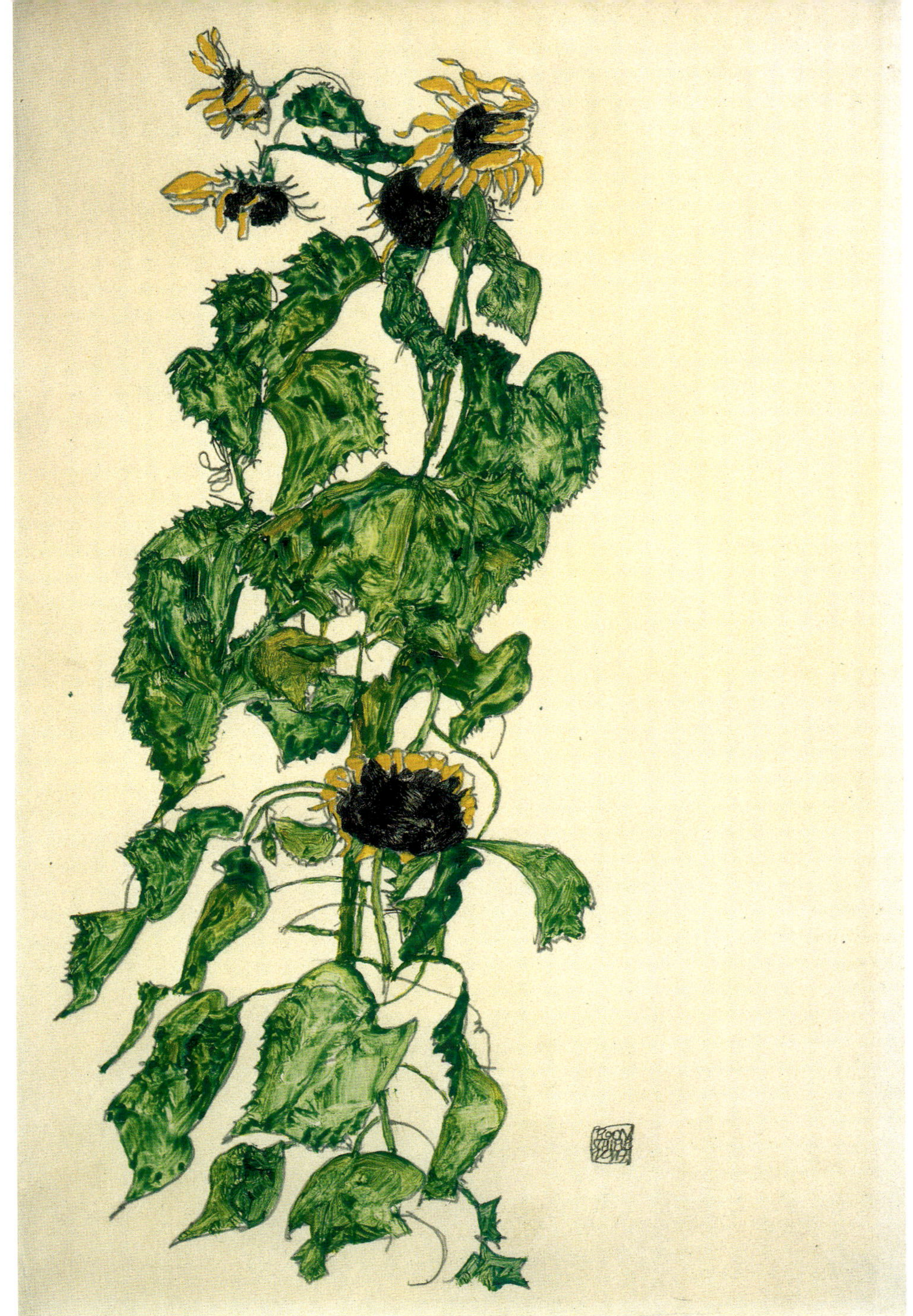

Lush green "I paint the light that comes out of all bodies," Schiele once said. Perhaps this is also true of his late flower pictures. Here there is no longer any trace of autumnal withering, as is found in his earlier sunflower paintings. The vibrant green foliage winds its way across the surface.

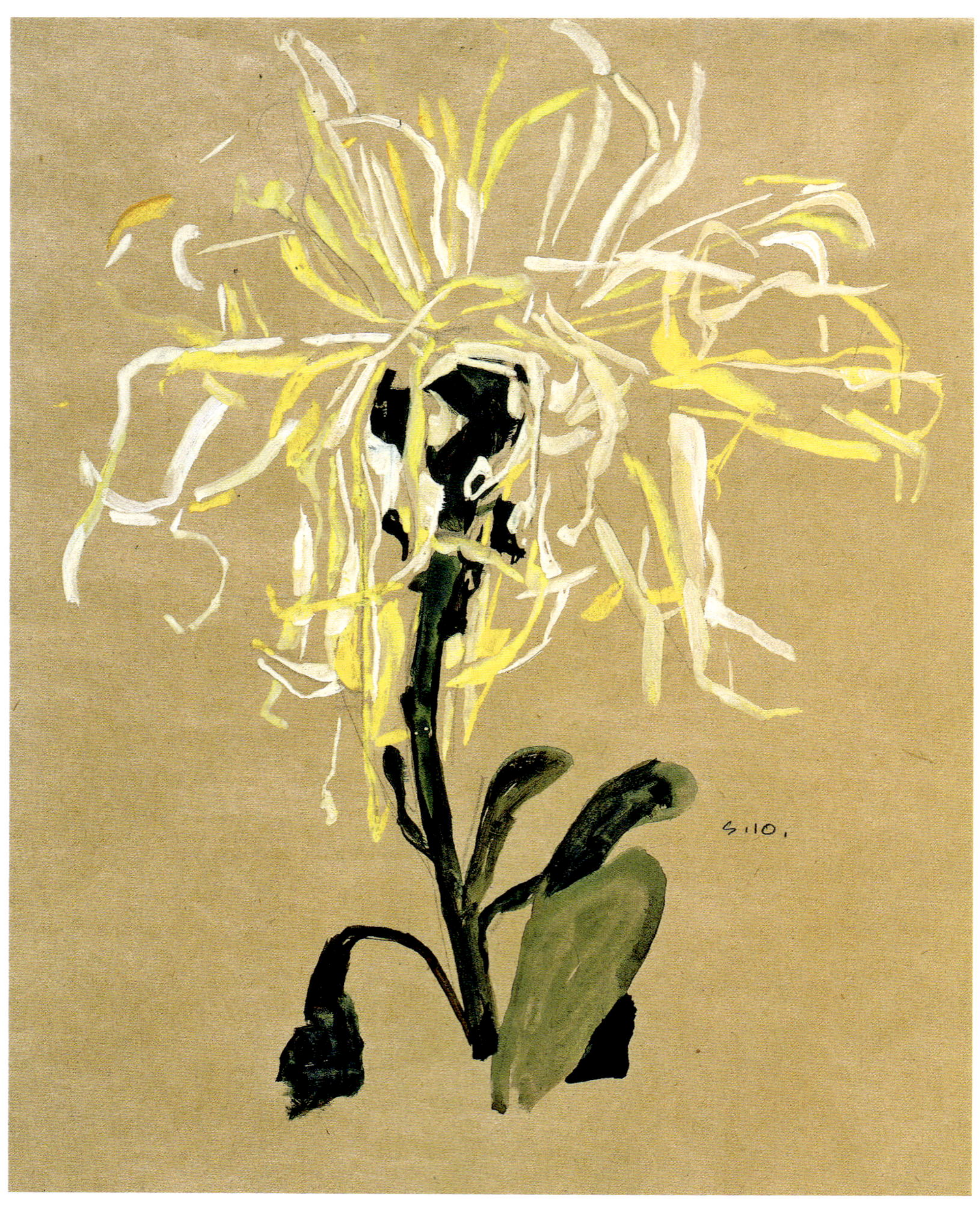

Chrysanthemums In 1910 Schiele created three watercolors of chrysanthemums as studies for a painting of the same name. While the yellow flower gives an impression of delicacy and lightness, the red chrysanthemum (facing page) almost leaps toward the observer in its fullness.

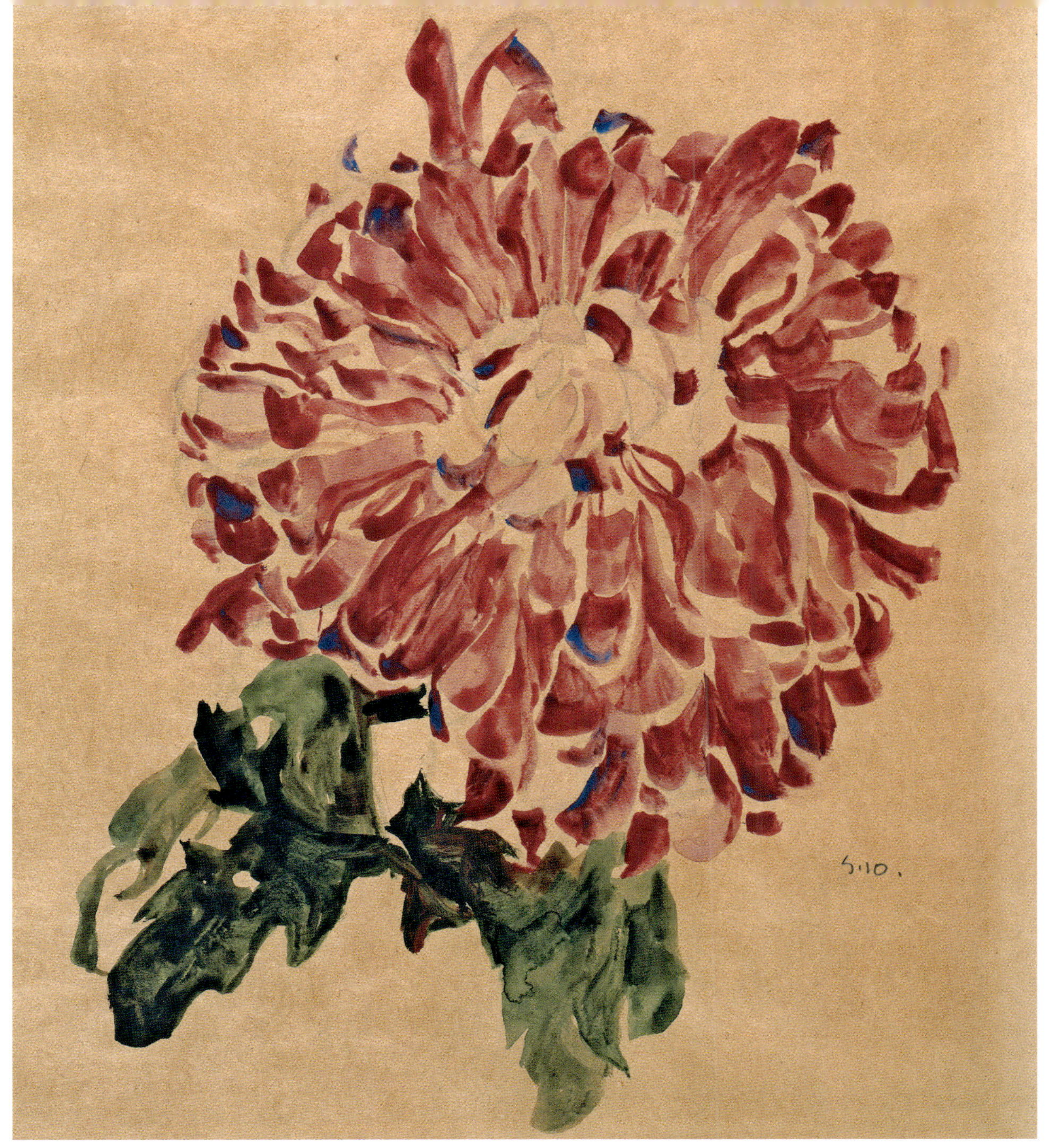

Plant study Even this brush drawing of a chrysanthemum blossom by Schiele manifests his Expressionism. The individual petals are not naturalistically rendered, but rather seem to express the very spirit of the vegetation.

Today

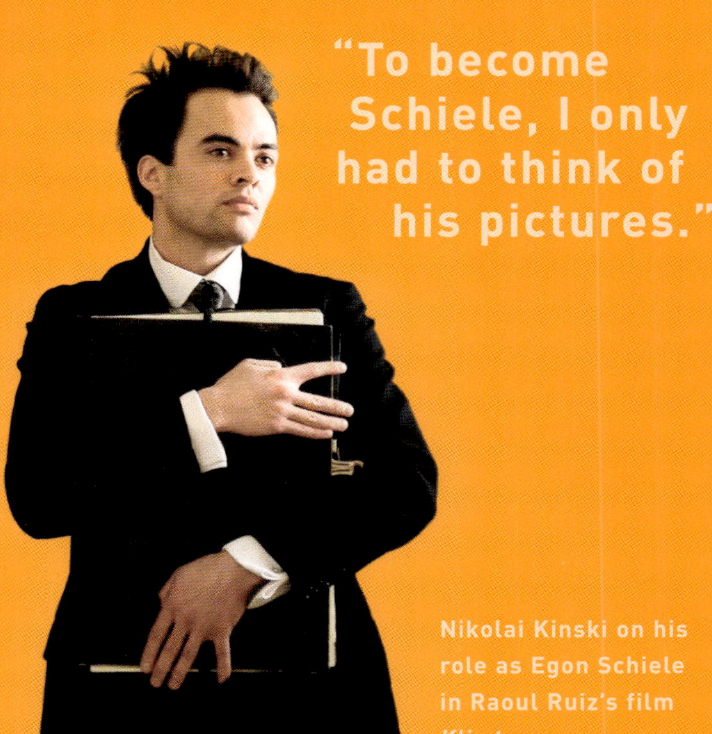

"To become Schiele, I only had to think of his pictures."

Nikolai Kinski on his role as Egon Schiele in Raoul Ruiz's film *Klimt*.

Ever-expanding ripples ...

... are made by Schiele's work—he was right: "Art cannot be modern; art is timeless." It took a little while before larger numbers came to know of his talent. Today his work is popular far beyond the borders of Austria. A veritable exhibition boom in the eighties was surpassed only by the record sums Schiele's paintings have fetched at auction.

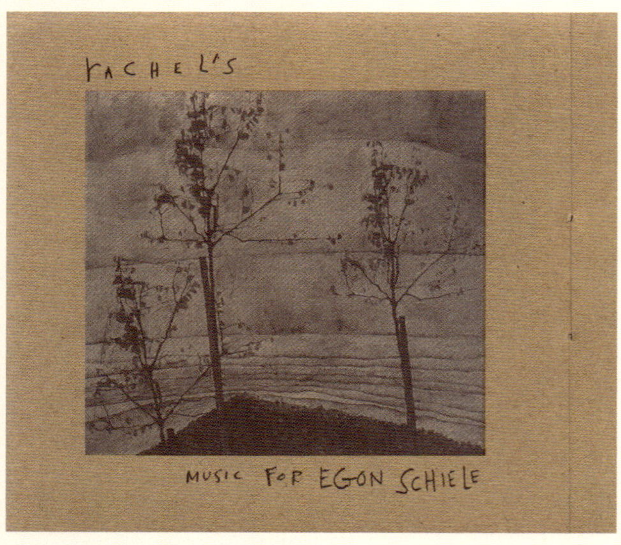

Raise the curtain

In America, Schiele has even made it to the stage—though only posthumously. In 1995, the theatrical dance production *Egon Schiele* by Stephan Mazurek premiered at the University of Illinois. Rachel Grimes's post-rock group Rachel's composed the score entitled *Music for Egon Schiele*. Some of the track titles are "Egon & Gertie," "Mime van Osen," and "Wally, Egon, & Models In The Studio." The tones of violin, cello, and piano take the place of colors on a canvas!

Vienna's museums ...

... are a must if you want to see Schiele's works in person.

→ The Albertina houses the Egon Schiele archive and possesses an important collection.

→ The Wien Museum has numerous works by Schiele.

→ Schiele's artwork also hangs in the Austrian Gallery Belvedere.

→ The Leopold Museum has a collection of 44 oil paintings as well as some 180 drawings by the master.

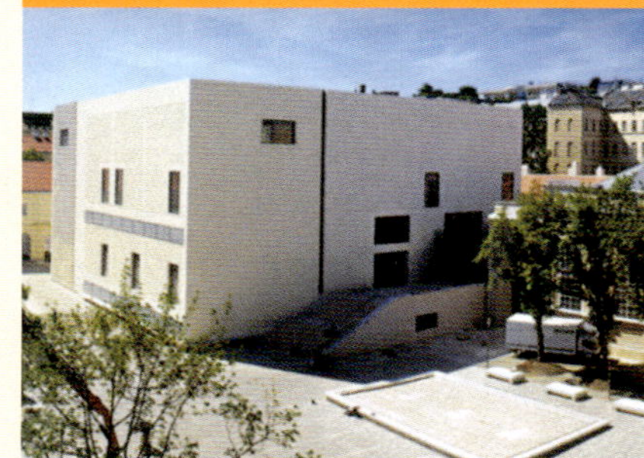

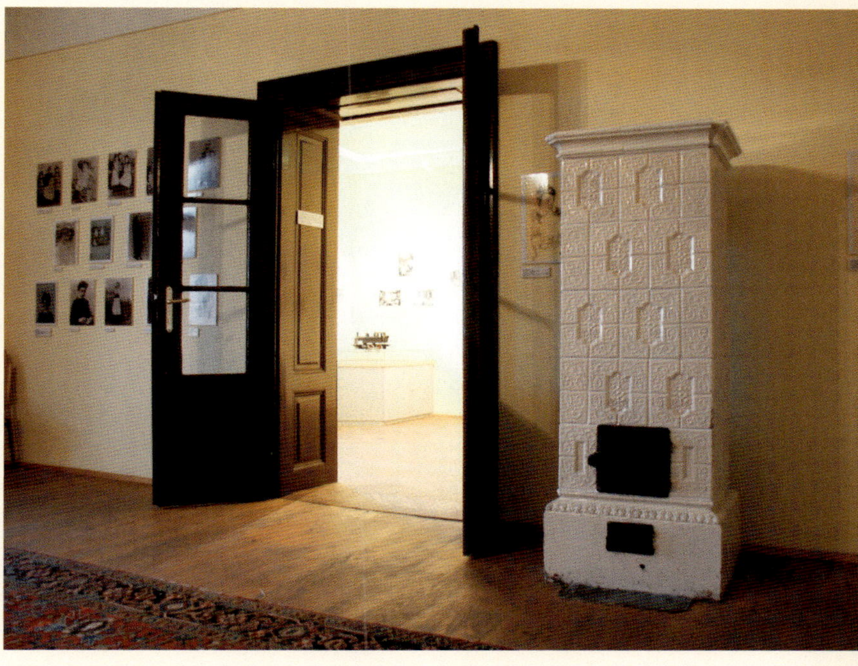

Behind bars

In tranquil Tulln on the Danube, the former prison has been transformed into a museum devoted to the town's most famous son. The 1990 inauguration was timed to coincide with Schiele's 100th birthday. No need to worry—his works can be viewed there without the need for handcuffs. One of the prison cells is a recreation of that which held Schiele at the court in Neulengbach.
The railroad station at Tulln is also used as a museum: the room in which Schiele was born and an adjoining room are furnished in turn-of-the-century fashion.

"Egon Schiele has always been an amazing source of inspiration for me. His paintings represent a very personal and revolutionary vision of the world, especially for the time they were created. Yet I still find his work incredibly modern. I particularly love the atmosphere he created in his portraits: glorious and distorted, a sublime and twisted celebration of sensuality."

Italo Zucchelli, designer for Calvin Klein

On the catwalk

In recent years, turn-of-the-century Vienna and in particular the works of Gustav Klimt and Egon Schiele have exerted a great influence on the world of fashion. The designers John Galliano and Wolfgang Joop have been inspired by Schiele, Calvin Klein and Marc Jacobs brought the Schiele style to the catwalk, and Nina Ricci even had an entire ad campaign in which works by Schiele and Klimt were juxtaposed with new creations. Ricci designer Lars Nilsson raves that "the sensuality, the emotions, and the modernity" of Schiele's work inspire him, which he then carries over to his designs. In the collections of the Italian house of Missoni, the patterns and bold colors of Schiele's images once again come to life (pp. 122–23).

A Rock Star

The Irish rock band The Frames was inspired by, of all things, the death of the artist. The final days of Egon and Edith under the pall of the Spanish flu that took both of their young lives spawned the group's song "Santa Maria," a memorial in sound that appears on the album *For the Birds*.

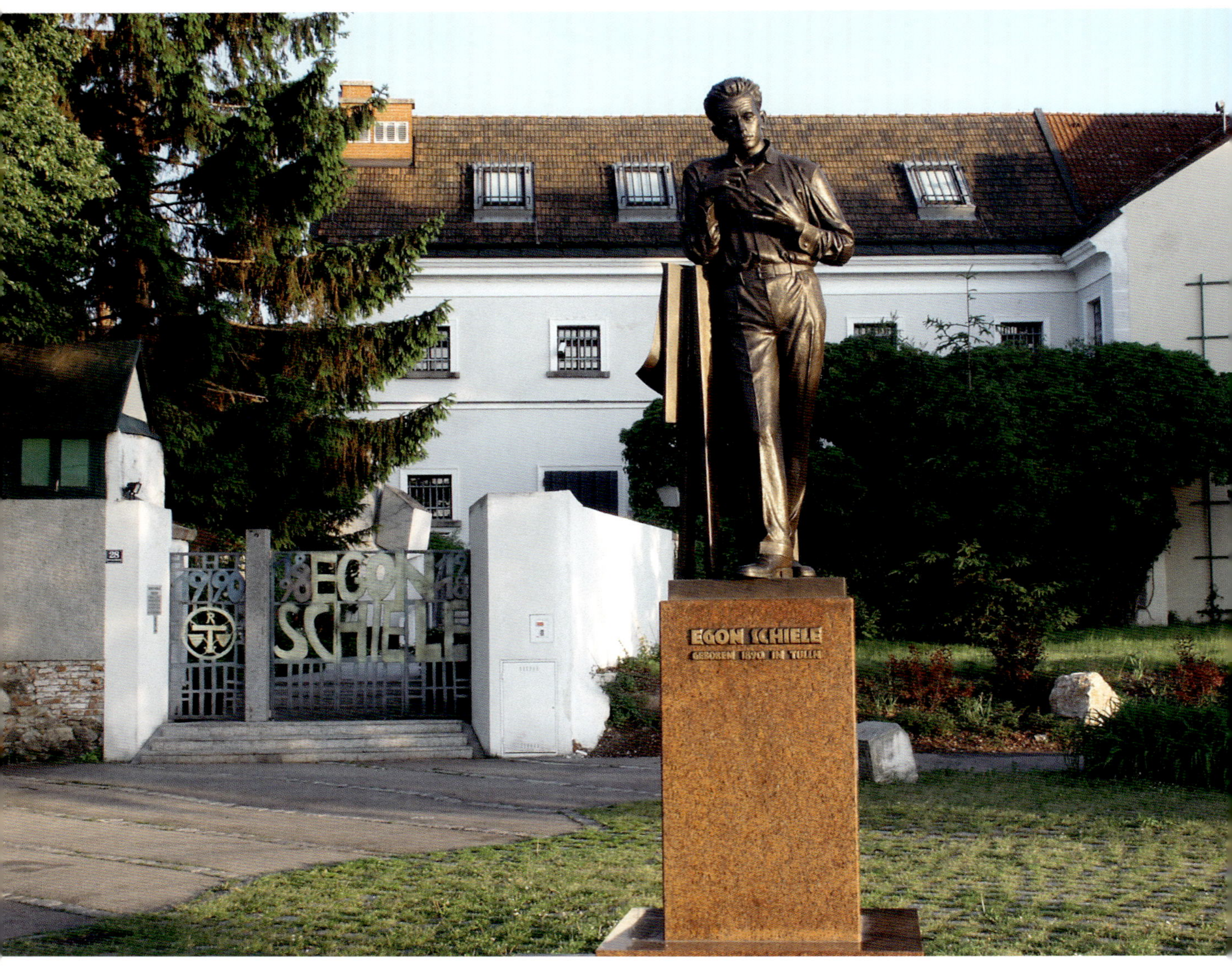

The artist's birthplace today houses the Egon Schiele Museum and is open to visitors.

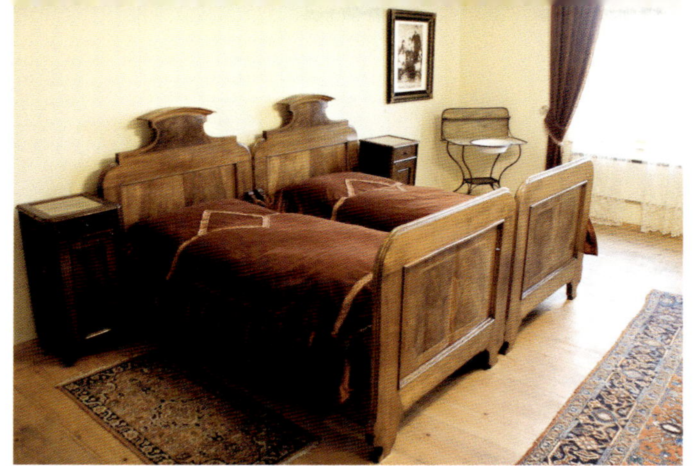

The room in which Schiele was born has been faithfully reconstructed.

Late Fame

Egon Schiele shared the fate of many artists: unrecognized in his lifetime, even faced with hostility, and forced to sell his works for sums that barely allowed him to eke out a living. He never did get his big break. If he could have known how highly valued his work is today, and the influence he was to have on the twentieth-century, it would have been well-deserved gratification.

Echoes

"For Schiele can indeed paint pictures, but only seldom can he sell them. Of course, this is his own fault. Why does he paint what he likes and not what people like."

Arthur Roessler, 1913

Five books about Egon Schiele were published in the four years following his death. Four of these were from the pen of his collector and friend Arthur Roessler. The enthusiastic journalist edited the letters and prose of the artist, and wrote a book on Schiele's time in prison, *Egon Schiele im Gefängnis.* And then, all fell quiet for a time. Schiele's work was always being shown, but until the sixties he remained, like Klimt, a marginal figure on the exhibition scene. It was then that Otto and Heinrich Benesch contributed substantially to Schiele's popularity. The art historian Otto Benesch inherited the spirit and enthusiasm of collecting from his father Heinrich—and became the director of the Albertina Museum in Vienna. Incidentally, Heinrich Benesch bequeathed most of his Schiele collection to the museum.

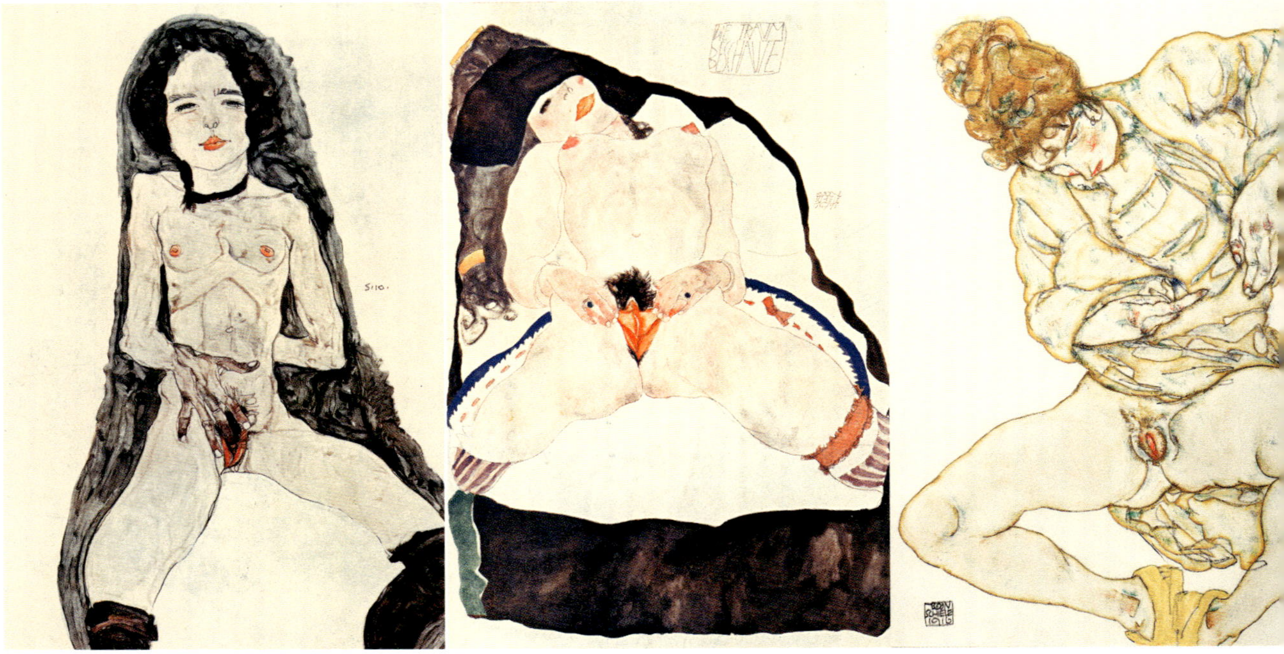

Schiele in America

Schiele, like most of the Expressionists, was ostracized during the Third Reich. At the time, many of his works—classified by the National Socialists as "degenerate art"—were sent to the United States, where the artist was still unknown. The first large sales exhibition including works by the Austrian painter, held in New York in 1941, brought meager results: art dealer Otto Kallir was only able to sell one of Schiele's pictures—for $250 dollars, paid in eighteen monthly installments of $13 each! A little more patience was needed before the name of Egon Schiele was being bandied around across the ocean. But there as well, superlatives have been used for decades to describe unconventional Schiele. He would certainly have been delighted!

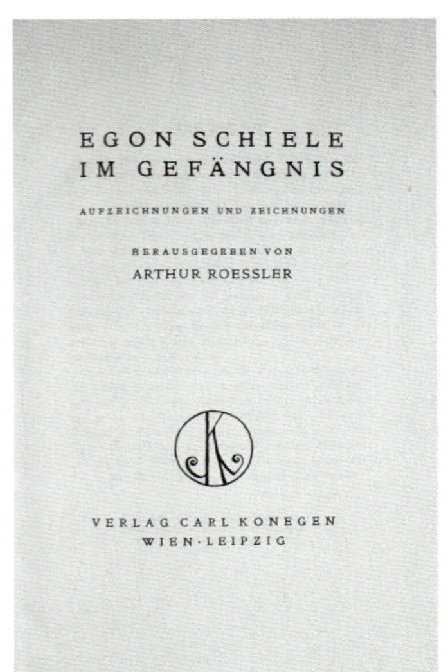

EGON SCHIELE
IM GEFÄNGNIS

AUFZEICHNUNGEN UND ZEICHNUNGEN

HERAUSGEGEBEN VON
ARTHUR ROESSLER

VERLAG CARL KONEGEN
WIEN·LEIPZIG

above: In 1922–23, the Viennese art dealer Karl Grünwald published a portfolio with these five color reproductions of Schiele drawings.

left: In 1922, Arthur Roessler wrote the book *Egon Schiele in Prison*.

The first major Schiele museum exhibition toured five major cities from Boston to Minneapolis in 1960–61. In 1963, Schiele's works traveled out to the west coast of the U.S. with the exhibition *Viennese Expressionism 1910–1924*. In Europe, the eighties witnessed a verita-

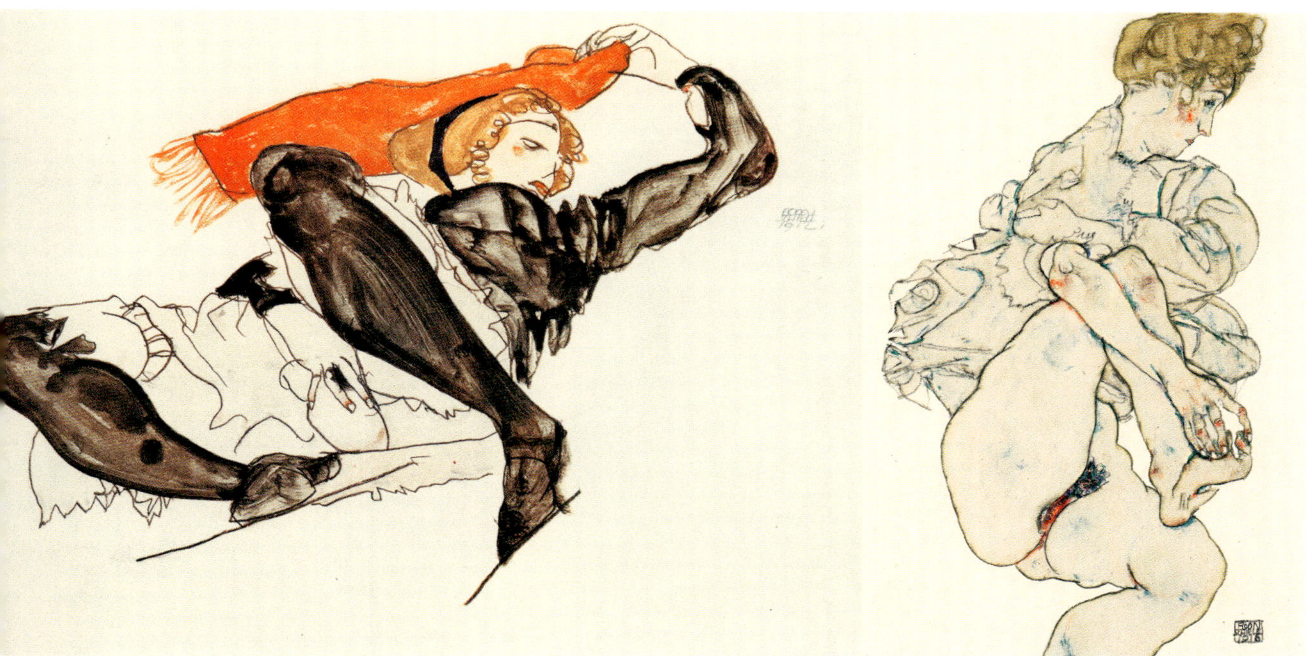

ble "Vienna around 1900" boom. In Hamburg, Edinburgh, Venice, Vienna, Paris, and New York, exhibitions dedicated to turn-of-the-century Austrian art of course featured Schiele as one of the protagonists.

Record-breaking?

The year 2003 saw record prices for two Austrian artists, Egon Schiele and Gustav Klimt. In June of that year, Schiele's *Krumau Landscape: Town and River* of 1916 sold in London for $21 million. The price was nearly double the previous record for a work by Egon Schiele—his portrait of the painter Anton Peschka went under the hammer for barely $11.3 million. With this sum, Schiele is already approaching the incredible $29.1 million fetched by Klimt's *Country House on the Attersee* in November of the same year in New York.

Bare facts

The collector Rudolf Leopold assembled in Vienna the largest collection of Egon Schiele's major paintings and drawings. In the Museum Leopold, the building most visited in Vienna's Museum District, Schiele's path from Jugendstil to Expressionism is reconstructed.

The exhibition *Naked Truth: Klimt, Schiele, Kokoschka and Other Scandals* of 2005 revolved around scandal as the impetus for the development of modern art. What was also potentially scandalous was the motto the museum chose for a hot July day: "Naked in the Museum," which was taken seriously by some five hundred visitors, some of whom waited outside in swimsuits. The worldwide reaction was tremendous—what a surprise!

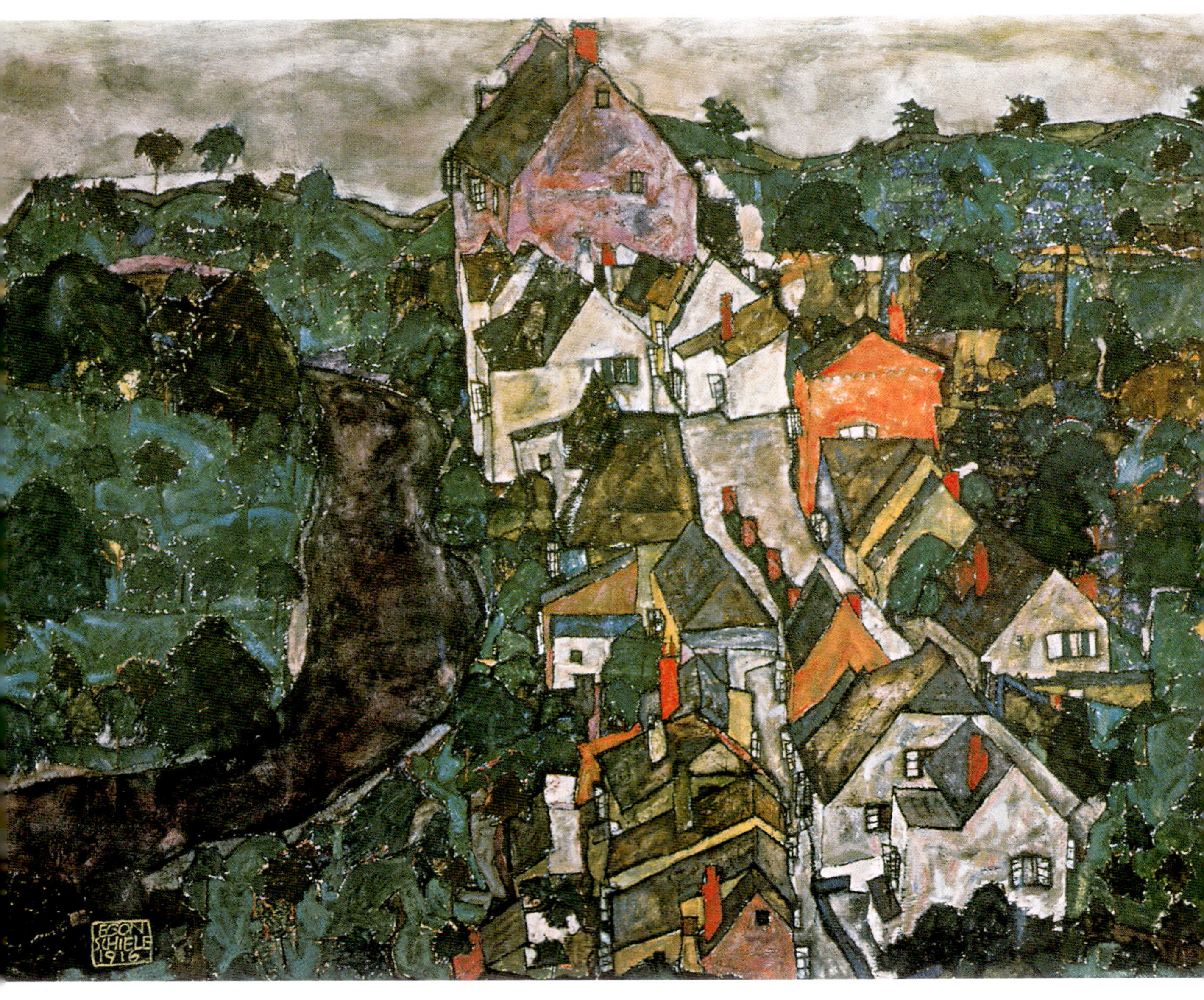

Top price All records were broken in 2003 by Egon Schiele's *Krumau Landscape: Town and River.* This painting of 1916 sold for $21 million to a bidder at a London auction, making it the most expensive Schiele of all time!

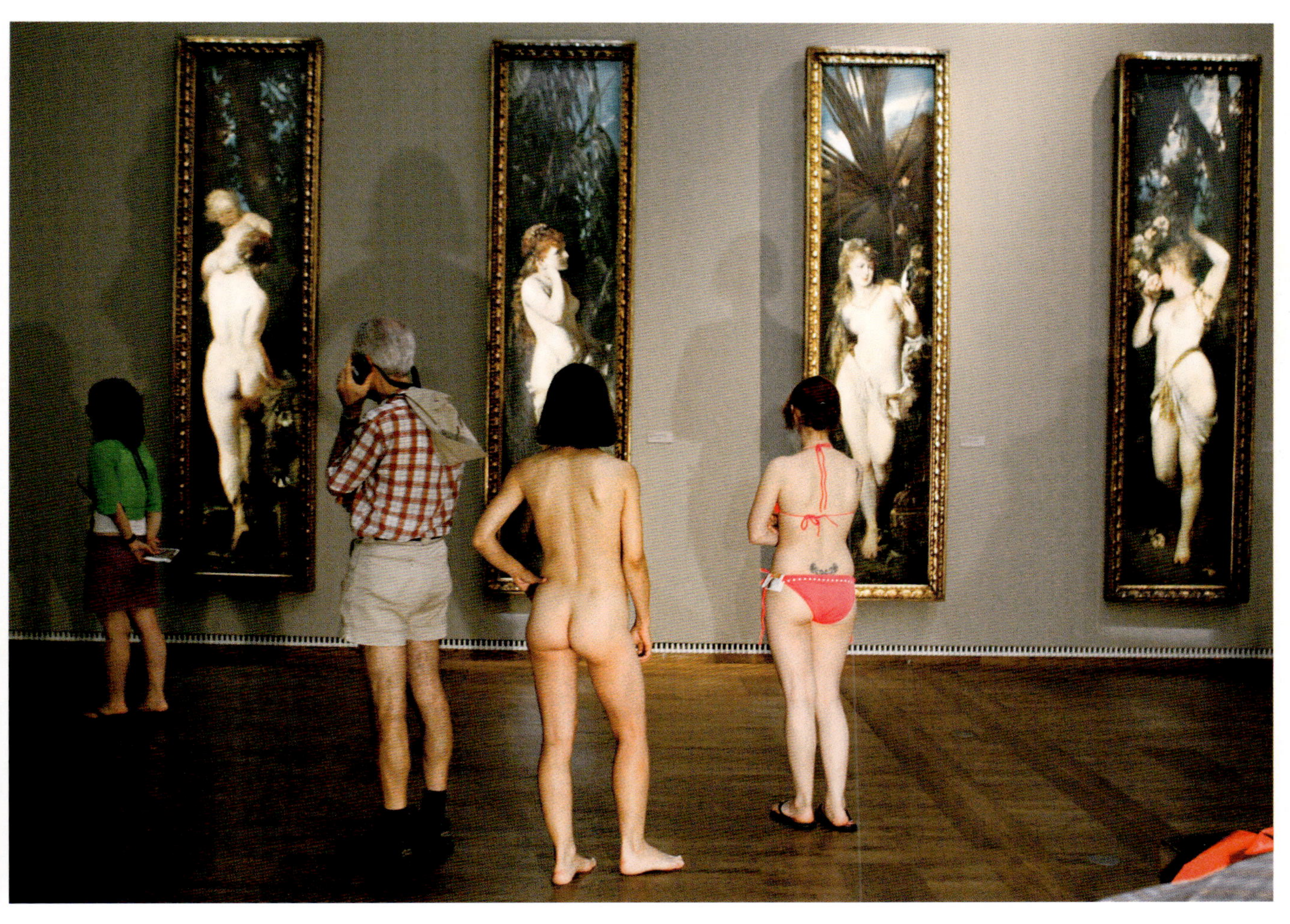

Bare facts In the summer of 2005, the collector Rudolf Leopold invited art lovers to visit his museum *au naturel* for his exhibition *The Naked Truth.* Some five hundred brave visitors followed his motto—here some of them stand in front of Hans Makart's *The Five Senses.*

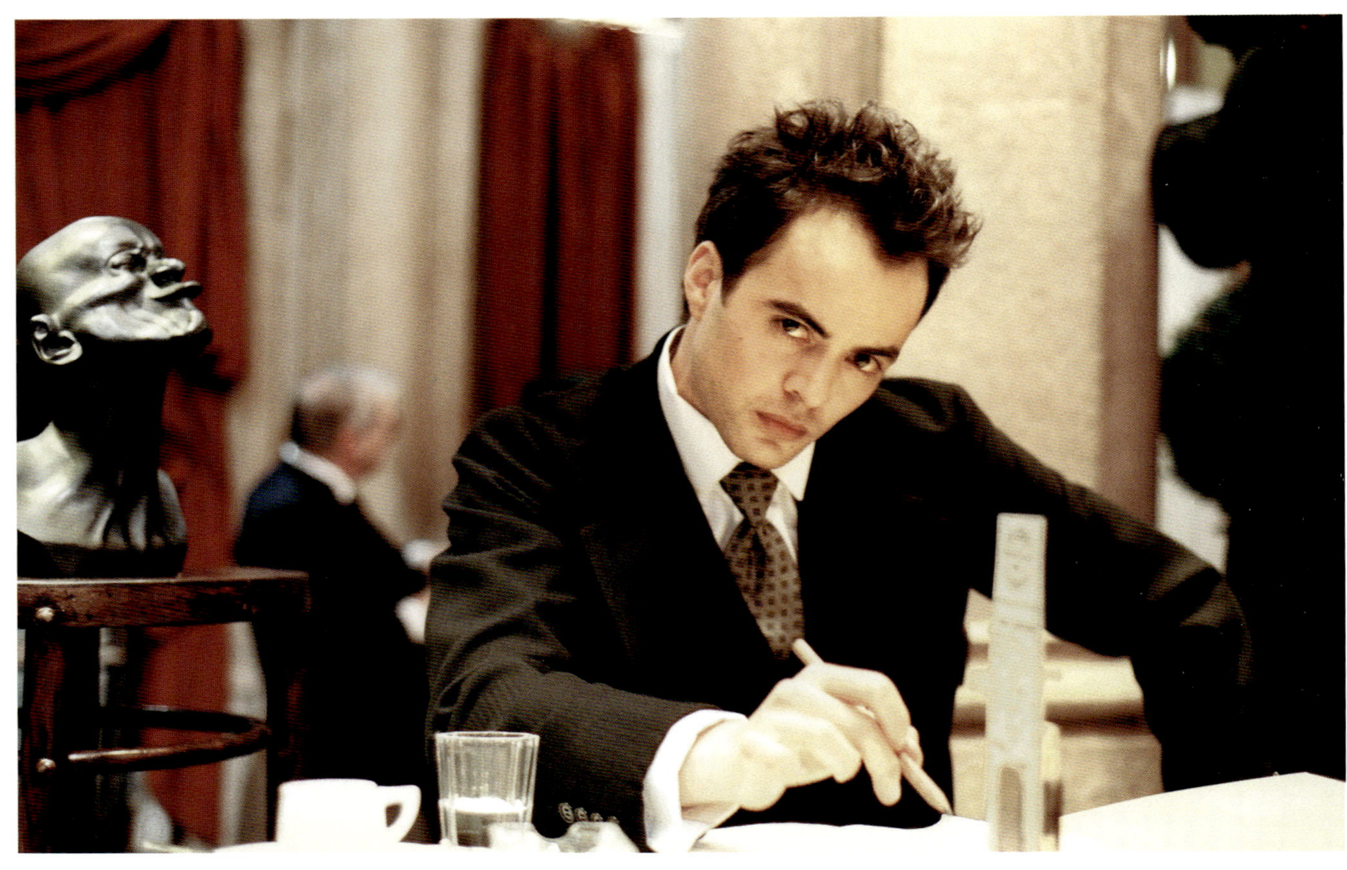

Star of the screen The Chilean-French director Raoul Ruiz filmed Gustav Klimt's life with John Malkovich in the title role. Nikolai Kinski, seen here, played the part of Egon Schiele. The actor became intensively involved in Schiele's work: "His lines burn holes in my subconscious."

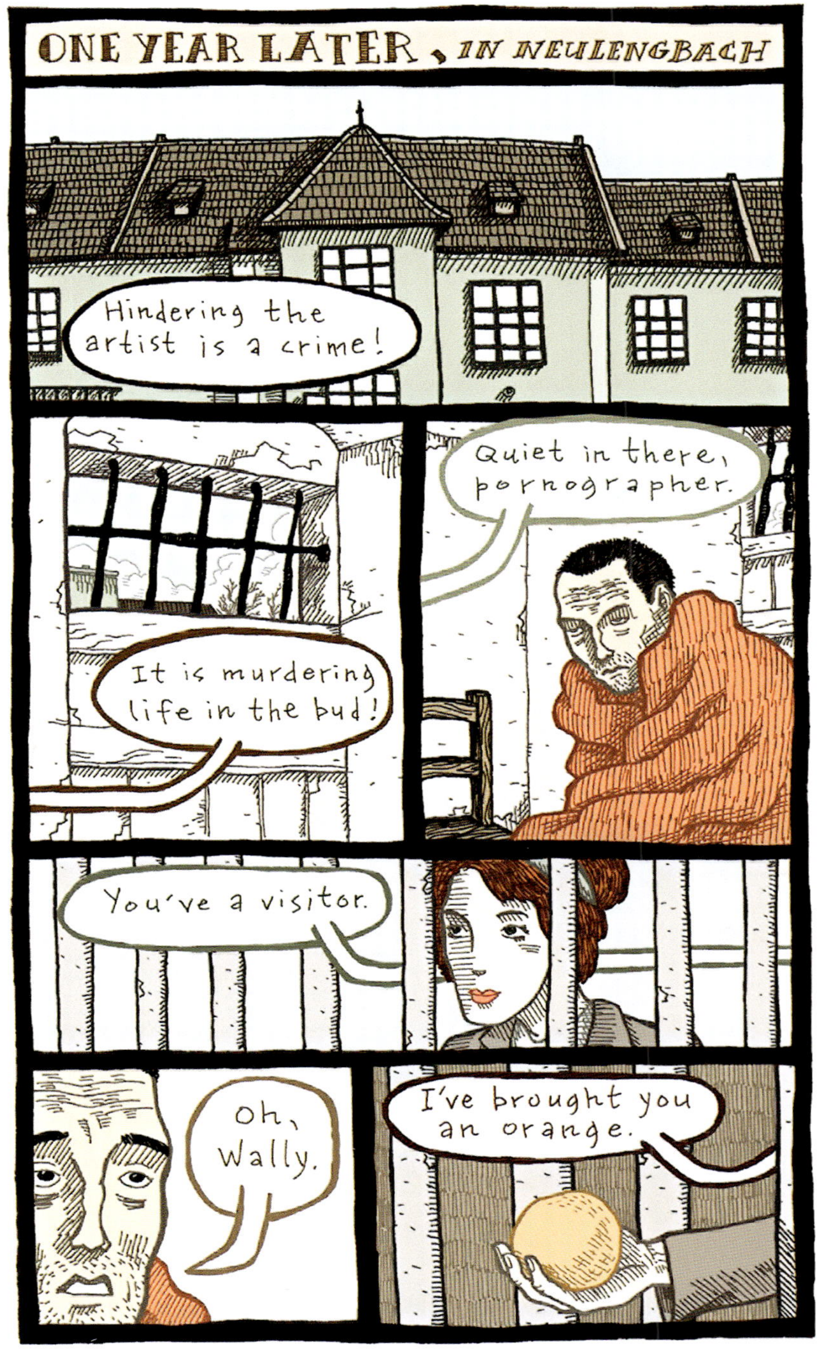

Comic strip In 2002, the artist Jamie Tanner dedicated a comic strip to Egon Schiele, "The Perpetual Child," consisting of biographical fragments. The scandal over Schiele's nude drawings and his stay in the prison at Neulengbach were of course included.

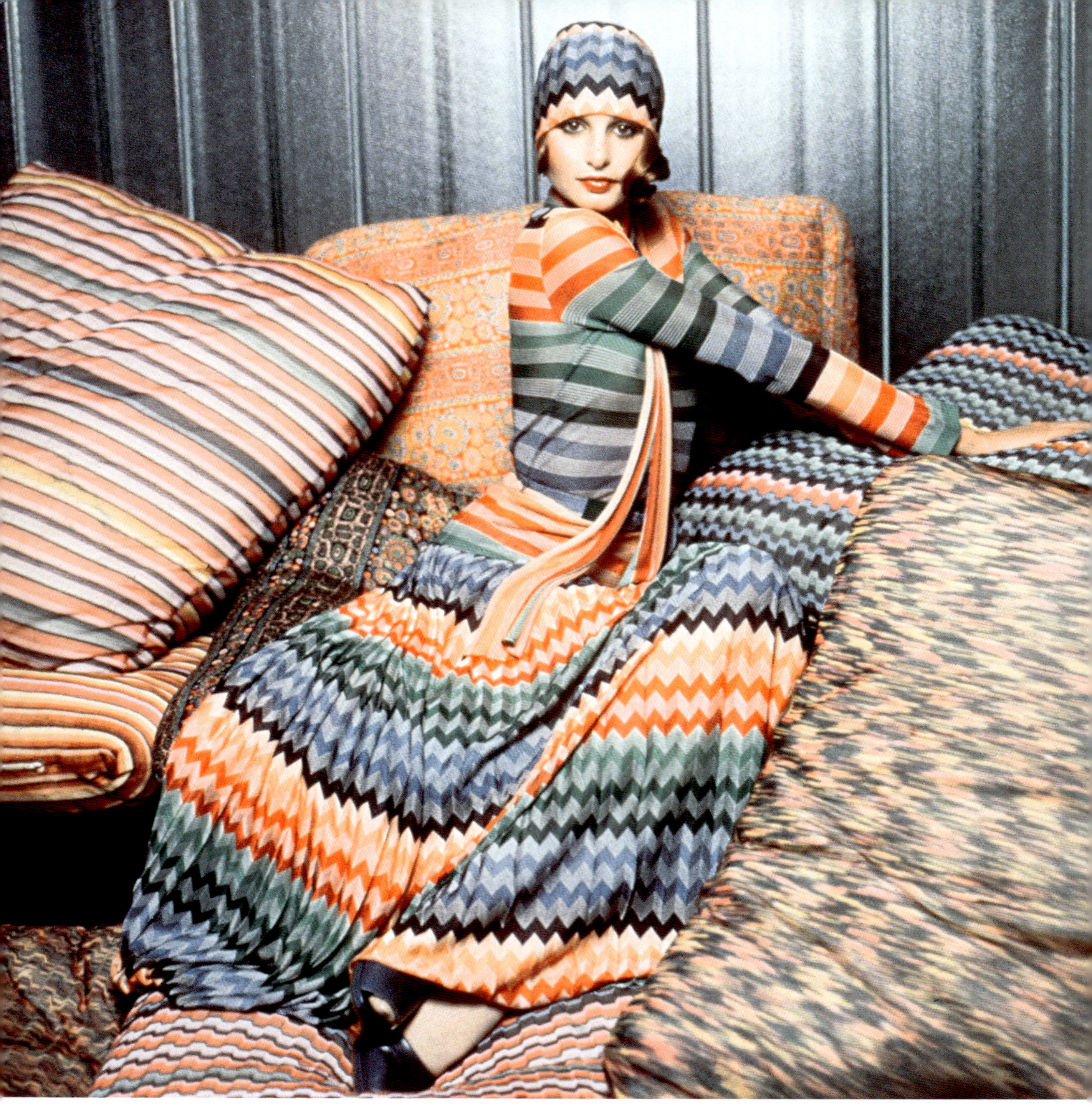

Rage of color The collections of the house of Missoni—in designs such as these from the 1970s—with their characteristic patterns and colors, are reminiscent of works by the artist.

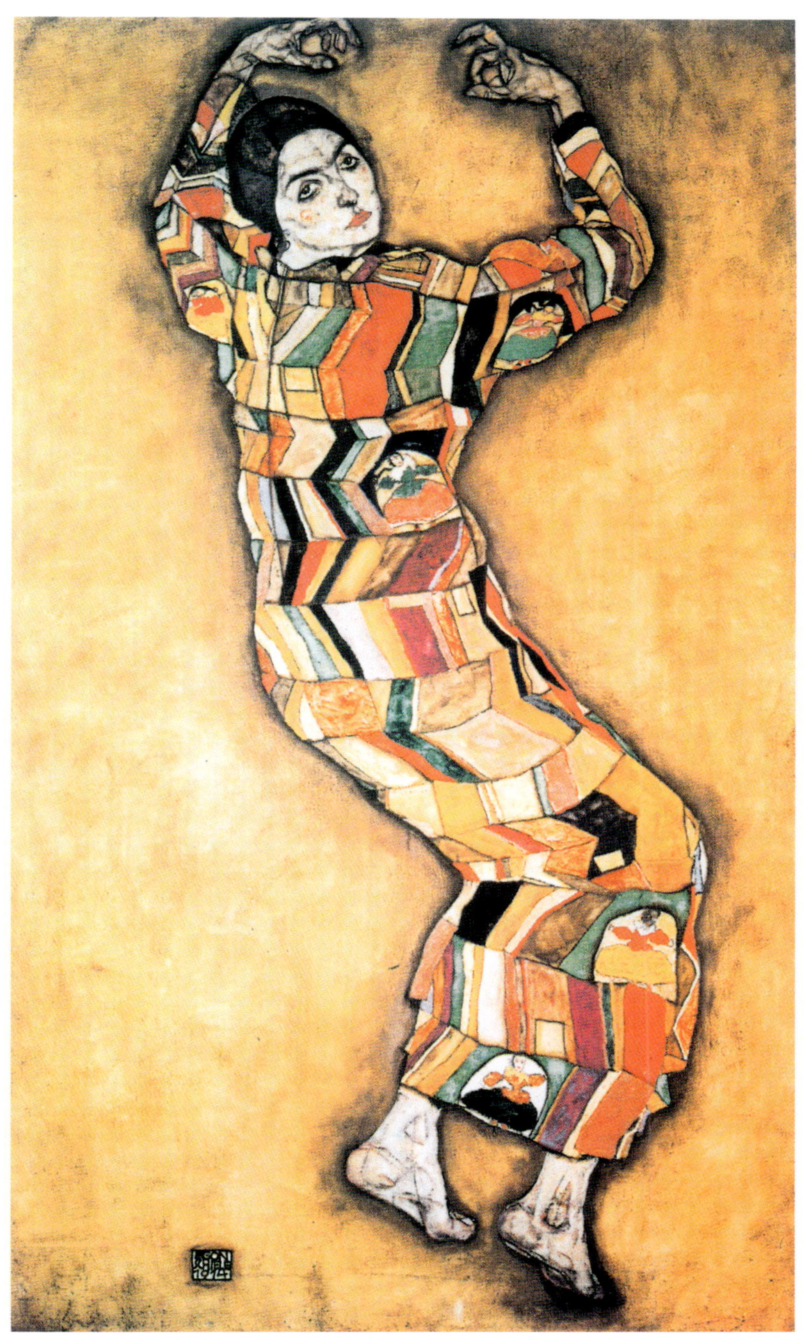

Inspiration The clothing of Schiele's models often contributes decisively to the effect of the works. Many contemporary fashion designers cite the artist as a source of inspiration.

Illustration Credits:

p. 1: Egon Schiele, *Self-Portrait* [Selbstporträt], 1912, gouache, watercolor, and pencil, private collection
p. 5: Moritz Nähr, Gustav Klimt with the artists of the Vienna Secession, April 1902, back row (left to right): Anton Stark, Gustav Klimt (seated), Adolf Böhm, Wilhelm List, Maximilian Kurzweil, Leopold Stolba, Rudolf Bacher; front row (left to right): Koloman Moser, Maximilian Lenz, Ernst Stöhr, Emil Orlik, Carl Moll
p. 6 left: Gustav Klimt, *Portrait of Emilie Flöge* [Bildnis Emilie Flöge], 1902, oil on canvas, 181 x 66.5 cm, Vienna, Wien Museum
p. 6 right: Hermann Drawe, crowded quarters in Vienna, 1904
p. 7 left: Joseph Maria Olbrich, Secession building, 1897–99
p. 7 right: Otto Wagner, Residence on Wienzeile, Vienna, 1898, external view
p. 8: Otto Wagner, Linke Wienzeile 38, 1898–99
p. 9: The opening of the Vienna *Kunstschau,* 1908
p. 10: Reinhold Völkel, *Das Café Griensteidl,* 1896, watercolor, 23 x 34.3 cm, Vienna, Wien Museum
p. 11 left: Maria Li Karz, advertising poster for the Wiener Werkstätte, ca. 1925, 19.8 x 20.6 cm, Vienna, Österreichisches Museum für Angewandte Kunst (MAK)
p. 11 right: Gustav Klimt, photograph
p. 12: Grete Wiesenthal in *Voices of Spring* by Richard Strauss, 1908–9, photograph, Vienna, theater collection of the Österreichische Nationalbibliothek
p. 13: Oskar Kokoschka, photograph
p. 14: Gustav Klimt, *Beethoven Frieze* (detail), 1902, casein paint on plaster undercoat, 2.2 x 24 m, Vienna, Österreichische Galerie Belvedere
p. 15: Gustav Klimt, *Beethoven Frieze* (detail), 1902, casein paint on plaster undercoat, 2.2 x 24 m, Vienna, Österreichische Galerie Belvedere
p. 17: Johannes Fischer, Egon Schiele, silver gelatin print mounted on cardboard, overpainted, Vienna, Albertina
p. 18: Egon Schiele, *Heinrich Benesch,* 1917, black chalk and gouache, 45.7 x 28.5 cm, Vienna, Albertina
p. 19 above: photograph by Anton Trcka, overpainted and signed by Egon Schiele, 1914
p. 19 below: Signature of Egon Schiele
p. 20: Egon Schiele posing, 1914, photograph by Anton Trčka
p. 21: Anton Faistauer, exhibition poster for the Neukunstgruppe in Vienna's Pisko Gallery, 1909, Zug, Stiftung Sammlung Kamm, Kunsthaus Zug
p. 22: Pisko Gallery, Vienna, ca. 1909
p. 23 left: Arthur Roessler, photograph by Pauline Hamilton
p. 23 right: Egon Schiele and Arthur Roessler in front of the Schloss Ort on the Traunsee, 1913
p. 24: Egon Schiele, *Portrait of Erich Lederer* [Porträt Erich Lederer], 1912–13, oil on canvas, 139 x 55 cm, Basel, Öffentliche Kunstsammlung
p. 25: Title page of the Egon Schiele issue of the magazine *Die Aktion,* September 1916
p. 26: Exhibition poster for the 49th Vienna Secession, 1918, color lithograph
p. 27: Egon Schiele in Neulengbach, 1912, photograph, Roessler Estate
p. 28: Egon Schiele, *Double Portrait of Heinrich and Otto Benesch* [Doppelporträt Heinrich und Otto Benesch], 1913, oil on canvas, 121 x 131 cm, Linz, Neue Galerie der Stadt Linz, Wolfgang Gurlitt-Museum
p. 29: Egon Schiele, *Max Kahrer in Profile* [Max Kahrer im Profil], 1910, pencil, black chalk, and body color on brown paper, 45.9 x 30.4 cm, Vienna, Albertina
p. 30: Egon Schiele, *Arthur Roessler,* 1910, oil on canvas, 100 x 100 cm, Vienna, Wien Museum
p. 31: Egon Schiele, *Edith Schiele,* 1918, oil on canvas, 139.5 x 109.2 cm, Vienna, Österreichische Galerie Belvedere
p. 32: Egon Schiele, *Embrace (Lovers II)* [Umarmung (Liebende II)], 1917, oil on canvas, 100 x 170.2 cm, Vienna, Österreichische Galerie Belvedere
p. 33: Egon Schiele, *Death and the Maiden* [Der Tod and das Mädchen], 1915, oil on canvas, 150 x 180 cm, Vienna, Österreichische Galerie Belvedere
p. 35: Egon Schiele before large studio mirror (detail), 1915, photograph by Johannes Fischer, Vienna, Albertina
p. 36: Egon Schiele, *Self-Portrait with Red Eye* [Selbstporträt mit rotem Auge], 1910, gouache, charcoal, and pencil, 44.6 x 30.7 cm, private collection
p. 37 above: Egon Schiele, *The Scornful Woman (Gertrude Schiele)* [Die Hämische (Gertrude Schiele)], 1910, gouache, watercolor, and charcoal with white heightening, 45 x 31.4 cm, private collection
p. 37 below: In front of the Academy on Schillerplatz, Egon Schiele standing in the second row, 2nd from right, June 1907, photograph
p. 38: Egon Schiele, *Four Trees at Sunset* [Vier Bäume], 1917, oil on canvas, 110.5 x 141 cm, Vienna, Österreichische Galerie Belvedere
p. 39: Egon Schiele, photograph from his Academy student card
p. 40: Life class at the Vienna Academy, photograph
p. 41: First volume of the magazine *Ver Sacrum* in the original fabric binding of the Secession, 1898, Vienna, Österreichische Nationalbibliothek, Emma Teschner Collection
p. 42: Moritz Nähr, photograph of Gustav Klimt, ca. 1910
p. 43: Egon Schiele, *Danaë,* 1909, oil and metallic paint on canvas, 80 x 125.4 cm, private collection
p. 44: Egon Schiele, *Portrait of Painter Anton Faistauer* [Bildnis des Malers Anton Faistauer], 1909, pencil, colored chalk, and body color on brown packing paper, 29.6 x 31.3 cm, Vienna, Albertina
p. 45 left: Egon Schiele, *Two Men with Halos* [Zwei Männer mit Nimben], 1912, India ink over pencil on paper, 15.5 x 9.9 cm, Vienna, Albertina
p. 45 right: Egon Schiele, transcript of the poem "Visionen" (Visions), 1914
p. 46: Egon Schiele, *Schiele With A Nude Model Standing in Front of a Mirror* [Egon Schiele, ein Aktmodell und sich selbst im Spiegel zeichnend], 1910, pencil on packing paper, 55.2 x 35.3 cm, Vienna, Albertina
p. 47: Egon Schiele, *Seated Woman in Chemise* [Sitzender Halbakt], 1914, pencil on paper, 45.7 x 30.8 cm, New York, The Metropolitan Museum of Art, Bequest of Scofield Thayer

p. 48: Egon Schiele, *Lesbian Couple* [Lesbisches Paar], 1914, pencil and gouache on paper, 31.2 x 47.9 cm, private collection
p. 49: Egon Schiele, *Striding Torso in Green Shirt* [Schreitender Torso in grünem Hemd], 1913, gouache, watercolor, pencil, and chalk on paper, 48.2 x 31.8 cm, Serge Sabarsky Collection
p. 50: Egon Schiele, *Portrait of Dr. Hugo Koller* [Porträt Dr. Hugo Koller], 1918, oil on canvas, 140.3 x 109.6 cm, Vienna, Österreichische Galerie Belvedere
p. 51: Egon Schiele, *Portrait of the Painter Karl Zakovšek* [Bildnis des Malers Karl Zakovšek], 1910, oil, tempera, and chalk on canvas, 100.3 x 90.3 cm, private collection
p. 52: Egon Schiele, *Mother with Two Children III* [Mutter mit zwei Kindern III], 1917, oil on canvas, 150 x 150 cm, Vienna, Österreichische Galerie Belvedere
p. 53: Egon Schiele, *The Family (Squatting Couple)* [Die Familie (Kauerndes Menschenpaar)], 1918, oil on canvas, 152.5 x 162.5 cm, Vienna, Österreichische Galerie Belvedere
p. 54: Egon Schiele, *End of Town (Krumau Houses III)* [Stadtende (Häuserbogen III)], 1917–18, oil on canvas, 109.5 x 139.5 cm, Graz, Neue Galerie am Landesmuseum Joanneum
p. 55: Egon Schiele, *Suburban House with Washing* [Vorstadthaus mit Wäsche], 1917, oil on canvas, 110 x 140.4 cm, private collection
p. 57: Egon Schiele, *Self-Portrait* [Selbstbildnis], 1914, pencil and gouache, 46 x 30.5 cm, Prague, National Gallery
p. 58: Gerti Schiele as fashion model, photograph
p. 59 above: Melanie, Gerti, and Egon with a toy train, ca. 1895, photograph
p. 59: Egon Schiele, *Self-Portrait* [Selbstporträt], 1914, gouache, watercolor, and chalk, 47.6 x 31.1 cm, private collection
p. 60: Egon Schiele at age 15, ca. 1905, photograph by Adolf Bernhard, Vienna, Albertina
p. 61: Handwritten résumé of the life of Egon Schiele, 1910, pencil, Vienna, Albertina, Egon Schiele Archive, Max Wagner Foundation
p. 62: Railroad station building at Tulln, photograph
p. 63 left: Adolf Schiele and Marie Soukup as fiancées, 1879, photograph
p. 63 right: Egon Schiele, *Snow-Covered Vineyard, in the Background Klosterneuburg in Fog* [Verschneiter Weingarten, im Hintergrund Klosterneuburg im Nebel], 1907, oil on canvas, 58.5 x 74 cm, Tulln an der Donau, Egon Schiele Museum
p. 64: Leopold and Marie Czihaczek in the music room, 1907
p. 65: Erwin Dom Osen with the dancer Moa at a mime performance, ca. 1910
p. 66 left: Egon Schiele's house in Neulengbach, photograph
p. 66 right: Egon Schiele and Anton Peschka in Krumau, 1910
p. 67: Egon Schiele, *Female Nude, Semi-Reclining* [Mädchenakt, halb liegend], 1910, pencil, 55.7 x 37 cm, Graz, Neue Galerie am Landesmuseum Joanneum
p. 68: Egon Schiele, *Self-Portrait* [Selbstporträt], 1906, charcoal, 45.5 x 34.6 cm, Vienna, Albertina
p. 69: Egon Schiele, *Self-Portrait with Brown Hat* [Selbstbildnis mit braunem Hut], 1910, charcoal and gouache, 45.4 x 31 cm, private collection
p. 70: Egon Schiele, *Self-Portrait as Prisoner* [Selbstbildnis als Gefangener], 1912, brush, watercolor, and pencil, 47.9 x 31.9 cm, Vienna, Albertina
p. 71: Egon Schiele, *Two Young Girls* [Zwei kauernde Mädchen], 1911, pencil, watercolor, and opaque white on paper, 41.3 x 32 cm, Vienna, Albertina
p. 72: Egon Schiele, *Standing Nude Boy* [Stehender nackter Junge], 1910, black chalk and watercolor, 45.3 x 23 cm, Budapest, Szépmüvészeti Múzeum
p. 73: Egon Schiele, *Two Women Embracing* [Zwei sich umarmende Frauen], 1911, watercolor and pencil on paper, 56 x 37 cm, private collection
p. 74: Egon Schiele, *Mime van Osen*, 1910, watercolor and charcoal on cardboard, 37.8 x 29.7 cm, Graz, Neue Galerie am Landesmuseum Joanneum
p. 75: Egon Schiele, *Self-Portrait* [Selbstbildnis], 1910, black chalk and watercolor, 44.5 x 30.8 cm, Location unknown
p. 76: Prison cell in Neulengbach
p. 77: Edith Schiele with her dog Lord, ca. 1917
p. 78: Egon Schiele with comrades from the prisoner of war camp for Russian officers, 1916, photograph
p. 79: Egon Schiele on his deathbed, 1918, photograph by Martha Fein
p. 80: Egon Schiele, *Self-Portrait with Arm Twisted Above Head* [Selbstbildnis mit Arm über den Kopf gezogen], 1910, watercolor and charcoal, 45.1 x 31.7 cm, private collection
p. 81: Egon Schiele, *Self-Portrait with Bare Stomach* [Selbstbildnis mit entblößtem Nabel], 1911, pencil and watercolor on paper, 55.6 x 36.4 cm, Vienna, Albertina
p. 82: Egon Schiele, *Self-Portrait as St. Sebastian* [Selbstporträt als Heiliger Sebastian], poster design, 1914, charcoal and gouache, 67 x 50 cm, Vienna, Wien Museum
p. 83: Egon Schiele, *Conversion* [Bekehrung], 1912, oil and chalk on canvas, 70.1 x 80.2 cm, private collection
p. 84: Egon Schiele, *Individual Houses (Houses with Mountains)* [Einzelne Häuser (Häuser mit Bergen)], 1915, oil on canvas, 109.7 x 140 cm, private collection
p. 85: Egon Schiele, *Bare Tree Behind a Fence* [Baum hinter einem Zaun], 1912, oil on wood, 32.5 x 41.2 cm, Serge Sabarsky Collection
p. 86: Egon Schiele, *City on the Blue River (Dead Town I)* [Stadt am blauen Fluss I (Tote Stadt I)], 1910, gouache and black chalk on paper, 41.2 x 30.8 cm, private collection
p. 87: Egon Schiele, *Russian Prisoner of War with Fur Hat* [Russischer Kriegsgefangener mit Pelzmütze], 1915, pencil and body color on packing paper, 44.6 x 31.2 cm, Vienna, Albertina
p. 88: Egon Schiele, *Seated Woman with Bent Knee* [Sitzende Frau mit hochgezogenem Knie], 1917, charcoal, watercolor, and gouache, 46 x 30.5 cm, Prague, National Gallery
p. 89: Egon Schiele, *Female Nude Lying on her Stomach* [Auf dem Bauch liegender weiblicher Akt], 1917, black chalk and gouache, 29.8 x 46 cm, Vienna, Albertina
p. 91: Egon Schiele, *Woman in Black Stockings (Valerie Neuzil)* [Frau in schwarzen Strümpfen (Valerie Neuzil)], 1913, gouache, watercolor, and pencil, 32 x 48 cm, private collection, courtesy Galerie St. Etienne, New York

p. 92: Egon Schiele, *Seated Pregnant Nude* [Sitzende Schwangere], 1910, black chalk and watercolor on paper, 45.1 x 31.1 cm, private collection
p. 93 left: Wally Neuzil in Altmünster, 1913, photograph
p. 93 right: Egon Schiele, letter to the Harms sisters of December 10, 1914, Vienna, Albertina, Egon Schiele Archive
p. 94: Egon Schiele, *Seated Couple (Egon and Edith Schiele)* [Sitzendes Paar (Egon und Edith Schiele)], 1915, pencil and gouache, 52.2 x 41.2 cm, Vienna, Albertina
p. 95: Egon Schiele and Wally in Neuzil
p. 96: Egon Schiele, *Nude Self-Portrait* [Aktselbstbildnis], 1918, black chalk on paper, 30 x 47.9 cm, Vienna, Albertina
p. 97: The Harms family
p. 98 left: Egon and Edith Schiele, summer of 1918
p. 98 right: The sisters Adele and Edith Harms as young girls
p. 99: Egon Schiele, *Edith Schiele,* 1918, chalk on paper, 44 x 29.7 cm, private collection
p. 100: Egon Schiele, *Two Girls on a Fringed Blanket* [Zwei Mädchen auf einer Fransendecke], 1911, watercolor, gouache, India ink, and pencil, 55.9 x 36.8 cm, private collection
p. 101: Egon Schiele, *Female Nude with Green Cushion* [Weiblicher Akt mit grünem Polster], 1910, charcoal and watercolor, 44.9 x 32.2 cm, Graz, Neue Galerie am Landesmuseum Joanneum
p. 102: Egon Schiele, *Standing Male Nude with Arm Raised, Back View* [Männlicher Akt mit erhobenem Arm], 1910, watercolor and charcoal on paper, 44.8 x 31.4 cm, New York, The Museum of Modern Art
p. 103: Egon Schiele, *Standing Woman in Red* [Stehende Frau in Rot], 1913, gouache, watercolor, and pencil, 48.3 x 32.4 cm, private collection
p. 104: Egon Schiele, *Edith Schiele with her Nephew* [Edith Schiele mit ihrem Neffen], 1915, black chalk on paper, 48.8 x 33.5 cm, Vienna, Albertina
p. 105: Egon Schiele, *Houses with Renaissance Gables* [Häuser mit Renaissancegiebeln], 1917, black chalk, 45.8 x 28.8 cm, Vienna, Albertina
p. 106: Egon Schiele, *Marguerites, Morning Glories, and Red Poppy* [Margeriten, Windling and Mohnblume], 1918, pencil, watercolor, 42 x 27 cm, Linz, Oberösterreichische Landesmuseum
p. 107: Egon Schiele, *Sunflowers* [Sonnenblumen], 1917, pencil, watercolor, and gouache on paper, 45.8 x 29.8 cm, Vienna, Albertina
p. 108: Egon Schiele, *Yellow Chrysanthemum* [Gelbe Chrysantheme], 1910, pencil, watercolor, and opaque white on brown paper, 45 x 31.6 cm, Vienna, Albertina
p. 109: Egon Schiele, *Red Chrysanthemum* [Rote Chrysantheme], 1910, pencil, and watercolor on brown paper, 29.7 x 25.7 cm, Vienna, Albertina
p. 111: Nikolai Kinski as Egon Schiele in Raoul Ruiz's film *Klimt*
p. 112 right: Rachel's, cover of the album *Music for Egon Schiele,* 1996
p. 112 left: Leopold Museum, Vienna, exterior view
p. 113: Interior view of the house where Egon Schiele was born, Tulln an der Donau, Egon Schiele Museum
p. 114: Exterior view of the Egon Schiele Museum, Tulln an der Donau
p. 115: Interior view of the house where Egon Schiele was born, Tulln an der Donau, Egon Schiele Museum
p. 116 / 117: Egon Schiele, portfolio: five drawings, Vienna, ca. 1920, five color reproductions, edition of 100, 50 x 32.5 cm
p. 116 below: Cover of the book *Egon Schiele im Gefängnis* (Egon Schiele in Prison) by Arthur Roessler, 1922
p. 118: Egon Schiele, *Krumau Landscape (Town and River)* [Krumauer Landschaft (Stadt and Fluss)], 1916, oil, tempera, and colored chalk on canvas, 110.5 x 141 cm, Linz, Wolfgang Gurlitt Collection in the Neue Galerie der Stadt Linz
p. 119: "Naked in the Museum" project, 2005, Vienna, Leopold Museum
p. 120: Nikolai Kinski as Egon Schiele in Raoul Ruiz's film *Klimt*
p. 121: Jamie Tanner, "The Perpetual Child" (extract), 2002
p. 122: Model in Missoni fashions, seated on Missoni cushions and blankets, 1975
p. 123: Egon Schiele, *Portrait of Friederike Maria Beer* [Bildnis Friederike Maria Beer], 1914, private collection

On the cover
Front of jacket: Egon Schiele, *Seated Woman with Bent Knee* (detail), 1917 (see p. 88)
Back of jacket: Egon Schiele in Neulengbach, 1912, photograph, Roessler Estate (see p. 27)
Front flap, inside above (left to right), Secession building (see p. 7); Venus of Willendorf; Willy Stöwer, sinking of the *Titanic*; Charlie Chaplin and Paulette Goddard in *Modern Times*; Gustav Klimt, photograph; below (left to right), the railroad station building at Tulln, photograph; In front of the Academy on Schillerplatz (see p. 37); Egon Schiele, *Danaë*, 1909 (see p. 43); Egon Schiele, *Two Women Embracing*, 1911 (see p. 73); Egon Schiele, *Double Portrait of Heinrich and Otto Benesch*, 1913 (see p. 28); Egon Schiele, *Lesbian Couple*, 1914 (see p. 48); Edith Schiele with her dog Lord, ca. 1917; *Die Aktion* magazine (see p. 25); Egon Schiele on his deathbed, 1918
Back flap, inside: (all works by Egon Schiele): left to right, Portrait: *Self-Portrait with Brown Hat*, 1910 (see p. 69); *Portrait of Erich Lederer*, 1912/13 (see p. 24); *Double Portrait of Heinrich and Otto Benesch*, 1913 (see p. 28); *Self-Portrait*, 1914 (see p. 57); Edith Schiele, 1918 (see p. 31); Landscape: *Snow-Covered Vineyard, in the Background Klosterneuburg in the Fog*), 1907 (p. 63); *City on the Blue River II* [Stadt am Blauen Fluss II], 1911, pencil, gouache and oil on wood, 37.2 x 29.8 cm, private collection; *Little Tree (Chestnut Tree at Lake Constance)* [Bäumchen (Kastanienbaum am Bodensee)], 1912, watercolor and pencil on paper, 45.8 x 29.5 cm, private collection; *Krumau Landscape (Town and River)*, 1916 (see p. 118); *End of the Town (Krumau Houses III)*, 1917/18 (see p. 54); Drawing: *Mime van Osen*, 1910 (see p. 74); *Seated Woman in Chemise*, 1914 (see p. 47); *Edith Schiele with her Nephew*, 1915 (see p. 104); *Houses with Renaissance Gables*, 1917 (see p. 105); *Edith Schiele*, 1918 (see p. 99)

If you want to know more ...

Schiele's correspondence, his war journal, and his poems can be read in Christian M. Nebehay's **Egon Schiele: 1890–1918; Leben, Briefe, Gedichte** (Life, Letters, Poems), Residenz Verlag: Salzburg, 1979. A short section of this book is dedicated to the people in Schiele's circle.

Schiele reveals much about himself in his sketchbooks, providing a great deal of information about his working methods. They are presented in Christian M. Nebehay, **Egon Schiele: Sketchbooks,** Rizzoli: New York, 1989.

Schiele's biography and his complete works have been collected by Jane Kallir, who provides an introduction to the turn-of-the-century Austrian painting: **Egon Schiele: The Complete Works,** Harry N. Abrams: New York, 1990.

Schiele's interest in illness and death was explored by Klaus Albrecht Schröder: **Egon Schiele: Eros and Passion,** Prestel: Munich, 2004. This Schiele expert looks at these themes against their contemporary background and also investigates the role of erotic and medical-psychological photography.

The catalogue **The Naked Truth** also offers rewarding information on the scandals, large and small, of turn-of-the-century Vienna—Schiele, of course, is included, along with Klimt, Kokoschka, and others! By Max Hollein and Tobias G. Natter, Prestel: Munich, 2005.

In a beautiful book of sketches, the "naked truth" itself is the subject: **Egon Schiele: Erotic Sketches / Erotische Skizzen,** Prestel: Munich, 2005.

The exhibition catalogue **New Worlds: German and Austrian Art, 1890–1940,** ed. Renée Price, Neue Galerie: New York, 2001, sheds light on the reception of Egon Schiele's work in America since 1939.

An exhibition in the Leopold Museum in Vienna was devoted to Schiele's little regarded landscapes: **Egon Schiele Landscapes,** ed. Rudolf Leopold, Prestel: Munich, 2010.

Paintings and drawings from the Austrian Leopold Collection can be duly admired in the catalogue **Egon Schiele: The Leopold Collection, Vienna,** ed. Rudolf Leopold, Prestel: Munich, 2009.

A representative selection of Schiele's works on paper, collected in an exhibition catalogue from the Albertina, offers insights into the artist's rapid development. Klaus Albrecht Schröder, **Egon Schiele,** Prestel: Munich, 2005.

The Wien Museum has made Schiele's relationship with one of his earliest patrons, the art critic Arthur Roessler, the theme of an exhibition: **Egon Schiele und Arthur Roessler: Der Künstler und sein Förderer,** Hatje Cantz: Ostfildern, 2004.

Imprint

Material was kindly made available to us by those museums and collections named in the illustrations credits, or are from the publisher's archives, with the following exceptions:
Albertina, Vienna: pp. 18, 29, 35, 44, 45, 46, 60, 61, 68, 70, 71, 75, 78 right, 81, 87, 89, 93 right, 94, 96, 104, 105, 107, 108, 109
Österreichische Galerie Belvedere, Vienna: pp. 14, 15, 31, 32, 33, 38, 50, 52, 53
© The Metropolitan Museum of Art, New York: p. 47
www.klimtderfilm.at, © Bernhard Berger: pp. 111, 120
© Rachel Grimes: p. 112
Egon Schiele Museum, Tulln an der Donau: pp. 113, 114, 115
Leonhard Foeger, Reuters Agency: p. 119
© Jamie Tanner: p. 121
Getty Images: p. 122

The excerpt from *The World of Yesterday* by Stefan Zweig is reproduced with the kind permission of Pushkin Press. Translation copyright Anthea Bell.

Prestel Verlag, Munich
A member of Verlagsgruppe Random House GmbH

Prestel Verlag
Königinstrasse 9
80539 Munich
Tel. +49 (0)89 24 29 08-300
Fax +49 (0)89 24 29 08-335
www.prestel.de

Prestel Publishing Ltd.
4 Bloomsbury Place
London WC1A 2QA
Tel. +44 (0)20 7323-5004
Fax +44 (0)20 7636-8004
www.prestel.com

Prestel Publishing
900 Broadway, Suite 603
New York, NY 10003
Tel. +1 (212) 995-2720
Fax +1 (212) 995-2733

The Library of Congress Control Number: 2010928217
Library of Congress Control Number is available; British Library Cataloguing-in-Publication Data: a catalogue record for this book is available from the British Library; Deutsche Nationalbibliothek holds a record of this publication in the Deutsche Nationalbibliografie; detailed bibliographical data can be found under: http://dnb.d-nb.de

Prestel books are available worldwide. Please contact your nearest bookseller or one of the above addresses for information concerning your local distributor.

Translation from the German: Christine Shuttleworth
Project management: Julia Strysio and Anita Dahlinger
Copyediting: Jonathan Fox
Production: Miriam Horwath
Art direction: Cilly Klotz
Design and layout: Sybille Engels, engels zahm + partner
Typesetting: Wolfram Söll
Lithography: ReproLine Mediateam, München
Printing: Druckerei Uhl GmbH & Co. KG, Radolfzell

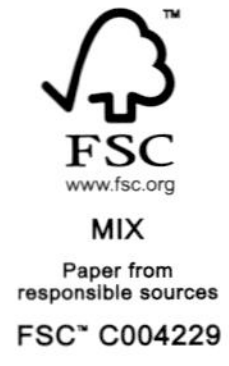

Verlagsgruppe Random House FSC-DEU-0100
The FSC-certified paper *LuxoArt silk* is produced by Sappi, Biberist, Switzerland.

Printed in Germany

ISBN 978-3-7913-4491-1